SUPERCOHERENCE
THE 7TH SENSE

SUPERCOHERENCE
THE 7TH SENSE

THRITY ENGINEER

HAY HOUSE

Australia • Canada • Hong Kong • India
South Africa • United Kingdom • United States

First published and distributed in the United Kingdom by:
Hay House UK Ltd, 292B Kensal Rd, London W10 5BE. Tel.: (44) 20 8962 1230;
Fax: (44) 20 8962 1239. www.hayhouse.co.uk

Published and distributed in the United States of America by:
Hay House, Inc., PO Box 5100, Carlsbad, CA 92018-5100.
Tel.: (1) 760 431 7695 or (800) 654 5126; Fax: (1) 760 431 6948 or (800) 650 5115.
www.hayhouse.com

Published and distributed in Australia by:
Hay House Australia Ltd, 18/36 Ralph St, Alexandria NSW 2015.
Tel.: (61) 2 9669 4299; Fax: (61) 2 9669 4144. www.hayhouse.com.au

Published and distributed in the Republic of South Africa by:
Hay House SA (Pty), Ltd, PO Box 990, Witkoppen 2068.
Tel./Fax: (27) 11 467 8904. www.hayhouse.co.za

Published and distributed in India by:
Hay House Publishers India, Muskaan Complex, Plot No.3, B-2,
Vasant Kunj, New Delhi – 110 070.
Tel.: (91) 11 4176 1620; Fax: (91) 11 4176 1630. www.hayhouse.co.in

Distributed in Canada by:
Raincoast, 9050 Shaughnessy St, Vancouver, BC V6P 6E5.
Tel.: (1) 604 323 7100; Fax: (1) 604 323 2600

© Thrity Engineer, 2008
The moral rights of the author have been asserted.

The author of this book does not dispense medical advice or prescribe the use of any
technique as a form of treatment for physical or medical problems without the advice of a
physician, either directly or indirectly. The intent of the author is only to offer information
of a general nature to help you in your quest for emotional and spiritual wellbeing. In the
event you use any of the information in this book for yourself, which is your constitutional
right, the author and the publisher assume no responsibility for your actions.

A catalogue record for this book is available from the British Library.

All the clients whose images are featured in this book have given their permission.

ISBN 978-1-4019-1584-1

Designed by e-Digital Design.
Illustration concept on p34-35 by Elizabeth Best.
Printed in the UK by CPI William Clowes Ltd, Beccles, NR34 7TL

To Patrick Richards, the genius inventor of the Luminator
and the founder of the life discipline that is Biolumanetics,
with deep admiration and heartfelt thanks

and

to YOU,

the infinite human full of possibility.

'The first step is to measure whatever can be easily measured.
This is okay as far as it goes.
The second step is to disregard that which cannot be easily measured
or to give it an arbitrary value.
This is artificial and misleading.
The third step is to presume that what cannot be measured
isn't really important.
This is blindness.
The fourth step is to say that what can't be measured
doesn't really exist.
This is suicide.'

Robert MacNamara

That which could not easily be measured can now be measured.

'Three Laws of Technology:

1. When a scientist states that something is possible,
he is almost certainly right.
When he states that something is impossible,
he is very probably wrong.

2. The only way of discovering the limits of the possible
is to venture a little way past them into the impossible.

3. Any sufficiently developed technology
is indistinguishable from magic.'

Arthur C. Clarke

Warning notice: Do not open this book if you are not
a believer in authentic magic.

CONTENTS

VI. The Unlimited Human

Preface

They say truth is stranger than fiction. The story I am about to tell you is true, though it will very probably stretch and challenge most people, from scientists to metaphysicians and everyone in between. I found myself a participant in this strange and extraordinary real-life science-'fiction' tale totally by 'accident' – on one level at least. Then it captured my interest and took over my life in the most unexpected way. This book is about my personal journey of discovery, as seen through the eyes of my humble Polaroid camera. From a fairly normal life, I was plunged without warning into a parallel universe where reality operated by completely different rules. Every single belief system that I held was challenged and my conceptual apple cart was not only upset, it was completely toppled and rearranged in the most thorough manner. I have never got over this event and now I have no inclination to get over it. It is the reality I know, trust and live by. Today, many years later, I can say with absolute certainty and confidence that this single fateful event has been the greatest gift that I have ever received from a benign and Supreme Intelligence. My life, which was ordinary before, cannot be considered ordinary by any standards any more. It has been transformed, transmuted and transfigured, healed and made radiant. It has also been and continues to be an incredible adventure full of surprises, gifts and shocks – and brilliant fun.

It did not start out that way. In 1990, through a series of 'bad' decisions in the space of two cataclysmic months, I lost most of my money and my marriage of 25 years. Up until then I had had a very normal life. I had had a secure and happy childhood and had been married with two children and a husband who rarely refused me anything. I had dabbled in antiques, qualified as India's first woman gemmologist and travelled the world, as my husband was an airline pilot. I had also invested quite successfully in property in the UK and made some money. At that point in my life what I wanted was £1,000,000 in my bank account, amongst other things. And, quite self-satisfied and very wilful, I got pretty much whatever I wanted.

From this 'happy' position I was plunged without warning into a hellish place where I did not know the rules. Losing everything was a monumental shock to the system. In the beginning there was a non-realization and a non-acceptance that it had happened – that the money was really, truly and irrevocably lost, that there was no way of getting it back from the man I had so trustingly and foolishly given it to, a man who had promised to make me richer than I had ever dreamed of. All my dear friends and my family had been able to see it happening, but had not been able to do anything to stop me in my madness. It really was a clear case of 'Whom the gods wish to destroy they first make mad.'

I was finally hit with the realization that I was not going to get my money back, that not only was I not going to be rich but I was going to be poor and that though I knew how to dabble in various activities, I did not know how to earn a living. By this time I had also divorced my husband. This had been done in an amicable way and we still considered ourselves friends. So I found myself in a foreign country with no support system and no one to rescue me. I was plunged into a terrifying and unfamiliar space. I became acquainted with fear and the paralysis that accompanies it, with despair, desperation, hopelessness, grief, sadness, guilt and regret thrown in for good measure, and for the first time a total loss of self-esteem. All the doors had been shut firmly in my face. Everything I had valued had turned to ashes. There was nowhere to go and no one to turn to. No money, no marriage, no viable options for earning a reasonable living. The dark night of the soul had begun. The turning point of my life had arrived.

Six months of total depression and dysfunction followed. I had lost it. My routine was to wake up in the morning, have a shower and go downstairs and sit in front of the telly the whole day. The telly was my only tenuous connection to life. It also anaesthetized the pain of being present in my life. It made the day pass until I could fall asleep fitfully again and wake again, with terror, hopelessness and despair, to repeat the cycle. I did not want to see, meet or talk to anyone. The only sane decision I made was not to resort to drugs or drink to dull the pain and not increase my smoking from the four cigarettes a day that I had smoked for years. In my twenties I had studied for eight years to be a psychoanalyst and the insights painfully gained so long ago now stood me in good stead. I remember my analyst telling me that it was OK to be depressed and that it would pass.

After six months of this hellish limbo existence, I had had enough. Something had to give. I decided that I could not carry on the way I was and that suicide would be a peaceful way out. I even explored the ways that would be the least physically painful for me. Two considerations stopped me. One was the pain I would cause my children, who had loved and supported me, and my darling mother in India, who would have been distraught. The second was the realization that suicide was not a way out of my suffering and would afford me no relief, just a continuation of that which I wished to end. Coming from the East, I knew that reincarnation was not an abstract theory but the way it was. So the final escape hatch was closed.

At this point I truly did not know what to do. I was at sea, completely lost. I finally said, 'I need help. Please help me.' This was not said to anyone in particular, just out aloud, yet those six magical words, which six months before I would have found impossible to say, at once brought a strange sense of relief.

I started looking at options like hypnotherapy and started reading books, especially of the self-help variety. More importantly, I started getting back in touch with friends again. They had not dropped me – I had dropped them. They were pleased and relieved I was approachable again.

One of my friends gave me a book called *The Silva Mind Control Method*. I read it from cover to cover in a day and was fascinated. The book recommended some mental exercises which I started doing the very same day and carried on doing regularly. I had not practised meditation or visualization before and knew nothing of different brain states. It was all new to me. I then took the Silva Mind Control course in London and a new world opened for me. Over two weekends I learned of the power of the right brain, the alpha state and the awesome non-linear nature of reality in a very personal experiential way. That changed my view of reality forever; it was the stepping stone to a totally new and radical understanding. It opened the door to a new life that until a few months before I had not had a clue about and would probably have dismissed out of hand had someone told me of it. As a result of this open door I became acquainted with a whole new world of books, courses and self-development. It felt as though I had died and been born again. To this day I call it my second life.

And life took off after that. In 1992 I was one of the first people in the UK to start doing aura photography, which is a colloquial name for biofeedback imaging. In aura photography a colourful image is produced of a person's face and torso using various biofeedback methods and an interpretation is given of what those colours mean. The camera cost US$10,000, which was an impossible amount for me – remember I had lost nearly all my money – but my daughter took out a loan for me. This started my interest in what I call 'the technologies of consciousness'.

At the end of 1994 my son asked me what my next step would be. He said he did not think aura photography would hold me forever and believed I would be looking to expand my knowledge. I have to say he was right. I do love the new – new ideas and concepts, new technologies, new ways of expanding consciousness. I knew a bit about colour through aura photography, but though I loved music, I did not know anything about sound. I decided that would be my next area of exploration.

I spoke to some friends about it and one of them pointed me in the direction of an article in a magazine called *Kindred Spirit*. It was about a discipline called Bio-Acoustics and Signature Sound. I got the magazine and was enthralled by the article. I wanted very much to do the two-module programme that was on offer in the US and had just enough money – a few thousand dollars – to do so. However, my life was beginning to settle and did I really need to spend all that money? After some hesitation and dithering, I resolved the internal deadlock with a simple question to myself: 'If it were not for the money, Thrity, would you do it?' The answer was an unequivocal 'Yes.' I decided to go ahead and do the modules and also attend the practitioner's conference, which fortuitously was tagged on to the end of the two courses.

So in May 1995 I went to the US and did the programme. I made some lovely friends and learned some very interesting new methodologies about the therapeutic uses of low-frequency sound. It was about what they called 'vocal coherence' and it was fascinating.

Then came the conference of Bio-Acoustic Sound practitioners. The venue was a beautiful national park near Columbus in Ohio. The talks, which were attended by practitioners from all over the country, further expanded my knowledge of the power of sound, its awesome effects on the shaping of physical reality and the many levels and layers of information available in the human voice.

It was mid-morning break time. I stretched my legs, strolled around the room and found myself standing in a corner having a chat with someone. I happened to hear a nurse practitioner in a group nearby mention the words 'aura photography' and was curious to hear what was being said about it. She was talking about a man who was doing it and I asked her what sort of equipment he used. I will never forget her answer: 'He uses an ordinary camera.'

I could not believe my ears, so to make sure I asked, 'Does he use an ordinary camera with biofeedback sensors attached?'

'No, it is just an ordinary camera.'

When the implications of that answer sank in, I could feel my excitement rising. What she had described was technically 'impossible', yet she was saying it was happening. I could hardly contain my excitement as I asked her for the man's name and phone number. She said his name was Patrick Richards and that he lived in Michigan. At this point I had never been to Michigan and had only the vaguest idea of where it was on the map.

The conference ended and I went to Colorado to stay with my brother and his family for a few days before coming back to London. As soon as I reached my brother's place I rang the number I had been given, got an answer phone and left a message. The next day, while we were out, Patrick phoned back and left a message for me. My name is unusual by American standards, so he apologized if he had garbled it. I rang back and – third time lucky – we finally spoke. I told him who I was and how I had got his name and finally asked the burning question: 'Is it true that you take aura photos with an ordinary camera?'

His reply took my breath away: 'Yes, I do, but we don't use them.'

I could not believe my ears. Here was someone who could do the impossible, yet didn't even use it. The mind boggled. Very tentatively I asked, 'Well, what *do* you do?'

When he started to tell me, I could feel the hair on the back of my neck and on my arms rising. Here was this quiet, low, grave American voice telling me science fiction had been made fact. I said mildly, 'It sounds like *Star Trek*.' He laughed and said it was a bit like that.

I have to say that the very first time I spoke to him, I felt that I had come home. All that I had been searching for, though not consciously – one could poetically say the soul was searching without the personality being aware – had now been found. The search was over for this lifetime. I knew what I had incarnated for. In that one fateful phone call my life was swept away by something much bigger than I had ever dreamed of – and I would have it no other way.

We talked some more. I asked more questions, he faxed me information, I got more and more hooked. I told him how much I wanted his system. However, there was a reality check: I had no money to speak of. I had spent the last few thousand dollars in my bank account on the trip and the Bio-Acoustics course. Heart in mouth, I asked him what the system cost. He told me. I had not expected it to be a few hundred dollars and it was not. There seemed to be no way that I could raise that kind of money.

I thanked him for the information and mulled it over. I wanted to use that system with every fibre of my being. So I did something that I would never have had the nerve to do for myself. I had only spoken to this man over the phone, we had never met, and yet somehow I plucked up my courage and asked, 'If I raise a certain amount of the total, will you give me credit for the rest? I will pay you the balance over a two-year period.'

What incredible joy and relief when he said he would! I know that in similar circumstances I would probably have said no and I can never thank him enough for that initial act of trust and generosity. In that moment I knew that the system was mine, though I could not see how I could raise even the initial amount of money.

Some years later Patrick told me that he too was at a turning point in his life when I made contact. As his system had not met with any acceptance, he had asked the universe to find a home for it on another continent and specified that he wanted some connection with the East. Our meeting fulfilled both those conditions in the most unexpected way.

I came back to London and got to grips with the question of how to raise the money. At that point my credit rating was terrible and even if that had not been the case I could not very well have gone to the bank and asked for credit to buy something that I had not seen and that was new on this Earth – that did not sound like a realistic option.

I had some very wealthy friends in India, to whom the required amount would have been small change. Should I ask one of them to guarantee a loan for me? But I was not looking for a handout. I decided against it because it simply did not feel right.

I made up my mind that if it was going to happen, it would happen with ease and grace or not at all. After all, the system had found me. What were the odds of my standing in that corner of that room in Ohio at the exact moment when aura photography was being mentioned by probably one of the few people on Earth who knew of the existence of Patrick's system? There was no way on Earth I could have known of Patrick's existence, nor he of mine, yet an Intelligence far superior had connected, with absolute elegance and simplicity, an unknown engineer in Michigan to an aura photographer from India who lived in London.

As soon as I let go of the head stuff and let go of the struggle, another option appeared. I thought, 'This is much bigger than I am. I want to share it.' Whom did I want to share it with? At that time a group of us who had (with one exception) done the Silva Mind Control course used to meet weekly at my place to meditate and try out our intuition. We were a personal-development group of sorts. I had only got to know these people after my cataclysmic life events and so I had not known any of them for long, yet they had become my dearest friends. None of them was wealthy, but I decided to ask them if they wanted to participate in some way. So I phoned each of them and the conversations went like this: 'I am going to invite you for dinner and I am going to ask you for money.' I also told them it was OK to say no, our friendship would not be in jeopardy. I told them I did not want an answer that day and would not accept it until they had thought about it and were sure that it was OK. I explained as much as I knew, which wasn't much, but my enthusiasm and their regard for me were enough. Every one of them (with one exception) said yes and I had the promise of the money in 10 days. I can never thank them enough for their love and their trust. This was ease and grace as far as I was concerned.

I phoned Patrick and told him I had raised the money – not just the deposit, but the full amount. He could not believe it.

To cut a long story short, the equipment was duly paid for and arrived in London in October 1995. By that time I had also gone to Michigan for training, accompanied by my doctor daughter. The greatest adventure and the steepest learning curve of this lifetime had now truly begun.

An odd 'coincidence' was that the name of the man who had cheated me of my money was also Patrick. When I realized the significance of that, I knew the circle of healing was complete: one Patrick had 'destroyed' my life and another Patrick had given it back. Today, many years later, knowing what I do about the multi-dimensional and holographic nature of reality, I ask myself who was that man who took away my money – my bitterest enemy or my dearest friend? It is clear to me that if he had not done what he did, my life's trajectory would have been completely different. Looking back on these events, it is absolutely clear to me that the 7th sense was in action throughout in the exquisite synchronicities that occurred during the whole process.

Ten years on, what have these life-changing events and this system meant for me personally? Since 1990 I have believed in personal development, self-empowerment and self-help and have done the best I can to live by that belief. I have known that I am the creator – no, I will amend that to co-creator – of my destiny. It started with the Silva Mind Control Method and was followed by creative visualization and the learning and practice of different methods of relaxation and meditation and the use of affirmations to gain insight into myself. These all helped me to gain an understanding of how I had been responsible for precipitating the calamities that had occurred in my life. I made strides using these methods and achieved some wonderful results, practising some form of meditation or visualization every day. This in itself was a huge change from my previous lack of consistency. Getting in touch with this incredibly wise and intelligent non-linear side of myself was new and wonderful.

I was not a believer in the power of pills, potions and machines as tools for transformation and believed I could and would do it all by myself without any external help from any mechanical or material source. This belief has been turned inside out, upside down and topsy-turvy since the reality that is the Luminator came into my life. Today, with the experience and insights of hindsight, I know that no amount of meditation or visualization or number of affirmations could have given me such access to those parts of myself that I knew existed within me and such understanding and control over them. It was as if there were unseen walls barring my way forward. I did not have the keys to open those locked doors within my being. I could try sincerely, yet there was a gap that would not close – there was a vital bit of information missing. The Luminator and VRIC imaging were the connections that closed the gap between my intention and my reality.

Since then the process has deepened and intensified and has transformed me in the most profound yet gentle way. The conditioned, conditional, controlling, fear-driven aspect of the mind is now beginning to lose its fear and therefore its grip. As a result, a very different aspect is emerging. Nothing has been lost and much has been gained. I am beginning to taste freedom, and it is comfortable. There is no loss of control and descent into chaos, only the emergence of a sense of rightness. This process has taken place with blinding speed, coupled with a thoroughness and power that simply have to be experienced to be believed. I have been turned inside out, stabilized, strengthened and renewed at every level and have not had to struggle. I have simply had to get out of my own way and let the process unfold. Humans have no frames of reference for this level of reality and therefore cannot even begin to conjecture the implications and possibilities that emerge from its manifestation on Earth.

My internal landscape has also changed dramatically. I feel calm inside, my self-confidence grows, the tenderness that I always valued in others and had been unable to access readily in myself has increased dramatically and is readily perceptible in the dramatic and beneficial changes in my close relationships with my immediate family. Long-standing patterns of anger and distrust have melted away, to be replaced by a greater openness in the sharing of painful feelings, a greater ability to listen to, understand and accept the pain of others without denial, flippancy or justification, and a readiness to repair and redress if necessary. Patterns of withholding love and making it manipulative and conditional have largely been replaced by an effortless tenderness that does not diminish even when the other is unable to reciprocate in the manner one would like.

A sense of generosity has also expanded and deepened, removing the unconscious necessity of always keeping count of favours done and the accompanying expectation of an immediate return in kind. This generosity has also extended to the emotional level, resulting in the ability to whole-heartedly appreciate, acknowledge and praise others, honour their struggle, their strength and their virtues, and be able to hear them be praised without feeling less oneself.

For many years after the cataclysmic loss of my money and the struggle that ensued to set my financial life in some semblance of order, I had developed the tendency to be very careful with the meagre financial resources at my disposal. With unpaid bills accumulating and a mortgage in arrears, I who had signed cheques for £50,000 without batting an eyelid became fearful of signing a cheque for £20. It became very difficult to be generous. Everyone in my family thought I was tight-fisted, and they were right. It has taken years, yet now I have succeeded in getting my financial life in order. I treat money with respect, but it is never my first consideration. Neither is it my last. I have become comfortable around it and it has become comfortable around me. It has become much easier to be generous, as my fear has been taken away as I have come to understand and trust the nature of the flow of Intelligence which is everything, including money.

Today I have many more choices than I could ever have dreamed of and the possibility of making the choices that produce results that I can be happy with. My life has meaning and is full of passion, purpose and infinite tenderness, combined with a clarity that enables me to see the magic in everyone I meet. My life is coherent (a lot of the time) and I am grateful.

I know with absolute certainty that I could not have come into this strong and peaceful place, certainly not within this short time frame, without the use of Biolumanetics and living in the field of the Luminator.

I realize this gift was given to me to share. I could not just say thank you, put it in my pocket and walk away, as a part of me would certainly have liked to. I have come to realize this is a life task that has been assigned and it is squarely on my plate. From the moment I encountered the system in 1995 my life has been fully and freely given to it. Though the hardware was not my invention, I have developed many of the methods and protocols described in this book, the software programs, so to speak, here in London. Now I would like to share this gift with you.

ACKNOWLEDGEMENTS AND THANKS

Where do I start? My heart is full. I know words can never convey my heartfelt gratitude for the gifts that I have received.

Whom do I thank first and whom later? This list of people that I wish to acknowledge and thank is not in any special order. I want to clarify this point, as each one of them is incredibly special to me and no one is more special than the others.

I wish to acknowledge my large extended family in India, who gave me a secure and happy childhood, my darling long-suffering parents, who had to put up with my wayward and wilful ways in my younger years, especially my darling gentle mother, who is an example to me of what an ideal mother can be. I also wish to acknowledge the financial help my brother Darius and my wonderful American sister-in-law Kay gave me when I was in serious trouble in my forties. I feel truly blessed with my immediate family, my darling ex-husband Pesi, who has always been my great friend and support, my son Rustam, who was my first teacher in energy medicine, and, most of all, the daughter of my heart Meher for her incredible generosity, support, honesty and clarity. Without her financial help I could not have started on this incredible journey.

I wish to acknowledge my Swedish associate Karl Ryberg, the creator of the Monocrom light-colour dome, which I consider one of the greatest life-enhancement technologies on Earth today, apart from the Luminator. I credit him for bringing colour and light healing into the twenty-first century.

I wish to thank the special friends Lucy, Ann, Phiroza, Jiten and

Annie, who loved and trusted me enough to lend me the money to buy the Luminator. I also remember with great gratitude the dear friends Janice, Agnes, Nigel and Lorraine, who came in later as investors into 3S when none of them was particularly wealthy. Without them, 3S would not exist.

My greatest thanks go to my clients, without whom this book could not have been written. They were the pioneers who decided to try something radical and new and, by some standards, quite expensive. They came when this work had not been written about or endorsed by authorities and experts. I offer them my deepest heartfelt gratitude for making this adventure happen. My most special thanks go to those clients who gave me permission to use their photographs for having the courage to expose their vulnerabilities, to enable you, the reader, to see the possibilities.

I thank my agent, the exceptional and extraordinary Marianne Gunn O'Connor, for being who she is and for her unstinting generosity, phenomenal ability and willingness to do whatever it takes with passion, enthusiasm and commitment, coupled with the tenderness that she extends to all her clients – a winning combination of the head and the heart. I honestly do not think this book would have seen the light of day without her unshakeable belief in the work and her commitment to getting the book out despite many setbacks and rejections.

Knowing the extraordinary nature of this process and the radical nature of the information in this book, I knew it would have its own unique journey. It is a book that does not easily fit a genre and it needed someone extraordinary in the publishing world to recognize its merit and act on it. It needed someone to fall in love with it. I had to wait for that special someone for a few years. Michelle Pilley from Hay House was that exceptional person. The moment she came to see me to experience the process, I knew she was the right one. She understood the process and its extraordinary nature, did not try and fit it into an old box and did fall in love with it. I knew the system had found the passionate advocate it needed and I felt I had come home when Michelle welcomed me into the Hay House family, which I feel privileged to be part of. Michelle also did me a great service when she assigned Lizzie Hutchins to be my editor. I really thank Lizzie for dealing with an unusual subject with exquisite understanding and consummate skill. The book is definitely better thanks to her work. It has been a joy to work with the UK team at Hay House, and I want to thank Jo Lal, Joanna Lincoln, Leanne Siu Anastasi, Jo Burgess and Megan Slyfield, the wonderful women I have been in contact with for this work. I also appreciate greatly the sensibility of Peter O'Dwyer, who designed the cover, which I love. He has succeeded in capturing the essence of what this book is about in visual terms.

A special word of thanks goes to my friend Elizabeth Best, who kept the thousands of VRIC images filed and in some semblance of order for many years.

INTRODUCTION

'The only thing that is permanent,' as the saying runs, 'is change.' That is very true today. Do you know we are living in exponential times? Even if you are not consciously aware of it, you have probably felt it. They say that new technical information is doubling every two years and it is predicted to double every 72 hours by 2010. One week's worth of information in the *New York Times* is more than a person was likely to come across in a lifetime in the eighteenth century. The amount of new information generated this year is estimated to be more than in the previous 5,000. There are 2.7 billion searches on Google each month. The top 10 jobs that will be in demand in 2010 did not exist in 2004. A person is likely to have had 10 to 18 jobs by the age of 38. On and on it goes – crazy, unbelievable, inexorable...

Ever since we entered the information age the rate of change has accelerated exponentially. Just a few years ago, before the advent of email, it took several days for a letter to reach its destination. Today we can reach any number of people across the globe instantly by just hitting a button on a computer. The times we live in are both exciting and exhilarating and challenging and exhausting. Nothing seems safe – what worked the day before yesterday does not work today and what was safe yesterday is destroyed today before our alarmed and uncomprehending gaze. Nothing and no one seems to be spared. Loyal and long service mean nothing today when it comes to job security and all of us feel the reverberations through the rise and fall of shares and the unpredictable goings-on in stock markets the world over. On a personal level, the rules of engagement between men and women are being drastically redefined and the stereotypical role-playing between the sexes is being seen as nonsensical and unacceptable. The patriarchal system that has held sway for millennia is in the process of a huge shift. In the workplace, too, the old authoritarian ways of fear, force and control are seen to be not only ineffective but counterproductive. Adrift in a changing world, we run from pillar to post, finding it harder and harder to keep still. Time is the commodity that is in scarce supply and most demand. Where are we going? What is our life about? What is the measure of whether it makes sense to us?

All of this takes its toll. Stress is the number-one killer today. Studies at the CDC (Center for Disease Prevention and Control) and the Stanford Medical School reveal the startling finding that stress is the cause of 80 per cent (CDC) to 95 per cent (Stanford Medical School) of all disease, no matter what the label attached to the presenting symptoms. Despite all the advances in technology, young and old today are stressed as never before, with burn-out, poor lame-duck performance and downright physical and mental illness. Information overload, a polluted food chain, unhealthy electromagnetic work and home environments and non-nourishing lifestyles do not help either. Ask yourself this question: as the rate of change speeds up, will stress levels rise or fall?

When the system is stressed, neither eating organic food nor taking super-vitamins nor working out at the gym will do you much good. No diet is going do it for you either. It may interest you to know that when the system is stressed, it cannot digest or assimilate food properly. It does not matter, therefore, whether the food you eat is organic super-food or not. Also, doing physical exercise when the system is stressed may result in an injury.

There is an uneasy knowing gaining ground that despite all the phenomenal technological advances of the twentieth century, things are not as they should be. There is an increasing awareness that we are in a crisis of unprecedented proportions. The old ways and quick fixes are seen not to work, but new ways have not yet emerged.

In the book *Presence*, published by SOL (Society of Organizational Learning, an outgrowth from the MIT's School of Organizational Learning), Alok Singh, a member of the global youth network Pioneers of Change, says, 'Our systems are failing, and their failures are coming to the surface: they do not serve people. The current crisis will not go away because we are just operating on the symptoms.'

Otto Schwarmer, one of the co-authors of *Presence*, says:

'This experience of the entire system as dying applies not only to health care but also to education, agriculture and government. People say that there are simply no high leverage strategies that will make any difference as long as we continue to avoid integrative approaches that involve all these areas. When I said I expected our current systems to hit the wall sometime within the next decade, almost no one agreed with me. Many said the system would crash much earlier, and some said that it was not going to happen in the future because it was already happening now.'

Can science help us out of this quagmire? Today we live in an age of great scientific and technological advance. We know more about the universe than at any time in the last several hundred, maybe several thousand years. Science seems to have discovered the very laws that govern it – gravity, electromagnetism, the field theory, quantum theory, relativity theory and the more exciting and interesting chaos and complexity theory, the string theory and the elegant multi-dimensional universe theory. But something seems to be missing – a vital X factor. There is no mainstream area of science that attempts to understand the whole human and what makes it tick. All the exploration has been of the external physical universe, while the 'internal' universe of the thinking, feeling, spiritual human has been *terra incognita*. How strange it seems that mainstream science seeks to understand the laws that govern the universe and makes no attempt to understand the one who is asking the question. How can one understand anything in reality without an understanding of the self?

Since the days of Galileo, Descartes and Newton, mathematical, logical, linear and now statistical proof has been needed to draw any 'scientific' conclusions that can be held as 'valid'. So science can observe, postulate and hypothesize, but cannot do the one thing that all humans do, in every act: assign a qualitative value of good, bad, enjoyable or not, as the case may be, to something in the context of their life. What, therefore, is the worth of this limited 'scientific' 'truth' and 'objectivity'? Ethics and love, two extremely important qualities valued by humans, including I daresay scientists, simply do not figure in the equation.

The fatal flaw is that science does not understand emotion and factor it into its model. Emotion is completely unpredictable and personal and is anathema to the scientific model of reality because of its subjective nature. But in making the linear intellect our god of gods and our final arbiter of truth, we lose something we all had as children – a sense of wonder and magic.

This story is about one of the most extraordinary technological breakthroughs in human history and it brings the magic back into science. With the advent of this new 'artful science', it is possible to explore the internal landscape of the feeling human with more precision than with the greatest measuring tools of twentieth-century linear science. It has an exquisite rigour and offers us 'objective' proof of the truth of our deep-feeling self. It gives us the possibility of *living* in truth. It gives us an unprecedented window into the deepest aspects of the self and it is a science where values are held paramount.

This new science, or rather what I would call a 'life discipline', turns the old limited reductionist science of the third dimension on its head and reveals how feelings, thoughts, emotions, attitudes, conscious awareness and the soul's journeys are the main factors that shape personal human reality as it relates to health, wealth and happiness. It is evidence-based, yet paradoxically it makes the linear intellect understand in the most unequivocal and irrefutable manner that it cannot be understood in simple linear terms. No technical gibberish, no fancy mathematics and no fancy statistics are necessary to prevent 'ordinary' humans from recognizing the truth about themselves.

If I ask myself what are the most important aspects of this science, I come to realize it is about two things: it is about truth and it is about love. And I will add a third: it is about pure authentic magic.

At one level, of course, there is no such thing as magic, only laws of reality that we do not yet understand. A hundred and fifty years ago, if someone had foretold of aeroplanes and rockets and space travel, of phones and mobile phones, they would have been laughed out of existence or burnt at the stake for being possessed by the devil. If 30 years ago someone had told you that you could put a phone to your ear with no wires and could talk to a friend on another continent also holding a phone with no wires, what would your response have been? Would you have said 'Wow!' or 'Impossible!'? Let us say that you were smart enough to have had the 'Wow!' response instead of the other one. But now let us up the ante a bit. Imagine you were living in the wilds of the Amazon rain forest the same 30 years back and had never been to a city or seen a phone of any sort. What would your response have been then? You would have said a mobile phone was magic, would you not?

Today, if you are not a believer in the extraordinary nature of reality, the claims that I will make may seem over-the-top and outrageous to you. But reality – and that includes your personal reality – is far more wondrous than anything you have ever dreamed of. Put another way, reality is not reasonable or mundane. It does not have to be. The possibilities that exist for you as a human are truly unlimited.

Any truly radical, new and revolutionary ideas will meet with resistance, of course. And it is one thing to enjoy magic in fiction and be thrilled by it – it is a pleasant escape – and quite another to find it applies to your body, your mind, your health, wealth and happiness. If I were to tell you that you were magic, mystery and miracle rolled into one, that you were a being of light wondrous beyond measure, what would your response be?

It might sound wonderful, but for millennia humans have resisted change and hung on to the *status quo ante* with as much force as they could muster. Ask yourself why most pioneers have a rough time. The more extraordinary and radical their work, the fiercer the criticism they face from their peers and contemporaries. People simply do not like change. To you, the reader, a question: How do you respond to change?

One thing is for sure: the rate of change we are seeing today is not going to abate. In fact, in my view we are seeing the culmination of great cycles and the Earth is in what is called a 'phase shift' in chaos theory. A phase shift is a change of mega proportions – when water changes to vapour or to ice, for example. What emerges is radically different from what existed before the shift. The forms seem to bear no resemblance to each other, but are nevertheless the result of totally lawful processes that are super-intelligent.

So you may well soon find the rules of success, safety and happiness have changed forever. Just being good by the old standards and keeping your head down will not be enough. Fighting and resisting will be equally futile. When the winds of change reach gale force, it will be too late to start learning new tricks. You will realize that you are on your own. There will be no one to consult or to blame – no guru, no teacher, no doctor and no expert. The wheel will have turned full circle and the power and the responsibility will be squarely back where they belong – with you.

Exhilarating, exciting and/or terrifying, it does not matter, it is round the corner – no, it is already here. Are you ready and able to handle what the universe has in store for you?

The system you will encounter in this book has the same quality of the impossible or the impossibly wonderful (take your pick) as the mobile phone would have done to a person in the Amazon rain forest 30 years ago. But looked at in the old way, this book will offer you no consolation. It is not written by a PhD or doctor of medicine. Neither is it written by an 'expert' or team of experts from Yale, Harvard, Princeton, MIT, UCLA, Oxford or Cambridge or any other great institution of learning. So you will not be able to fall back on any of your old assumptions or give away your power to experts because you mistakenly assume that they know much more than you do. In the past I have trusted financial experts and medical experts and found that they did not know as much as I thought. They were not incompetent or uncaring and yet the results did not meet their promises and rosy projections, or my expectations.

The age of self-responsibility and self-accountability has dawned and there is no escape and no excuse for anyone. One can rail, rant and rave at the powers that be, it will help not one whit. Without talking gloom and doom, the times that are coming are going to be more challenging and full of surprises than we can possibly imagine. And the skills and tools we will need for these testing, trying, troubled times of great opportunity will be radically different from anything generally known today.

Yet those tools are already here now. We all have an instrument with which to understand the universe: our unique bodymind. Our success and happiness depend on the extent and quality of that understanding. The bad news is that 99.99 per cent of us know and use less than 5 per cent of our capabilities and capacities, with the resulting consequences. The good news is that there are resources hidden within us that are far greater than we can imagine.

Supercoherence is in my view the discovery of a 7th sense that we have always had but have not had access to in any objective, systematic way. It holds the key to self-knowledge and super function that lie beyond the distortions of personal perception and it has a quality of truth that is simply unobtainable in any other manner, for now, on Earth.

Finding the Way

I have reflected and asked myself, 'Why am I writing this book and whom am I writing it for? Who is going to read it? Who will understand and appreciate it?'

After putting myself through this useful-useless exercise in the analysis-paralysis mode for a short while, I found the answers, when they came, were simple: it would go where it was needed and be read by whoever read it and it would always be perfect and right. I was not in charge or in control of the universe, something much more intelligent than I ever could be at the linear rational level was in total control, and I could rest easy in that understanding. I did not and could not know who was going to read, understand or appreciate the book, but I need not worry. That would unfold as, how and when it did.

My only real desire was that I wanted it to be understood by anyone and everyone who could read and not to contain any equations, technical jargon or 'technical gibberish', as my great associate Patrick Richards calls it. I know how ignorant I feel when I read a computer magazine. Like a lot of people, I also find technical stuff sometimes tedious and boring. Instead I wanted to use the language of the heart-full mind and the mindful heart. Eventually I realized I would just write my way – there was really no other way for it to be authentic.

When this book is complete and out there in the world, then my job is done, at one level. Let the chips fall where they may.

On another note, this book is not filled with scientific references, footnotes and addenda, impressive though they might appear. The chapter on the research and exploration that I undertook will help those who wish to explore various aspects in greater detail, but essentially I have attempted to stay within my personal experience and the insights that I have gained as a result of my direct involvement with my work, which is outlined in the main body of this book. As such I take full responsibility for any and all opinions that are expressed in it.

A very important point to clarify is that many of the case studies in this book talk about the 'diseases' and 'dysfunctions' that clients come labelled with. However, this system does not either 'diagnose' 'disease' and 'dysfunction' or make claim to effect miracle 'cures'. If you want to be 'diagnosed' and 'cured' you should see a medical doctor or other practitioner. The case studies used in this book simply serve to illustrate the point that re-establishing coherence can and often does give the body-mind the opportunity and the energetic wherewithal to restore health, vitality and much more.

On another level, when I see the extreme simplicity of the system and its profound implications for humanity, I cannot fail to realize that there is an extreme Intelligence that had a conscious intention when it enabled the creation of the Luminator and VRIC imaging through the agency of Patrick Richards. It becomes more and more obvious to me that this exquisitely simple, infinitely complex tool is for the 'ordinary' human. Its truth can be experienced by anyone if they simply participate through their desire and their intention. The great truths of the wisdom traditions have been made available, just for the asking, to 'ordinary' suffering humanity in a gesture of exquisite generosity and mercy. In writing this book I wish to honour, as best I am able, the central intention of that Intelligence in making truth, authenticity and harmony available to all who seek them in the most direct, objective and personal way that has been possible in living memory.

In many wisdom traditions there is the concept of having known perfection and lost it. There is the fall from grace, Adam and Eve's ejection from the garden of Eden in the Western tradition, the concept of Sat Yug (a golden age) and Kali Yug in the Indian wisdom tradition, and Sukhavati, the pure land of the Buddhist and the Samurai. Somehow many of us, in some deep part of ourselves, know this heaven, remember this state of being and long for it. We look for it in a myriad different ways on this Earth plane, most of them unsuccessful. We have been in the cycle of suffering for millennia and know it, and yet do not know the way back to that place of pure happiness.

Thirty degrees off Earth magnetic there is a parallel universe. It is a universe that has probably always been there, but has not been seen and therefore known to us. It lies outside the boundaries of the five-sensory reality, yet now, for the first time since our fall from grace, it has become visible to the five-sensory reality. In my view this is a momentous event and heralds the changing of an epoch – a paradigm shift of unimaginable magnitude. This work is about my exploration of this mysterious universe, It has started yielding its secrets and it may guide us back to what we have lost: ourselves.

LIFE IS LIGHT

'What we call real is made of things that cannot
be called real.'
Niels Bohr, quantum theorist

'The universe is not only stranger than we imagine,
it is stranger than we can imagine.'
Arthur Eddington, astronomer and physicist

'As far as the laws of mathematics refer to reality,
they are not certain, and as far as they are certain,
they do not refer to reality.'
Albert Einstein

CHAPTER 1

WHAT IS COHERENCE?

WHY IS IT IMPORTANT?

The most important concept of this book can be encapsulated in one word: 'coherence'. It is important to understand this with some clarity. 'Coherence' is not a word most of us use very often. If asked to define it, many of us would have some difficulty in doing so adequately. Even the *Oxford English Dictionary* does not do a very good job of it, defining it as follows:

> *'Coherence: 1) the ability to speak intelligibly and articulately,*
> *2) of logical and consistent, easily followed argument,*
> *3) of cohering or sticking together.*
> *4) In physics it means having a constant phase relationship.'*

I had not thought much about this word myself before my radical life shift took place. Today, many years later, it is a word I use many times a day and think about even more.

In the simplest terms coherence is the opposite of chaos or confusion. Politicians and businesspeople alike talk of a 'coherent strategy'. For a concept or plan to be coherent, it has to make sense, to hang together. Coherence is a form of recognizable order, a harmonious mixture of seemingly unconnected factors coming together and working together to produce a pleasing result.

Coherence is also the invisible force that holds the universe together. It has the quality of intelligence, harmony and order, yet mostly it cannot be quantified. It is the quality of coherence that makes each cell in our body do what it is supposed to do, rather than something else. When our bodies and/or our lives descend into chaos or illness, the quality of coherence is lost; some part of our bodymind is troubling us, not behaving as it should and causing us discomfort, be it emotional or physical, or more likely both.

Up until now there has not been a way to assess this quality of coherence or measure it in an acceptable manner. It does, however, become specific, precise and measurable when it comes to the phenomenon we call light. In 1960 there was a momentous event for humans when the laser was invented, a new facet of the awesome nature of light was revealed and a new set of possibilities unfolded as a result.

The Laser and the Light Bulb

Most of us have heard of laser light. It has two properties that make it different from normal light, be it sunlight or the artificial light we have in our homes: laser light is coherent and monochromatic. Normal light is incoherent and polychromatic.

For now we need not concern ourselves with the monochromatic/polychromatic quality of light but can stay with the difference between coherent and incoherent light. Incoherent light is light moving in countless different directions – it is omni-directional. In technical terms it is unpolarized and out of phase. In one sense incoherent light is unordered or unorganized light. The light on Earth, for as long as we have known it, has been incoherent. With the invention of the laser, however, it was found that light could acquire completely different characteristics and behave completely differently. When the vibrations of light were polarized and in phase, light became coherent (*see Figure 1 on next page*). 'Polarized' means uni-directional and 'in phase' means that the peaks and the troughs of the electromagnetic wave match exactly. This characteristic of light was unknown until the laser was discovered.

In my view, at this juncture what we do not know about the phenomenon called light far exceeds what we do know. However, let us see what happens when light is organized. A normal 100-watt light bulb (incoherent light) can light a small room, whereas a powerful laser can put a spot of light on the moon. A hundred watts of coherent laser light can cut through steel and do all kinds of other incredible things that cannot be done with incoherent light. Apparently a 1-milliwatt (one thousandth of a watt) laser is 1,000,000 times brighter than a 100–watt light bulb. Laser light also has the quality of extreme precision, as the laser effect can only happen when each photon is in exact lockstep or alignment with the other photons.

The key point here is that the same amount of light energy, differently organized, has totally different capabilities and gives an exponentially different result.

Light and Life

In both the ancient esoteric traditions and modern quantum physics there is general acceptance of the fact that all life is simply a modification of light. In fact, light is the irreducible substance of all phenomena. David Bohm, the great physicist-philosopher, says, 'All matter is frozen light.' Richard Feynman, the Nobel Prize-winning physicist, concurs that all physical phenomena occur as a result of the interactions between photons and electrons (the smallest 'particles' of light and energy). Georg Feuerstein, the renowned yoga teacher, says, 'We have not yet assimilated this century's most far-reaching discovery; namely that energy or light is

Figure 1: From a 100-watt light bulb to a 100-watt laser – the power of coherence!

Incoherent light	Coherent light
(Light on Earth)	(Light in the field of the Luminator)
Light that is omni-multi directional – moving in countless different directions – is called incoherent.	Light that is polarized (uni-directional) and in phase (where the peaks and troughs of the electromagnetic wave match exactly) is called coherent.
Incoherent light is unorganized or disordered light.	Coherent light is organized or ordered light.
Incoherent light is unfocused.	Coherent light is focused.
An incandescent (ordinary) light bulb is an example of incoherent light.	Lasers are examples of coherent light.
A 100-watt light bulb will light an average room.	A 100-watt laser will cut through steel.
The same amount of light differently organised gives an exponentially different result	

the principle underlying all manifestation. In other words we have not yet grasped that we, our bodies and our minds, are light.' Parmahansa Yogananda, the great Indian mystic, affirms that 'If our senses conveyed the whole truth to us, we would see the earth as rivers and glaciers of electrons, each speck of dust as a rolling mass of light.' For me, the greatest and probably the best-known physicist of the last century, Albert Einstein, really put this insight on the map when he discovered that matter and energy were the same with his famous equation of $e=mc^2$.

It is necessary to have a minimal understanding and acceptance of this very important point in order to understand the concepts we will shortly be exploring. Quite simply, light is the source 'material' from which we are made and is the fundamental level of expression of life in all its myriad forms.

In the 1920s Alexander Gurwitsch, a Russian scientist, discovered that biological life actually emitted light. Subsequently several scientists in various countries confirmed this discovery, especially after the Second World War, when photon multipliers became available. These devices enable the measurement of very small quantities of light. These cell or biological light emissions are termed 'bio-photons' and their study is termed 'bio-photon research'.

The next exciting and significant insight came in the 1970s. This brought together the concepts of light, coherence and energy as they applied to humans and specifically human health. A German biophysicist called Fritz-Albert Popp sought to prove that not only did cells emit light and communicate with each other via that light but, even more importantly, he discovered that the coherence of the light emission was a significant factor in assessing the vitality of the lifeform. The greater the coherence of the photon emission, the greater the vitality. Coherent light and vitality were intimately and inextricably interlinked. If one was changed or affected, the other would follow suit. So it would follow that loss of coherence could lead to disease or disorder. Conversely, it makes sense that an increase in coherence could lead to health, vitality and the establishment of order in the energy system at the most fundamental level of expression. If we go back to the example of the 100-watt light bulb and the

100-watt laser and recreate the effect for the human, what possibilities would emerge for health, vitality and much more? What would this coherent human-energy laser be capable of?

Why, you may ask, has it not been done? What is holding us back from gaining this phenomenal increase in energy, vitality and orderly function? As you may guess, this exciting potentiality is not so easy to actualize in reality. Popp's insights were gained in controlled conditions (a very dark room) in a laboratory using cells, cucumber seedlings, fruit flies and a photon multiplier. Popp says that the weak radiation, or UPE (ultra-low photon emission), emitted is the equivalent of seeing a candle at 10 kilometres. What do you think the chances are of seeing a candle at 10 kilometres, let alone assessing whether the light signal from that candle is coherent or incoherent? Not a lot. Popp also makes it clear that it is not possible to assess the coherence or otherwise of complex living systems.

So, I hear you ask, why are you telling me about these incredible possibilities and then telling me it cannot be done? Am I leading you up the garden path, or more accurately a dead end? It may all be good theory, but what if it can only be applied in the next 100 years? What good is it to me right now?

Fortunately we do not have to wait 100 years, and our road leads not to a dead end but to a new beginning and to opportunities for health, happiness and success that we have not even dreamed of. This book is about the invention of a technology so utterly extraordinary that its like has not existed on this Earth plane in living memory. This ground-breaking technology has led to the creation of an entire new model of understanding, a whole new system of assessment, and applications for the enhancement of human function based on the very principles we have been exploring: light, energy and coherence. As a result of this technology, for the first time in history we have been granted access to the quantum dimension through the five-sensory reality. Please reflect for a moment on the magnitude and the implications of this event. We can now actually see that energetic reality and see for ourselves that we are truly Photo sapiens, beings of light. The science of Einstein and Popp and the principles of ancient mysticism have come together and come magically alive in the parallel universe of the Luminator.

CHAPTER 2

THE FREQUENCY UNIVERSE
LIGHT-ENERGY-INFORMATION

The frequency universe is an extremely strange place and operates by even stranger rules. The physical world that we experience through our five senses and the rules that govern this world, or rather this material dimension, make no sense in this other invisible energy-information realm and have to be completely put to one side. High and low, soft and hard, pretty and ugly, big and small, old and new – all the distinctions and definitions that are completely accurate and appropriate in this world, all the measures and measuring instruments that we use to live our everyday lives in the physical reality, become disconcertingly redundant and irrelevant when trying to understand the frequency universe and the rules which govern it. You and I understand the words 'high' and 'low', for example, and we know that Mount Everest is the tallest mountain on Earth and 29,000 feet plus is higher than 2 feet, but at the frequency level there is no distinction, only vibration.

This vibration is neither random nor meaningless just because it is invisible. This nano and sub-nano domain is the reality that underpins the solid physical reality of the five senses and holds it together. It is a world of the very small – a nano metre is one billionth of a metre. Let us examine what happens in this world of the super small.

This is from a *Computer Shopper* magazine of 2003:

'Scientists at the University of Oklahoma have come up with an intriguing method of storing information at densities previously considered impossible.

The team has shown that the 19 hydrogen atoms of a single organic molecule can be used to store 1024 bits of information. The data is stored at sub-atomic level by manipulating a property of single protons that form the heart of each hydrogen atom. What the research team has managed to prove is that data can be successfully stored and retrieved from a system at the sub-atomic level. If you were to try to store the entire contents of the Encyclopaedia Britannica *using such a system the space that would be required for the number of molecules used would fit comfortably into a grain of sand.'*

How small is a grain of sand and how many volumes is the Encyclopaedia Britannica? Which is big and which is small? Reality has been turned topsy-turvy and language fails us when we try to understand the indescribable nature of this other reality. Do you begin to comprehend the awesome power that is available in this unseen realm of the super small?

This realm is composed of light, energy and information, which do not operate separately but are inextricably intertwined, which means that light is energy and is also information. Imagine the many volumes of the *Encyclopaedia Britannica* reduced to a couple of CDRoms, which, as you know, involves laser technology – the world of light, energy and information again. Today this is commonplace, but a few years ago it would have sounded as impossible as the previous example.

On a more down-to-earth level in nature this power is apparent quite readily. Think of a mighty oak tree with a little acorn lying in its shade. That little acorn contains within it the power to become that mighty oak.

Looking at it or cutting it up into tiny bits does not give you a clue to the awesome power hidden within it. Putting it under a microscope would never reveal an oak tree.

To take another example, how do a sperm and an egg coming together create a human baby containing trillions of cells in just a few months? From two to trillions – that is efficient energy management. You cannot see, smell, hear or access this level of unseen intelligence but only experience its potent force in the incredible end result.

I love flowers and their scents. I use essential oils for massage and other uses. To extract an ounce of essential oil, one has to crush many pounds' weight of flowers. A lot of flowers, a lot of input, results in a small output. Of course the oil is concentrated and much stronger than the scent of a single flower, so it makes sense. That is the reality of energy consumption at the physical level. So if I were to tell you that it took just one flower to make an almost unlimited amount of a flower *essence*, it would seem that the rules of energy consumption had been turned upside down. It would sound incredible, but it is the truth. You cannot taste or smell flower essences, nor can you see them as anything other than the water in which the 'energy signature' of the flower is carried, but they are far more potent than essential oils. This has been evidenced on innumerable occasions using the new system that is explored in this book.

Many people are using flower essences today, but in general we have very little understanding of how to harness the vast hidden power of the frequency universe. We confine ourselves to the physical level accessible to the five-sensory reality and this limited view is the main reason why we have been unable to explore and use this potentially unlimited resource. This blinkered view has led to a huge and heedless misuse of the physical, finite resources of the Earth, which has resulted in the despoiling of the environment. Carrying on the way we are, we are reducing the trillions to two. We are heading in the wrong direction.

So often we assign value to having more and more material things and admire and aspire to physical beauty and brawn. Our heroes and heroines are sportsmen and women or film heroes who subdue everyone and everything with their physical might. There is nothing particularly heinous about these things, except that there is no acknowledgement of the far more potent forces that also reside within each of us. To ascribe importance only to the dense, gross and very real physical level leads to an unintelligent mindset resulting in unintelligent behaviour, where the essence of who we are is unrealized and a huge, potent and precious resource is left untapped.

Take the Empire State Building, Buckingham Palace, the Taj Mahal or St Paul's cathedral – solid, spectacular and impressive, each in their own way, and very real. Yet they could not exist without a plan. That plan was created by a person, who conceived it in the mind, at the level of thought. Which is more real and more potent, the invisible thought or the solid and so very impressive structure that came as a result? Where is the power?

Taken a step further, what does a thought weigh? How many atoms make up a thought? Is a thought real and can you prove that it exists?

Quantum theory tells us that once we approach the atomic scale our common-sense view of reality fails us. Things we'd describe as impossible suddenly become possible. Sub-atomic particles can, under certain circumstances, be in two states or two places at once. Quantum mechanical tunnelling is similarly weird. The theory states that if something is small enough and moving fast enough, it can pass through a solid barrier. And that isn't by making a hole in it, as a bullet might pass through a sheet of paper – it will appear on the other side of the barrier while the barrier remains intact.

As the rules that seem to govern the physical universe seem to dissolve before our eyes, the mind boggles at the magnitude of the reality that it is faced with. It has to understand in real terms that this other reality is, if you like, more real, more fundamental and further up the chain of causality than the so-solid reality perceived by the five senses. How does it work?

The Law of Resonance

The frequency universe operates according to the law of resonance, also called the law of attraction. Resonance is an energetic phenomenon. It is nature's way of efficient energy exchange. It is a seamless, effortless, totally precise and exact process. It can be demonstrated quite simply with two tuning forks that are tuned to the same frequency. If one strikes or resonates the first tuning fork, it will start to 'sing' or emit a sound. Almost immediately the second tuning fork will also start to sing, even though it is not touching the first one. Another tuning fork, if tuned to another frequency, will be inert and will not respond.

The law of resonance precedes, supersedes, overrides and subsumes the laws of the gross, physical, seemingly solid universe we appear to live in and have to make sense of. It is in fact a governing law.

Resonance connects the inner and the outer reality. It is how the inner you communicates with the outer world. At the frequency level there is actually no inner and no outer, only resonance – an exchange of information. This is where the world of the very large – the galaxies – and the world of the very small – the atomic, sub-atomic, info realm – meet, connect and interact. Though they appear to be impossibly different and totally unconnected, they are in fact the same, a flow of information rather than anything else. This may seem incomprehensible, but it is so.

However, it is not quite as simple as that. If it were, life would be seamless, effortless and effective. Is your life simple, seamless, effortless and effective? How do you resonate with the universe and how does the universe resonate with you?

15

In the case of the tuning fork it is relatively simple to understand. Frequency is measured in scientific terms in Hertz accompanied by a number. So 640 Hz means it resonates at 640 cycles per second. It is possible to measure and/or calculate the frequency of any substance that exists at the physical level in mathematical terms and therefore define it in frequency terms. The frequency at which the substance or element resonates is called its 'resonant frequency' and it has an 'energy signature' that differentiates and defines it from everything else.

However, if we take a step further, the picture gets far more complex (other words for 'complex' are 'confusing', 'confounding', 'contradictory' and 'non-linear'!) than it was using the analogy of the tuning fork. When two frequencies combine, an energy-information exchange takes place and the result is called a 'harmonic frequency'. This will have completely different characteristics and bear no resemblance to its two constituent frequencies.

The Extraordinary Human Bodymind

Let us venture further down the rabbit hole. Everything resonates – thoughts have a resonance, feelings have a resonance, memories have a resonance. How can these be measured in mathematical terms? You cannot see your thoughts in the five-sensory reality, but you know that you think, you know that you feel and you know that every thought and feeling has a direct and global effect on the physical level, right down to the cellular level, as the book *The Molecules of Emotion* by Candace Pert clearly demonstrates. Can you start to imagine the level of complexity of this realm and its constant interaction with the physical realm of the body? Each of us is a frequency universe and has a unique resonant frequency and energy signature, but because our 'internal' universe is always interacting with the 'external' universe, our frequency is always fluctuating.

In my view, assessing this level of complexity has been beyond the remit of mathematics or science as we know it, until now. But now we have the tools to start to get sense and meaning out of this infinite, dynamic flowing process, this ocean of information that is a human being.

The numbers are staggering. Science tells us that the human body comprises around 50 trillion cells. That is the number 5 followed by 14 zeros. Each of those 50 trillion cells has hundreds of thousands of molecules (they say that there are more molecules in one human body than there are stars in the sky), and each of those molecules contains innumerable atoms. Each atom itself contains electrons and protons and even smaller units, including probably some not yet discovered.

The even more amazing, incredible fact is that though the body seems solid and stable and your hands and your legs and your eyes and your ears remain in the same place as they were yesterday and the day before and the day before that and if you look in the mirror you will recognize your face, this seeming stability and solidity is neither really stable nor solid at the energetic level which underpins it. If you think about it, you look in the mirror every day and see yourself every day. If you are 40 years old, go and take a look a photo of yourself at 15 or 20 and you will see just how much you have changed. But you did not see the process of this dramatic change as it happened to you moment by changing moment. When and how did you 'morph' from your 20-year-old self to your 40-year-old self? Would you recognize your 20-year-old self if you saw yourself walking down the road? I am not sure.

Whatever our age, we are in flux. Each of our cells, molecules, atoms, electrons and so on is in constant movement. They vibrate, oscillate and exchange information continuously and keep the vast interconnected and infinitely complex network that is the bodymind functioning intelligently. In effect they talk to each other continuously, communicating, co-operating and collaborating in a way that a mere six billion humans on Earth seem incapable of doing. Do you begin to understand that you are a bundle of infinity?

The system presented in this book is an exploration of this super-powerful, super-small reality as it applies to us. It gives us the possibility of harnessing this super energy to enhance our lives.

CHAPTER 3

PEERS AND PIONEERS
RESEARCH AND EXPLORATION

When I began to write this book, I decided that I needed to know a bit more about what was going on in the field in which I worked, so that I was writing from a reasonably informed perspective, even though I did not understand mathematics or physics or other sciences in any depth. I wanted to find out who the other people working in the field were, what they had achieved and whether there was any other modality or discipline that could do what we did.

I used the Internet as my medium for exploration, coupled with books. My reasoning was that most of the people I wanted to find out about would have their latest information on the Web. I also explored the different computer modalities for vibrational medicine and found about other approaches to using light for healing. This chapter is about that exploration and the understanding I gained as a result. As mentioned earlier, I do not like footnotes and addenda, so this will also serve readers who wish to explore my line of thinking further. It is in no way comprehensive, and I find as a result that I am a little better informed and a little less ignorant.

The World of Books

I have loved reading since early childhood and when I was catapulted into my 'second life', I did a fair bit of reading in the personal-development genre. Then I discovered the works of Dr Deepak Chopra and I was enthralled. I avidly read *Quantum Healing, Unconditional Life and Ageless Body, Timeless Mind* and they made a deep impression on me. Even today they resonate with everything that I do in my work. They were the first books that made sense to me at many different levels of myself. The skilful mix of modern medical scientific insights seen through the eyes of the ancient wisdom of the Upanishads made me understand for the first time the nature of the quantum reality in very personal terms – that I was other than my physical body, that I was consciousness.

The books that were very important and relevant for me were many. The most interesting and appealing from my point of view were the excellent *Energy Medicine: The Scientific Basis* by James Oschman, *Vibrational Medicine* by Dr Richard Gerber and *Virtual Medicine* by Dr Keith Scott-Mumby. Candace Pert's groundbreaking book *The Molecules of Emotion* also enhanced and deepened my understanding. (Further details of all the books mentioned here can be found in the Recommended Reading section.)

Light Medicine of the Future by Jacob Liberman, *Light Years Ahead*, edited by Brian Breiling and others, and John Ott's *Health and Light* contributed significantly to my understanding of the use of light, colour and technology in the process of bodymind healing and the enhancement of human function.

I also loved the work of Fritjof Capra, with his *Tao of Physics* and *Web of Life*, and Gary Zukav's *Dancing Wu Li Masters* and *The Seat of the Soul*, and of course James Gleick's *Chaos* and Danah Zohar's *Quantum Self*.

The interesting work of the Santa Fe Institute, described in the book *Complexity* by M. Mitchell Waldrop, made a huge impact. I found this book of particular interest as it let me see what some of the greatest scientists on Earth had been puzzling about, what questions were being asked and what new theories were being postulated. It was clear that scientists had now gone beyond the work detailed in *Chaos*, which had so captivated me when I had first read it.

I also read *Genome* by Matt Ridley, about the research into the genome project. In my view, though interesting, it is incomplete. My own work has shown that you are not limited by your genes, that you are more than your so-called 'selfish genes', more than a 'survival machine'. If anything we are 'love machines' and 'superconscious beings'. So, while the information about the genes is not inaccurate, in my considered view future research will show that we can learn to change our genetic inheritance by changing our consciousness.

Inspirational Figures

The persons whose work I found particularly interesting and relevant were Fritz-Albert Popp, Mae-Wan Ho and Herbert Fröhlich for their pioneering research in the field of coherence and quantum coherence, Rupert Sheldrake for his theory of morphogenic fields and morphic resonance, and Dean Radin of the University of Nevada for his research with REGs (random event generators) and his excellent and courageous book *The Conscious Universe*. I found the information on superconductors on the Internet and Hal Puthoff's paper on the zero-point field fascinating. My strong conjecture is that in Biolumanetics we have direct working access to the zero-point quantum field through the medium of VRIC imaging in the parallel universe of the Luminator. But to set the scene, here is some information about the work of these inspirational figures.

Fritz-Albert Popp

As already mentioned, since the 1970s Fritz-Albert Popp has been working with the theory that lifeforms emit light and the coherence or incoherence of that light signal is related to the vitality and health of the lifeform. His research indicates that light is the principal information carrier that tells each of our 50 trillion cells what to do on a continuous basis and is responsible for the orderly performance of the infinitely complex activities of the human body. Light is certainly a known carrier of information. You may not know that one fibre optic cable thinner than a human hair can carry an incredible 200,000 conversations simultaneously.

Popp's work has made clear the vital importance of the coherence of the photon emission as regards human health. Using this system, his team has been able to evaluate the energetic quality of various foods and assess whether they are vital, energetic, full of light and therefore life or are lifeless and not worth eating. They also work with cancer tissue and are able to tell what will cause the cells to behave in a more normal manner. I find their work fascinating. However, all their research is done with cells, cucumber and potato seedlings and fruit flies, and they readily concede that they do not have the equipment or the means to assess the coherence of a complex living system such as the human bodymind system. They assert that there is no system that can assess and enhance the state of quantum coherence of humans. However, that system has existed since 1978 when Biolumanetics was born with the invention of the Luminator and VRIC imaging.

The reason why scientists are not aware of the capabilities of that system may be because the research was conducted by a single genius and not at some august university or research institute. Big does not mean better; the greatest inventions and creations are often the work of individuals from nowhere in particular and without the requisite PhDs after their name. Dismissing such work is a standard error made by many scientists, journalists and others who gain their knowledge of such research through second-hand information and who then write about it in a similar vein, so that the error is compounded and prevents recognition of the individual involved. It reminds one of the old boys' network and the necessity of belonging to the right club. If one's face does not fit, then entrance to that club remains securely barred. This is certainly true in the West, but does not seem to be the case in the former USSR, where there seems to be greater collaboration and co-operation between scientists of different disciplines, and this cross-fertilization of ideas has benefits for all concerned.

To return to Popp's work, the International Institute of Bio-physics in Germany is where the research is being carried out today and there are 40 other laboratories all over the world that are involved in the research. The International Institute of Bio-physics also holds annual conferences. You might be interested to look at their website: www.lifescientists.de.

Mae-Wan Ho

Mae-Wan Ho is what I call a scientist of the future. She is very knowledgeable, clear-thinking, deep-feeling, proactive and passionate, and is the founder of the Institute for Science in Society. She has written what I consider to be the best paper on quantum coherence, an important theory that is discussed in Chapter 10. The paper is called 'The New Age of the Organism' and is written in a lucid yet passionate style that is accessible to the layman and not filled with equations and calculations. I would strongly recommend it to readers who want to know more about quantum coherence (see www.i-sis.org.uk).

Bruce Lipton and David Baltimore

In 2006 I discovered the work of Bruce Lipton, a cellular biologist from Stanford Medical School, which confirmed what I had always known.

Lipton's research has soundly debunked the myth of genes controlling our destiny, as he has clearly shown that genes are subject to other controls and that consciousness is a major factor in creating our personal reality.

More surprisingly, the pernicious prevailing dogma of genes controlling our lives has been further demolished by the Nobel Prize-winning biologist and leading geneticist David Baltimore, who makes it clear that the answers do not rest with the DNA. In a paper written in 2001 he states:

'But unless the human genome contains a lot of genes that are opaque to our computers, it is clear that we do not gain our undoubted complexity over worms and plants by using more genes. Understanding what does give us our complexity – our enormous behavioural repertoire, ability to produce conscious action, remarkable physical co-ordination, precisely tuned alterations in response to external variations in the environment, learning, memory, need I go on? – remains a challenge for the future.'

Well, the future is now and the 'ghost in the machine' has been located and is available for contact.

Harry Oldfield

Another pioneer whose work I admire uses an unusual imaging system called PIP and treats the human energy field directly. His treatment modalities are completely different from those I use (he uses crystals and coloured light) and there is a degree of interpretation involved in his method, but there are similarities in our approach and he too endeavours to address the whole human rather than confine himself to the physical aspect and does not address the symptoms of the illness directly. He also shares the central idea of reorganizing the energy field to heal the physical body. His name is Harry Oldfield. For those interested in finding out more about him, a book called *Harry Oldfield's Invisible Universe* makes interesting reading and is written in simple English as opposed to technical jargon.

Masaru Emoto

In 2001 I was given the wondrous book *The Message from Water* by Masaru Emoto in the original bilingual Japanese–English edition. I was wonderstruck at the exquisite images of the water crystals that showed in clear visual terms that water reflected human consciousness and could read and respond to words and feelings. Since the human body is 70 per cent water, the implications of Emoto's work gives us new hope and new insights into the way we impact each other and our environment. The amazing magical nature of the interconnected superconscious universe has been revealed to us through the work of this great pioneer – a true science of the twenty-first century. His book and Bruce Lipton's work, in particular, gave me the courage and the confidence to finish my own book.

Valerie Hunt

The pioneer I admire by far the most is Dr Valerie Hunt. I had the pleasure of hearing her speak at the Sound Colloquium in Colorado in 1997 and reading her book, *Infinite Mind*.

Valerie Hunt did her research at UCLA in the 1970s, many years before conventional science ever had heard of this hidden dimension of humankind, let alone set out to explore it. Her research was truly original (which a lot of research is not) and gave new insights, gained through science and measurement, into the human electromagnetic energy field. She further discovered that the condition of that invisible but vitally important parameter of the human had vast implications for health and disease in the physical body and the mind and much more. This is the closest science has ever come to assessing the whole human. This, coupled with her understanding of what she calls the 'coherency' or 'anti-coherency' of the whole energy field, makes her work enthralling, breath-taking in its vista and highly courageous. It stands the test of time, even after so many years have elapsed. Remember, this work was done at a time when you wouldn't have caught a card-carrying 'good scientist' within a million miles of admitting belief in such 'esoteric nonsense'.

Come to think of it, the position probably has not altered much even today. Very few doctors have heard of Hunt's work and fewer still have done anything to integrate it in any way with their core discipline. It is based on an understanding of the whole rather than making assumptions about that whole based on laboratory research into small parts of it such as various cells and molecules. The whole is and always will be greater than the sum of its parts, and Valerie Hunt recognized that and took it into account in her work. In effect, here was a card-carrying scientist saying, 'You are not your organs, cells and molecules. You are not a biochemical, mechanical machine but something more – much more.'

Which brings me to Valerie Hunt the mystic. Most scientists get mealy-mouthed when it comes to acknowledging their own and therefore anyone else's spirituality. Even so-called consciousness researchers are trying to find where consciousness resides in the human brain and talking of microtubules and the like being responsible for the phenomenon. It seems that somehow – anyhow – we must find all that we are at the physical level and it does not matter what idiotic intellectual hoops we jump through as long as we are able to avoid acknowledgement of anything beyond it. An acknowledgement of that which is greater than anything the intellect can conceive of – an acknowledgement of our connection to the Supreme Intelligence – is left for the metaphysicians, the philosophers and 'naïve New Agers'. The most important aspect of ourselves is considered a no-go area; you enter at the peril of losing your scientific credentials and possibly your career. The schism that has existed since the 'Age of

Reason' between religion and science is alive and well, and both sides have a contempt for and mistrust of each other, to the detriment of both.

The greatest scientists, however, are not prone to this error. Einstein, one of the greatest scientists of the last century, said, 'Science without religion is lame; religion without science is blind.' The only change I would make to that statement would be to substitute the word 'spirituality' for the word 'religion'.

Similarly, Valerie Hunt speaks openly, unequivocally, of the importance of the evolution of the being in line with its soul's purpose and the need for each person to find their divinity. She openly says she is both a mystic and a scientist, and she uses colour, sound, hands-on healing and addressing the issues of past lives to rebalance a person's energy field. I consider her work and the work of Fritz-Albert Popp and the quantum coherence researchers the most direct forerunners of the work I am doing today. While there is no similarity in the technologies and methods for either the assessment or the healing used by Hunt at UCLA or by Popp in Germany and the technologies and protocols that I use, the insights and conclusions arrived at by all these methodologies are strikingly similar.

Therapies and Technologies

As I knew that emotions had a direct relationship with physical health, I also explored the newish therapies that addressed the emotions directly, namely Thought Field Therapy, the energy-based EFT (Emotional Freedom Technique) and the synergistic ETT (Emotional Transformation Technique), which uses coloured light with eye-movement desensitizing techniques and psychotherapy. All of these go way beyond traditional psychotherapy and are powerful and effective, but there are caveats with all of them.

The other aspect of my exploration led me to find out more about the new computer-based technologies for assessment and vibrational healing that are explored thoroughly in Dr Keith Scott-Mumby's excellent and knowledgeable book, *Virtual Medicine*. I cannot say that I have looked at all the systems, but I have explored some. They are useful and effective and give the practitioner a view of another not so obviously apparent level of the client, going beyond the usual fix-the-symptom-based approach. In the hands of a skilled practitioner, they are undoubtedly effective and their non-invasive approach to healing can only be welcomed. My caveat is that all of them address the level of complexity and there is an endless plethora of information, which will always be the case when you look at that level, and therefore the results obtained depend on the interpretive skill of the practitioner. There is accuracy at some level, but the perception of the practitioner does play a key role, and the inevitable variability of this important factor can leave a gap between the results desired and the results achieved.

At the end of the day, after all the research at many levels, my considered conclusion simply confirms what I knew but could not have substantiated the first time I heard Patrick describe his system on the phone: that it is a breakthrough and a landmark and is way beyond the furthest frontier of any theory or science of this limited third dimension. It is also not only about theory *per se*; it is primarily about application in the here and now. Fancy theories and intellectual constructs on quarks, gluons, leptons, superstrings and baby universes are all very well and perhaps necessary, but they cannot be of much use to you and me until they leave the world of the intellect and become grounded in the living, throbbing reality that we know as life. They miss a vital factor, the 'What's in it for me?' factor. How is this useful, practical or relevant on a personal level?

II

FROM CHAOS TO COHERENCE

'Let the mind be enlarged according to its capacity to the grandeur of the mysteries, and not the mysteries contracted to the narrowness of the mind.'
Sir Francis Bacon

'Something deeply hidden has to be behind things.'
Albert Einstein

'In every culture and in every medical tradition before ours, healing was accomplished by moving energy.'
Albert Szent Gyorgi, winner of the Nobel Prize for Medicine

CHAPTER 4

THE LUMINATOR
WHERE DIMENSIONS MEET

It was 1978 and the energy crisis was at its peak. The price of oil had sky-rocketed and the oil embargo was on. In those troubled times a lone genius decided to find a solution to the problem. He was an American engineer called Patrick Richards. He was in his forties, had just sold a million-dollar consulting company and needed a new project to get his teeth into. He did not think in the normal way, 'in the box' so to speak, but decided to have a crack at the problem in a completely different manner.

His thinking was at one level very simple. In a normal environment heat rises, so it is hotter nearer the ceiling of a room and colder lower down. Patrick figured that if heat were redistributed more evenly, there would be a huge saving of energy. He designed a device to balance air temperatures to enable this efficient distribution of heat. This was the Luminator.

At the time the US government was sponsoring all types of incentive programmes to save energy, some of which were simply phenomenal. Industry could get a tax advantage simply by including an energy-saving device. In many cases the government would pay half the cost of the device and even homeowners would get half the cost. But unfortunately by the time Patrick had his device designed and working, the government programmes had ended and there was no longer any advantage in having an expensive piece of machinery to balance temperatures.

What Patrick found, however, during that period of time, from 1978 to roughly 1982, was that when the device was tested, unexpected health changes happened to the people who were in its vicinity, or field. Primarily they involved a reduction in stress, less eyestrain and the resolution of gastrointestinal challenges. Because Patrick had invested so much money in the device, he thought, 'Let's change the direction from balancing temperatures and saving energy and take advantage of the health improvements.'

A Mystery and an Enigma

Patrick's original intention was, however, achieved: temperatures were balanced in the field of the device when it was operating. Temperature sensors placed at one-inch intervals from floor to ceiling and wall to wall verified this.

More unexpectedly, an altered magnetic field was also created. A compass reading revealed a 30-degree deviation in the field of the device.

The third and most important alteration in the environment in the field of the Luminator was not readily apparent until some time later. This was that the light field of the room changed from an incoherent to a coherent one – a 'null field' or 'zero field'. The implications of this were far-reaching.

The invention of the Luminator was in fact a quantum leap of a magnitude similar to Galileo's discovery in the sense that it completely overturned the prevailing paradigm. But not even its inventor really understood it. Many years after its invention, I asked Patrick exactly what it did and got a really surprising response from him. He admitted that although it seemed to create a hole in space-time, he never had figured out how and why it did so. At one level the Luminator is a mystery and an enigma; the important point is that we do know a little of what it does and how to work with it and it permits us to unfold its mysteries as, how and when it sees fit. Over 12 years of working with it have given me a healthy respect for it and I know that if I work with it every day 24/7 for the rest of my life, I will uncover only a minute portion of its limitless possibilities.

I believe in time the Luminator will be recognized as one of the greatest inventions of the twentieth century. Yet for Patrick the opportunity that he had counted on to make his fortune faded away when he could not market the device in the way he had intended and recoup some of his large investment in time and money. The universe had other plans and the next part of the adventure was just beginning.

Patrick is a very practical idealist, dreamer and doer who calls himself an engineer-researcher. He is a great researcher and original thinker, but above all an applications man. There is a lot of research going on today, but much of it is not original and most of it has very few practical applications, only conjectures and possibilities which may or may not come to fruition in the distant future – loads of theory with no practical application. Patrick's incredible system, the like of which humans have never glimpsed before, not only has practical applications but it has not received a cent of funding from any institution and has been entirely self-funded by this incredible genius and benefactor of humanity. This greatest of pioneers has created a system that is incredibly comprehensive and far-reaching in scope, an integrated model that is radical, revolutionary and truly new.

While the invention of the Luminator was an 'accident' (if you believe in 'accidents'), in that Patrick set out to invent something else altogether, when he found the 'anomalous' effects of the device, he had the insight, intelligence and curiosity to explore them further. He started working with various health practitioners, including allopathic doctors, chiropractors and others, to find out what was going on. One day when he was photographing clients, the flash of his simple Polaroid camera failed. When he

WHY AND HOW THE VRIC EFFECT OCCURS

The illustrations below are a simple simulation of a very complex phenomenon.

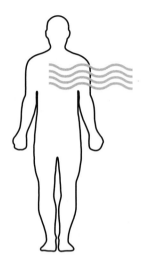

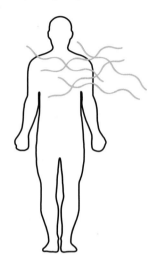

Life-forms emit a continuous and continuously changing signal of light. The figure shows a coherent, orderly light signal.

The figure above shows an incoherent, unorganised light signal.

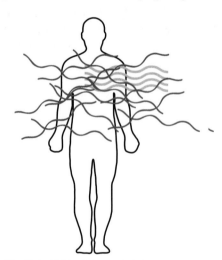

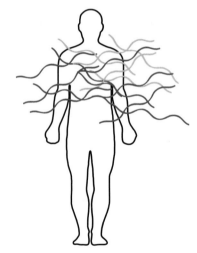

The light field of the earth is incoherent (in purple). In an incoherent field the coherent cell light emission (in orange) from the life-form would be masked and there would be no VRIC effect. You would get an ordinary photo.

The illustration above shows the light field of the earth and the light emission from life-form to be incoherent. The result again would be an ordinary Polaroid photo.

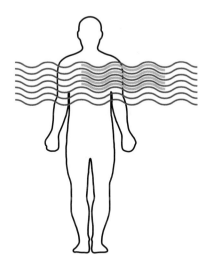
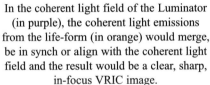
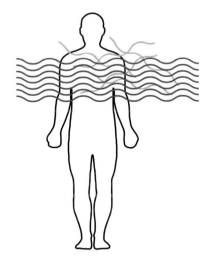

In the coherent light field of the Luminator (in purple), the coherent light emissions from the life-form (in orange) would merge, be in synch or align with the coherent light field and the result would be a clear, sharp, in-focus VRIC image.

In the coherent light field of the Luminator (in purple) an incoherent organised chaotic light emission (in orange) would be out of synch or misaligned with the coherent light field and would register as an interference. The result would be a fuzzy incoherent VRIC image.

saw the resulting photograph, he could not believe his eyes – the image was strange and fragmented. He was puzzled and fortunately did not throw it away. Instead he masked the flash with black tape and photographed the client again. The same thing happened. Something very strange was going on.

Though he did not know it, Patrick had inadvertently made visible a parallel universe. He had discovered that one could photograph the hidden reality of an individual.

VRIC IMAGING - ENTERING THE REALITY OF THE QUANTUM DIMENSION
PENETRATING THE MASK OF MATTER
THE PARALLEL UNIVERSE OF THE LUMINATOR

'Solid' body of the physical five-sensory reality	Quantum energetic body – field of fluctuation, flux and flow of light-energy-information – constant change

Shocked? Can't believe your eyes? Impossible? No, it is NOT camera shake. This is the truth and the reality that lies beyond the reach, remit or access of the reality of the five senses – until NOW. Small offer of consolation: after well over a decade I still find these images almost unbelievable at one level, I sympathise and can understand what a jolt they are to the belief system of humans.

CHAPTER 5

VRIC IMAGING
ENTERING A PARALLEL UNIVERSE

It was September 1995. My daughter and I were in Grand Haven, Michigan, having flown in from London. We were full of expectancy. I was really excited at the prospect of seeing this extraordinary 'science fiction-made-fact' device.

Patrick met us at the airport and took us straight to the centre where he practised. I couldn't wait to see what the Luminator would look like. He had made three devices. To me, two of them looked strange, almost alien. The third one looked more innocuous, more 'normal'. Patrick asked me to choose one. I chose the 'normal'-looking one.

It is impossible to describe the impact of experiencing the Luminator for the first time. Quite simply, Patrick took some photos of my daughter and me individually and together. Then we were photographed – or 'imaged' – holding various test tubes containing what looked like water. To my amazement, the photos kept changing. In fact in some of them it was difficult to recognize myself.

Every notion of reality as I had known it was completely overturned – 'life-changing experience' seems a very mild understatement. 'Magic' was the word that came most to mind, yet patently there was no trickery involved. I was smart enough to know that I was witnessing something that was extraordinary beyond measure. I could not get over the fact that two completely different realities existed, intertwined with each other, and this remarkable device could show it by means of a simple photograph.

The Power of the Image – Images of Power

VRIC (Visual Reference of Image Coherence) imaging is the term for the unusual photos taken in the field of the Luminator. The Luminator is not connected to the camera in any way, it is simply present in the room. It does not touch the client or the practitioner-photographer and is several feet away from both, yet the VRIC phenomenon could not take place without its presence.

VRIC images have awesome power to affect us. All images may in fact affect us more than we realize. Eighty per cent of the information we receive is processed through the visual sense. The remaining 20 per cent is divided between the rest of the senses. In essence, seeing is believing for most of us. In contrast, we may believe what we hear and we may not. We filter what we hear through our knowledge and experience of the past. But seeing is our most direct way of accessing and understanding reality. Images are read and responded to by both the linear cognitive brain and by the non-linear, non-verbal 'primitive' brain. Words and ideas, powerful though they are, have to be processed and filtered through the cognitive brain, which will always be at a disadvantage when compared to the instant visceral response of the 'primitive' feeling brain. (Malcolm Gladwell explores this phenomenon in his excellent book, *Blink*.)

The image is a powerful and universal means of communication and the most powerful image for each of us, by far, is our own image. Down the ages people have used the power of the image through paintings and self-portraits and today the advertising industry sells to us using the power of colour and the image to communicate to our unconscious – in effect we buy with our eyes. Even more significantly, the photography industry is more popular than ever and millions are spent on recording memories of who we are and what we wish to remember.

VRIC images of ourselves can be shocking and unbelievable because we have never seen this aspect of ourselves in 'glorious Technicolor'. They bypass the reasoning, linear mind and speak directly and instantly to the part of us that sees the truth – the non-linear, non-verbal aspect of mind. You cannot explain them, nor can they be denied. The message is simple, direct and unequivocal. Over the years I have seen people gasp with shock and relief at making the acquaintance of a side of themselves that they knew existed but had never been able to see before. To see the fragmented, suffering self in its simple truth and then to have the relief and pleasure of seeing it made whole again is an experience beyond words. It is never to be forgotten. Years afterwards, I am told again and again how VRIC images have affected people and how their lives have changed as a direct result. They cannot be used lightly, though they are simply light images. So let us explore what VRIC imaging is in some depth and detail.

VRIC Imaging

All VRIC imaging is done with a simple fixed-focus Polaroid camera in the field of the Luminator. There is one modification to the camera: the flash is masked with opaque black tape. In a normal imaging session, photos are taken from a fixed distance to create controlled conditions. The photographer stands approximately 12 feet away from the subject; there is a simple marker on the carpet to indicate the photographer's position.

Some useful tips on how to look at VRIC images:

• It is useful to have a magnifying glass to view the images.
• See whether the image of the subject/s is clear, sharp and in focus or fuzzy and fragmented. We call a sharp in-focus image 'coherent' and

a fuzzy or fragmented image 'incoherent'.

- Look at the eyes in particular. They are the windows of the soul and can give a lot of information.
- It is important to understand that small differences in the photos can and often do have vast implications. Sometimes the differences are visually dramatic and other times they are subtle. Remember the *Encyclopaedia Britannica* fitting on the grain of sand.
- Tongue in cheek, before viewing VRIC images and trying to understand their awesome implications you should have done the exercise recommended by the White Queen to Alice: 'Believe six impossible things before breakfast every day.'

Viewing these ordinary and yet utterly extraordinary images is confusing and confounding for most people. There is an obvious and glaring disparity between what the eye sees and what the camera sees. Over the years I have observed with some amusement the various reactions of people as they try and figure out how to make sense of the phenomenon. Scientists and of course photographers have the greatest difficulty. They know cameras and they know photography, but they do not know the Luminator and the altered field.

'The silly question is the first intimation of some totally new development,' according to Alfred North Whitehead. The standard questions are: 'Is it the camera?' 'No, there is nothing special about the camera.' 'Is it the film?' 'No, the film is standard Polaroid 600 film.' 'Is it camera shake?' 'No, it is not camera shake.' The most intriguing question is: 'Why can't I see what the camera is seeing?'

I once said to Patrick, 'As an engineer, you must have had a real problem with your system.' He told me he had spent three years trying to disprove it. Because by all known laws, this phenomenon should not have been taking place. Yet it patently was.

The fact is that there are unknown laws operating here. Any true scientist knows that the universe is lawful, even if they are not able to understand what a particular law is or how it operates. Meanwhile the befuddled intellect goes round in circles and finds it has nowhere to go and finally the 'expert' has to say the magic words: 'I don't know why or how this is happening.'

The beginning of wisdom is to know that you don't know. No one, however knowledgeable, can be an expert on the new. One has to have an open, clear mind (the 'beginner's mind' of Zen) and eyes full of wonder, as a child does, to see, understand and appreciate the truly new. Children generally have no problem understanding the VRIC images and their radical implications. Their parents have a much tougher time. In general, women find it easier to understand and accept than men. This may be because women are often not particularly interested in how technology works, but simply use it. In general men are more interested in finding out how the Luminator works than what the images mean.

The difficulty arises because the deceptively simple Polaroid camera and the instant images it produces are things everybody thinks they understand. A fuzzy photo is a fuzzy photo is a fuzzy photo. And a fuzzy photo happens when the camera shakes. Everybody knows that, especially photographers. They are the experts and to them a fuzzy image is simply a demonstration of slight carelessness, a bit of inefficiency. How else could one get a fuzzy photo? There is simply no other way. Right? Wrong!

If the imaging were done with an expensive technological gizmo invented by hundreds of august scientists at a great university, we would instantly 'understand' how it was possible and would accept how extraordinary it was. It is the coming together of the totally ordinary Polaroid photo and the utterly extraordinary images, with their radical implications, that makes the process truly confounding.

To add to the confusion of the intellect, the altered coherent light field in the room, without which the imaging could not happen, cannot be recognized as different by the five-sensory reality. The Luminator room looks like any other and people simply have to take one's word for it that the light field has been reorganized. We have no frame of reference for an altered field and had no means of creating it, as far as I know, until the Luminator came along. So it feels like trying to explain an apple to an alien from Mars.

I have found that when the VRIC effect is seen by a client for the first time and they realize that there is no trickery involved, that no Paul Daniels or David Copperfield could duplicate the 'magic' that is happening before their very eyes, they are filled with genuine amazement. However, something curious then happens. They go away all excited and tell their friends or family about their extraordinary experience and then they find that they are not believed. They say, 'Nobody believes me. They think there must be some trick or I am imagining it,' or 'I tried to explain, but found they couldn't understand what I was talking about.'

Scientists are not much better in the manner of their response. In the beginning I was perturbed by this lack of understanding, but then I began to realize why the imaging shook people's reality to the extent that it did. The vast implications of actually seeing a subtle parallel universe that is usually invisible to our eyes is extremely disconcerting, to put it mildly, for even the most advanced scientist, let alone for ordinary mortals. However, something strange happens when the sceptic comes to experience the system directly: scepticism is replaced by amazement as they see their own image change.

VRIC imaging is a clear demonstration of how thin the line is between 'ordinary' reality as understood through previous experience and knowledge and the utterly extraordinary. It is a cosmic joke played on the 'knowledgeable' ones who cannot get past the 'impossibility' of it.

'Knowledge' can be a bar, a wall, a blind spot that will prevent you from recognizing the reality that is. You think you know the rules, and you do up to a point; however, there is so much that none of us will ever know through the linear mind. And opinions, be they ever so well-informed, will avail you none when a quantum leap is present before you.

How and Why the VRIC Effect Happens

So what is actually happening? In a normal Earth environment, light is incoherent, which means it travels in a myriad of different directions. These are the standard conditions of the electromagnetic environment on Earth. In this normal incoherent environment the subtle fluctuations of a person's electromagnetic light-energy field exist, but cannot be differentiated or imaged. Because of their exceedingly subtle nature, they are just jumbled along with all the other chaotic light signals. However, in the field of the Luminator, for the first time in known human history, the electromagnetic environment becomes coherent or organized, which means that the light field is polarized and in phase and not moving in countless different directions. So even though there is no physical laser present, the environment has mysteriously acquired the characteristics of a laser. In this organized light field any change in the behaviour of the light field of the human will register as interference and be picked up by the camera as a clear or fuzzy image (see diagram on pages 34-5).

What Exactly Are We Seeing in the VRIC Phenomenon and Why Is It Significant?

As I understand it, what we are seeing in a VRIC image is a light phenomenon. In fact, we are seeing the light bulb-laser effect as it applies to humans. A clear VRIC image represents the laser effect, or coherent expression, being expressed by the human light-energy system and a fuzzy VRIC image represents the light bulb effect or incoherent expression of the system. So in effect the human energy system at the most fundamental level of expression fluctuates between only two extreme and extremely different energy states, i.e. chaos (light bulb or unorganized) or coherence (laser or super-organized).

This enables us to understand the radical difference in meaning between a clear and fuzzy image and can give us an idea why such huge changes happen when a photo changes from clear to fuzzy or vice versa. Small, seemingly insignificant changes in the images can have huge implications if you remember that a laser is a million times more powerful than a light bulb of the same wattage.

The Mystery and Paradox of Light

Light, physicists tell us, exists as particle and wave – two seemingly contradictory states. The mystery is that it is actually both particle *and* wave and what you see in a light phenomenon depends on what you look for. So if you do certain experiments it comes across as a particle and if you do a slit-lamp experiment, it manifests as a waveform.

What I believe we are seeing in VRIC imaging is the sum total of the harmonics of all the waveforms emitted by each cell, so what we are looking at is the wave aspect of light. What we are seeing is something unique and unprecedented: the actual harmonics and the resultant interference patterns between the different frequencies emitted by the cells. So we are witnessing the effect of what 50 trillion cells are doing on a continuous basis. All this vast and complex information is magically, amazingly, incredibly computed and reduced to one signal, which in any given moment fluctuates between only two states, chaos or coherence. This enables us to see the bottom-line effect on the totality of the lifeform that is us.

Essentially what we are seeing in VRIC is the qualitative and the quantitative aspect of the light emission of lifeforms. I recently came across a new word which is a combination of 'wave' and 'particle': 'waveicle'. I think in VRIC we are seeing the waveicle aspect of light.

Is It the Aura? Other Imaging Systems and VRIC Imaging

People sometimes ask if it is the aura that one is seeing in the VRIC images. The human aura is the individual field that is made up of the different colours and levels of light that are manifested by each person. Most of us know that sunlight, when put through a prism, is seen not to be white but to be made up of the visible spectrum from violet through to red. Aura readers can actually see these colours in the human aura and understand what they reveal about the mental or emotional state of the subject. Valerie Hunt's pioneering work at UCLA with the healer Rosalyn Bruyere has shown clearly in scientific terms that this process is real.

There are several imaging systems today which claim to see the auric field, including Harry Oldfield's PIP scan, aura photography or biofeedback imaging, Kirlian photography and Korotkov's GDV (an advanced form of Kirlian photography with a computer interface). All of these systems (apart from direct Kirlian photography) use a computer as an interface to interpret the information obtained through the biofeedback device and extrapolate that information through a computer software program to give us a visual representation of the field. While they are useful – and the point of this is not to devalue these systems – it is important to understand clearly the difference between these and VRIC imaging, where there is no computer program and no digital manipulation, as only an ordinary fixed-focus Polaroid camera is used. As Dr Keith Scott-Mumby said in describing this system in *Virtual Medicine*, there is 'no smoke and mirrors'. VRIC is not complicated – a child can understand it. It is very literal and 'in your face': there is either a clear or fuzzy photograph – no complicated interpretation required.

In the VRIC images we are not seeing the colours of the aura. We are in fact seeing the reverse process – all the colours of the rainbow combined to make up white light. We are seeing not the sum of the parts but the whole. To sum it up simply, though by no means completely, the aura reader is seeing the colours, we are seeing the white-light aspect.

What about the Chakras and the Meridians?

Another question that sometimes arises is whether these images show the invisible systems of the 'energy body' known as the chakras and the meridians. The rather paradoxical answer is that the information in these images is and is not about them. Though these systems are factored into the final light signal, VRIC images show a more fundamental level that holds those systems together. They portray the level that is in constant interdependent interactive communication with all the systems that go into the shaping and making of the indivisible person. After all, the chakra system and the meridian system cannot exist on their own; they are held together or come together and hold a person's energy body together when they decide to manifest in a physical form. This begs the question of what or who holds these systems together? You do, but this is not the you that you as a personality have any knowledge of. You are primarily that spark of superconscious light made life, held together by the invisible but potent forces of desire, intention, information and super intelligence.

Seeing Another Reality

To me as the photographer and the seer, VRIC images are the clearest evidence of how my mind is conditioned. It does not permit me to see the reality that is, even in the coherent light field of the Luminator. I have to concede that I am blind to this level of reality, and the limitation has nothing to do with my eyesight, which is pretty good, but with my perception.

It must be clearly understood that while the five-sensory reality of the physical or third dimension is very useful and important, it is also extremely limited. Yet paradoxically it is the only reality most of us know and believe in and therefore live by. The analogy comes to mind of the invention of the microscope, which allowed us to see a universe of germs and bacteria that had never been seen before by human eyes. This was purely through the relatively simple ability to magnify an object several hundred times. When the microscope was invented and the reality of germs and bacteria was revealed, a lot of doctors and surgeons refused to believe that such tiny creatures invisible to the naked eye could have an impact on human health. Yet today we know differently.

In a way nothing has changed since that time. Scientists, after all, are prone to the same prejudices as most other humans. Today this prejudice is glaringly evident when it comes to the Western medical orthodoxy as regards energy or vibrational medicine. The Luminator and VRIC are the modern-day equivalent of the microscope in that subtle energy or frequency medicine can no longer be dismissed as a figment of the imag-ination or the 'placebo' effect, powerful and real though the placebo effect is. There is now convincing visual 'proof' that small – invisible, in fact – 'un-measurable' 'non-things' can have powerful effects. However, I am not holding my breath for a mass conversion, given the plight and ordeal by fire of the pioneering scientist Jacques Benveniste. His landmark experiments demonstrated the ability of water to hold information and therefore validated homoeopathy, but this got him into serious trouble with his peers. Though homoeopathy has been around for a couple of hundred years and is the treatment of choice of many millions in many countries in Europe and India, it is still largely dismissed by the Western medical orthodoxy. I am reminded of my great hero Einstein's saying, 'Only two things are infinite, the universe and human stupidity, and I am not sure about the former.'

Humans are certainly not kind to pioneers and Patrick himself, who is sensitive, has borne the brunt of that unkindness, lack of understanding and non-acceptance of his life's work. As a result, he can be an expert doubter and often does not have much trust in people. This can sometimes lead to a world view that is not particularly optimistic. Yet I believe that in time we will understand that we owe a large debt of gratitude to this man, whom I consider one of the greatest benefactors humanity has known.

CHAPTER 6

LUMANETICS
POWER TOOLS OF THE INFORMATION REALM

Another of Patrick's gifts to humanity is the Lumanetic system. This is the frequency toolkit of Biolumanetics, which is used to create coherence. It contains the insights and knowledge of the disciplines of homoeopathy, acupuncture, crystal healing, chelation therapy, colour therapy, the Lumanetic emotional frequencies, flower remedies in Lumanetic form, the hormone frequencies – the list goes on and on. It is an open-ended system capable of growing and evolving, of endless newness. In fact, most of the healing knowledge of the past few thousands of years, from the ancient to the ultra-modern, has been integrated into this easy-to-use form and raised to another level of potency, effectiveness and power, creating a synergistic whole that is greater than any of its constituent parts.

Lumanetics come in three different forms: transceiver frequency pads, topical creams and drops. These pads, creams and liquids contain the vibrations or the energy signatures of various substances. This bears a passing resemblance to homoeopathic remedies. However, there are radical differences between homoeopathic remedies and Lumanetics. In homoeopathic remedies the frequency signature of the substance is broadcast or transmitted into the energy body of the person taking the remedy. The remedies are frequency transmitters. Lumanetics are different in that they are frequency *transceivers* – they deliver the required frequency-energy signature into the field of the person, and also bind with toxins and neutralize them. This makes them receivers as well as transmitters. This is done by introducing a negative magnetic charge into the 'master carrier' fluid that holds the energy signatures of the different Lumanetic frequencies. Toxins carry a positive magnetic charge and Lumanetics carry a negative magnetic charge.

Another difference is that Lumanetics frequencies are carried in distilled water – homoeopathic frequencies are carried in alcohol or in sugar pills. Lumanetics will hold their energetic information indefinitely, whereas homoeopathic frequencies can lose their charge if exposed to magnetic fields or X-rays in airport security scanning machines. Lumanetics are created in an altered magnetic field which is different from the magnetic field of the Earth and similar to the altered field of the Luminator, but not the same. Because of this, X-rays and airport scanning machines do not affect them. They can only be changed in the magnetic field in which they were created. This makes them stable. The normal magnetic field of the Earth does not affect them. They are locked frequencies, if you like. This has not been possible on Earth until now.

The most important difference to note is that Lumanetics are not used to diagnose or even to address dysfunction, but to enhance the function of the whole being (with exquisite precision and total specificity thanks to VRIC) and to enable the energy system to metabolize light more effectively. That is their fundamental aim. In effect they are light enhancers and coherence creators. For me this is the single most important point of their efficacy, power and elegance.

The *Materia Medica* contains many thousands of remedies and the Western pharmacopoeia has many thousands of medicines. The Chinese and the Ayurvedic systems each have a huge number of different herbs and other animal and mineral substances in their respective healing toolkits. The results of the case studies described in this book have been achieved using a vibrational toolkit using 160 different Lumanetics frequencies, transceiver pads containing three different energy signatures and eight topical creams, which between them contain not a single physical molecule of any medicinal substance other than that of the carrier (i.e. the distilled water or the cream used to carry the relevant energy signature). However, it may amaze you to know that with just 160 frequencies there are not simply 160 options available but 160 x 160, 159 times – virtually an infinite number.

How Are Lumanetics Applied?

Despite the huge range of options available, the application of Lumanetics is relatively straightforward. A Lumanetic frequency vial(s) is held in the hand and a VRIC image is taken. When the right frequency vials are held, the image becomes coherent. You do not feel anything, yet the image shows a difference.

How does this happen? If you think of yourself as a field of energy and information with a resonant frequency and think in terms of an energy exchange, it will be easier for you to understand that any change is immediately registered in the energy field before the physical senses are aware of it. The field is a far more sensitive sensing mechanism than your five senses. Energy exchange at that level is instant and real, but your five senses are not sensitive enough to register the change, let alone the effect of the energy exchange or transfer. So while you will feel nothing, your energy field senses and processes information far faster than your brain can compute and the changes at this supra-sensory level can be seen through VRIC imaging. So another level of reality, another level of knowledge, is revealed.

Once we have arrived at a vibrational solution to restore coherence, in most cases we ask the person to apply a trace of certain vibrational creams to various parts of the body, cover a part of the body with a small plastic patch containing a vibrational signature and/or to wear on their person a vial of liquid containing information or carry a vibrational cream.

The response from clients when we instruct them on what they have to do varies from polite acceptance to total incredulity to complete disbelief. They may start laughing when I tell them to keep a little bottle tucked in their bra or place a plastic patch on their solar plexus.

I remember a young client who was extremely blunt in his speech voicing his doubt: 'Are you trying to tell me that if I put this on, I am going to be well?' He was suffering from severe panic attacks and I had instructed him to put two Lumanetic plastic frequency patches on each of his wrists and apply a Lumanetic energy-information cream under his eyebrows. Of course he could not see the potent information that the cream or the patches contained and so he could not believe that doing something as innocuous as that could make a difference to his panic attacks. No injections, no pills, no counselling, not even a homoeopathic remedy to swallow – what on Earth was this woman up to?

A fortnight later when he came back and I asked him how he was, his smile and cheeky humour were back: 'I feel human again, but I feel in a bad mood – can you fix my mood?'

CHAPTER 7

BIOLUMANETICS

A NEW LIFE DISCIPLINE

Biolumanetics is a relatively new word for a new life discipline. The word did not exist before 1996; neither did the words 'Luminator' or 'Lumanetics'. From the early 1980s to 1996, Patrick called the Luminator the 'Null-field Generator'.

I had some part to play in the naming of the system. The very first time I met Patrick and saw the system in its awesome entirety, I asked him, 'What do you call it?'

He said, 'VRIC – visual reference of image coherence.'

I was not satisfied and persisted, 'VRIC is a process – the imaging process at the heart of the system. What do you call the whole system? It is more than a process, much more. It is a whole new system, a whole new concept, a new model of understanding.'

Some months later, Patrick asked me if I could think of a new name for the Null-field Generator. After a couple of days the word 'Luminator' popped into my mind. Patrick liked it enough to rename the subtle energy device accordingly. I was also delighted when he named the unique subtle-energetic frequency healing system 'Lumanetics'. So it was that the system got a name, acquired an energy form and became a new model of under-standing.

Biolumanetics, the science of life-light and coherent intention, is the coming together of two stand-alone systems, the Luminator and Lumanetics. Both systems can be and are used on their own and are powerful and effective in their own right. However, it is only in the coming together of the two that one sees the real awesome power of Biolumanetics. Also, there are processes and protocols in Biolumanetics that simply do not exist outside it and cannot be copied or reproduced in any other life discipline or science. In my understanding, using either the Luminator or Lumanetics without the other cannot be called or considered to be Biolumanetics.

In Biolumanetics we are working with the most fundamental level of expression of life in the most direct, objective manner – the interface-point where the energy that is light transforms into the matter that is life.

The quantum leap that is Biolumanetics has vast implications and innumerable applications and the possibilities of synergizing with and enhancing the fields of energy medicine, consciousness studies, family therapy, psychotherapy, the human potential movement and the world of business.

3S: Subtle, Sacred, Scientific

When the Luminator entered my life I knew that this was a momentous event as far as I was concerned. I consider myself immensely lucky and privileged to have encountered it when I did.

I needed to have a vehicle that would reflect the concept of what the Luminator was about. For me from the beginning it was obviously a tool for transformation and I wanted the company name to reflect its extraordinary nature. I asked myself what made it so different, so incredible, so unique and such a landmark in human history. I thought a lot about it for many days and then it was suddenly clear and the three words 'subtle', 'sacred' and 'scientific' came into my head and would not go away. For the first time there was the possibility of these three seemingly conflicted yet important vital aspects of reality being reunited in the most incredible way, giving humanity an unprecedented opportunity to realize the whole truth about its nature in a manner acceptable to all. An additional consideration was my own name, Thrity. Another way of writing it would be '3T'. There was a three in my name and in esoteric traditions three is a highly significant number – the Holy Trinity and so on. So the name '3S' is a combination of me and what I consider the purpose of the Luminator to be.

The 3S Approach

The 3S approach to 'illness', 'disease' and healing is a radical one. While we do take a 'case history' and clients can come with a list of 'symptoms' as long as one's arm, we do not attach a great deal of importance to the disease labels. So why do we record the 'symptoms'? It is done primarily as an *aide memoire*, or a marker of change. It helps the client to recognize that change has taken place. Once a symptom disappears, it often happens that the client forgets that they ever had it.

We also do not attach much significance to any so-called 'diagnosis' and 'prognosis'. Our view is that while we may have a symptom or a full-blown 'disease' at one level, there is another level within each one of us where there is no disease or dysfunction. This level is always present, but we had no direct access to it before the advent of the Luminator and VRIC imaging. Also, 'My doctor says so' and 'The professor said so' can create a sense of certainty in the client's mind as to the outcome and actually hinder progress.

In our view a diagnosis is inherently incomplete and inaccurate at many levels. It is largely based on incomplete information, no matter how many tests have been carried out, as it cannot factor in the infinite variability or the complex multi-factoral processes, the causal chains that underlie and underpin any 'symptom', given that every single cell is inextricably interconnected and communicating with every other of its 50 trillion counterparts in every single milli-second. Also, whilst it is being very slowly recognized that the catch-all 'stress' can cause illness, how is this very important factor assessed, let alone addressed in a conventional surgery, which is the first port of call for the vast majority in seeking relief from their suffering? One cannot fault the practitioner, when they have less than 10 minutes per patient.

So the approach question at 3S is not 'What is the problem?' no matter how seemingly serious or intractable it appears to be, but 'What will raise the vitality and the coherence of the whole bodymind system?' The 'problem' very often disappears, dissolves or is discreated when the bodymind is restored to optimum function at the quantum informational level. The solution may in fact seem to be totally unconnected to the symptom, which can be rather confusing for the client and disconcerting for practitioners of other healing disciplines.

What Happens in a VRIC Assessment at 3S?

People become clients at 3S for a variety of different reasons, to meet needs which may or may not be directly health-related. Some may come to repair broken relationships or to let go of addictive dysfunctional ones, for family therapy, for conflict resolution, to establish coherent intent or for many other reasons. Many of them come because of serious health challenges. This chapter does not go into the details of all the different methodologies we use for assessment and is written in a simple manner to give some idea of what one can expect to experience during a VRIC assessment at 3S.

For the initial assessment we ask clients to bring along photos of their parents, even if they have passed on, and their partners, spouses and children. We also ask them to bring photos of themselves as soon after birth as possible, as children and before and after significant life events such as the onset of an illness, the break-up of a relationship, the death of a loved one or a serious accident. In fact, what we want is a life history in pictures. This is the ideal. If there are no photos available, it is still possible to do a lot, but having the photos is definitely preferable.

We also ask them to bring along every single medication, supplement or remedy of any sort that they are currently taking.

At 3S we do not carry out a physical examination, but take note of their stated complaints and their list of symptoms. Most clients are eager to give a long and detailed list of symptoms, which are noted. I am equally or more interested in their life story, the significant events, deaths, divorces, what upsets them and their professional and personal relationships. Most people, when they become comfortable and learn to trust, will give a lot of in-depth information about themselves. I want to know what they want out of the process and I apprise them of what they can reasonably expect from it.

I never sit across a table from a client; we always sit facing each other with no barrier in between. I want them to relax and be as comfortable as possible. The room where we do the assessment is not clinical or intimidating in any way. It has paintings on the walls, a comfortable sofa, is painted in neutral colours and has loads of plants and flowers. Of course the Luminator is present in a corner of the room.

This initial 'getting to know you' process, where I get to know the client and the client gets to know me, can take up to an hour.

After that we do the imaging. You will remember that all VRIC imaging is done with a simple fixed-focus Polaroid camera with a masked flash.

The first image, which we call the 'baseline image', is taken with the client holding nothing at all. If the assessment is of a family or more than one person, each person will have a baseline image taken.

The next step often is for the main client to hold various photographs of themselves or significant others in their lives in each hand and then be imaged. From that we can determine what or who presents the greatest energetic challenge to the system of the client and this takes us well beyond what the client thinks, says or feels. In fact, clients are often extremely surprised about which events or persons present the challenge. Thus it is the bodymind system that establishes the priority of what needs to be handled and it is not reliant upon the practitioner's knowledge, insight or intuition or the client's opinions or demands. Then, using certain methods, we choose the Lumanetics to resolve that particular challenge.

The next step is for the client to be imaged holding the photo that created the greatest incoherence along with the selected Lumanetic creams or frequency vials until coherence is seen to be established with a clear image. In this way both the client and the practitioner can see that the challenge has been neutralized in the energy system.

Finally, once we have arrived at the appropriate energetic solution as evidenced through VRIC, we ask the client to hold the relevant Lumanetic solution(s) plus their allopathic medication or supplements or homoeopathic remedies and re-image them to see if they can be factored in and to establish that they combine well as a total solution for the client.

The client is then instructed how and where the Lumanetics that made their image coherent are to be applied or carried.

An assessment at 3S can take up to two hours and in general clients come once a month for an assessment.

This is the bare bones of the process, so to speak, and just gives some idea of the mechanics of it.

Science of 'Miracles'

Over the years at 3S I have been witness to what can only be described as miracles. I have been left standing in wonder and awe at the awesome intelligence that resides within the body and the power of the extraordinary, radical new system that is Biolumanetics.

The Biolumanetics process can, however, sometimes be confounding for clients. I know for sure that the cosmic joker had a hand in its creation when I see the awesome power that it demonstrates and the impossibly simple-looking tools that hold this power. A fuzzy photo and a plastic patch containing 'nothing' creating radical changes at every level? My brain simply cannot compute it to this day. I have to remind myself of the difference between the light bulb and the laser effect and the *Encyclopaedia Britannica* and the grain of sand. So I can understand why it is hard for people to come to grips with the idea and understand that applying a cream to an eyebrow or between the toes or wearing a plastic patch on their solar plexus can create radical and profound physical, mental, emotional and behavioural changes as quickly as they do.

Children and younger people, who are generally clearer and less brainwashed and conditioned than older people, do not have the same problem. Most people are conditioned and believe that when they are ill, they have to do something equally unpleasant like take bitter medicine or have an injection or, in a worst-case scenario, have surgery to get better. So it is possible to understand their confusion when profound and powerful changes happen in an incredibly innocuous way. It is even more mind-bending when they ask what the 'medicines' contain and I tell them that they contain nothing physical at all, simply a frequency or an energy signature.

I remember a client in his fifties asking me if it was possible for his eyesight to improve so quickly. He told me that as soon as he had applied the Lumanetic cream to his eyebrow ridge, he had felt a change and there had been a significant improvement in his vision. Yet it had been difficult for him to believe it. A little eight-year-old boy who had used exactly the same cream had no such difficulty. He had told his teacher that he could read and write better when he applied the 'magic' cream to his eyebrow. His parents, though, had not made the connection until the teacher had asked them about this 'magic' cream.

I remember another instance that illustrates this point even more dramatically. The same adult client had received enormous benefit from the Biolumanetics process and had been rapidly healed from the symptoms of 'MS'. The Lumanetic frequency pad had worked wonders for him and he knew and acknowledged that. One day his curiosity got the better of him. He decided to find out what it contained. So he cut it open and found nothing in it. Straightaway he was on the phone to me in confusion. He told me what he had done and asked me if I was using what he called 'reverse psychology' on him. I told him the pad contained a frequency and one could not see a frequency. In fact we could only know it contained something, or rather should I say 'non-thing', through VRIC; it was not within the remit of the five-sensory reality. I also reminded him that he had felt the tangible benefit and that all his symptoms had disappeared.

Short Case Studies Using Lumanetics
One of the general misconceptions that I come across from clients and from persons who ask in a spirit of genuine enquiry how the system works is that this is a spiritual system which fits spiritual needs, and so does not affect the physical level and may not be able to help greatly in alleviating physical challenges. There is a genuine schism in people's minds, so that even those who supposedly believe in vibrational healing often cannot get their heads around the fact that energy medicine can have very real, tangible and palpable physical effects. There is also

often the misconception that energy medicine takes longer to work than allopathic medicine. These short case studies are presented with a view to clearing those erroneous and somewhat nonsensical misconceptions, which are largely due to ignorance of the fact of the interconnectedness of the whole.

PE was 27 when she came to 3S. An aspiring actress, she had been diagnosed with 'polycystic ovary syndrome'. She had not had proper periods since she was 13 and was terrified she would not be able to have children. In her words she did not 'feel like a woman'. She had been to see a healer and six months prior to coming to 3S she had had a proper period, but then her periods had disappeared again.

Within three months PE started getting light periods and now she has had regular 'proper' periods with no breaks for over a year. I still remember how delighted she was when she got her first 'proper' period. She phoned me very early in the morning to tell me the news and I remember being quite grumpy at someone calling me so early until I realized how delighted and thankful she was and could join in her joy.

Only Lumanetics energy-information tools were used for PE.

JM was 24 when she came to 3S. Extremely perceptive and insightful, she was also very troubled and dysfunctional in many ways, by her own account. She felt her family was extremely dys-functional and she suffered from 'polycystic ovary syndrome', with periods that were very irregular. She had also abused drugs, alcohol and food in earlier years and had a turbulent and troubled history. Her periods regularized very fast and to her dismay she found herself unexpectedly pregnant.

Again only Lumanetics were used.

AMc was 27 when she came to 3S. She was having extremely painful periods and had been diagnosed with 'endometriosis'. She got relief from the pain almost immediately after starting at 3S and scans taken after using Lumanetics for four months revealed that she had healed completely, though I am told that there is no 'cure' for 'endometriosis'. Today, after a couple of years, she is still completely free of period pain.

SL was in her mid-fifties and suffered from extremely severe hot flushes and night sweats that left her drenched every night. These were accompanied by palpitations and she was having a very difficult time of it. She worked very hard and led a very stressful life, and was either unwilling or unable to change that. We gave her a Lumanetic frequency pad after her first Biolumanetics assessment. She could not believe that the very first night she wore this little plastic frequency pad on her body, she felt cold and could sleep again.

BZ was 17 and came from an orthodox religious background. He looked about 12 years old. He suffered from a congenital blood disorder causing anaemia, yet could not take iron. He was highly intelligent, mature and motivated, but was always tired, sleepy and unable to undertake his studies with the concentration that he would have liked.

After wearing the Lumanetic frequency pad for a month, he found his energy levels had improved beyond all recognition. This was acknowledged by his mentor, who had brought him to 3S. Today he still has to continue wearing the frequency pad, but his blood count has improved, much to his doctor's surprise. He is now much happier, as he can study with the seriousness that he had wanted, and he does not need as much sleep as before.

Over the years I have seen clients arrive in extreme distress or crisis, physical and/or mental, and leave two hours later looking and feeling completely different.

This incident occurred when Patrick came to London in 1996. The subject was a doctor in his early forties. I had only made his acquaintance very recently, so I was surprised to receive a call from a friend of his to say that he suffered from terrible migraines and was having an attack and had not been able to shake it off for the last two days. He was throwing up and was prostrate from the unbearable pain. Could Patrick help?

The doctor was driven over by his friend and when he appeared at my door he had one hand over his eye and was doubled over with pain. We helped him onto the massage table and Patrick massaged the Lumanetic cream into his light receptors on the bony ridge under the eyebrows, at the back of the ears and at the base of the neck. He was also instructed to change his breathing and breathe from the belly.

In 20 minutes or less, he was OK. He could stand up straight, carry on a reasonable conversation and the pain was considerably alleviated, so much so that he decided he could attend a meeting that very afternoon, which would certainly not have been a possibility just half an hour back.

In his case no imaging was done. For me it was a demonstration in real terms of the power of Lumanetics.

LM was a 50-year-old woman. When she came to 3S she had been ill for ten years. Her challenges included severe digestive food allergies, frozen shoulder, irritable bowel, constant headaches, very poor memory, severe depression, low back pain and thrush. In her own words, she felt 'toxic'. She had been treated with homoeopathy, allopathy, nutritional therapy, acupuncture and cranio-sacral therapy and had been seen by at least 10 practitioners. She was extremely distressed, desperate and less than hopeful. She desperately wanted to visit her son in Colorado, but her condition made it impossible.

Using VRIC and Biolumanetics, however, she made a full recovery. After four assessments she was able to leave for Colorado and even managed, to her surprise and mine, to go climbing in the Rockies.

LC was 57 years old. She had been diagnosed five years before as suffering from a rare genetic disorder called Anderson-Fabry disease. She was a gifted hands-on healer and had done all she could to help herself. She worked very hard and had a fairly challenging relationship with her second husband. She described her symptoms as follows: low back pain, joint pain and stiffness, allergies, cold and tingling extremities, diarrhoea, constipation, haemorrhoids, heart problems and ankle swelling, plus vision and dental problems.

The following is an abridged version of her account of the changes that happened to her since she started treatment using Biolumanetics:

'As a Fabryite one of the symptoms is that you don't sweat and this can be very painful as the toxins stay in the body and you feel aches and pains and can get very bloated. Now I sweat.
I can now eat most things in moderation without the Fabry pain in my hands and feet.
My skin no longer feels raw. It used to feel as though I had no skin at all and it was painful to touch.
My stamina has increased, despite a particularly taxing 18

months. I know that under similar circumstances with my previous record I would probably have had at least six Fabry attacks under this kind of stress and during this time I have not had the slightest problem.'

TS was almost 20 when she came to see me at 3S. Five months previously she had been involved in a serious accident when her car had overturned on the motorway at high speed. She had been alone in the car and she had luckily not been injured. However, since that time her periods had become totally erratic and now she was bleeding every few days. The bleeding would stop for several days and then restart. She said she was feeling very low and washed-out. In medical terms she would have been diagnosed with PTSD (post-traumatic stress disorder). Her doctor had told her there was not much she could do except put her on the pill, which TS was not happy to accept.

At her first Biolumanetics assessment she told me she was going away for several months to South America in less than two months. She had already booked her ticket and was not willing to change that. I was nonplussed, as I could not see how her health challenge could be addressed in such a short time. I also wondered at the wisdom of going to an unknown country with an unresolved health issue that was not necessarily going to get better. I mentioned this to both TS and her mother and said I could not give any guarantee as to the time frame, but I was willing to go ahead if this was clearly understood. They both accepted this and wanted to go ahead and engage in the process.

TS came for four Biolumanetics assessments over the next six weeks. By the third assessment she had experienced a three-week break from the bleeding, which was the longest break she had had since the accident. Her system had calmed down and was starting to behave normally. By the time she left for South America the periods had regularized, to everyone's relief and amazement. They remain regular to this day, a couple of years later.

Only Lumanetic frequency tools were used in conjunction with VRIC imaging to achieve this result.

The important point to note here is that in none of these cases was a diagnosis made at 3S in the conventional sense and at no time were the symptoms addressed directly with the fix-it approach. There was only the awesome power of light, energy and information, applied to the nth degree of precision.

My Journey of Exploration and Discovery

When I first went to Michigan in 1995 my daughter and I stayed for 15 days and were trained in the use of the Luminator by Patrick and his chiropractor associate Dr Carolyn Szutarski. I had come with great curiosity and was very keen to learn all I could.

Patrick shared his many years' experience and successful VRIC case studies of clients with very serious intractable 'illnesses' with labels such as 'chronic fatigue', 'PMS', 'ADD and ADHD', 'diabetic neuropathy', etc. On the one level I was very impressed, but on the other hand I was not greatly interested, as I had no real interest in disease or miracle cures. In fact, if I had known that I was going to be handling those kind of 'illnesses', I probably would never have engaged with the system, as I had no inclination whatsoever in that direction. My thinking had veered in a completely different direction. I knew immediately that this system was a tool for the human-potential movement and it was my intention to use it in that way. Patrick's experience, however, was to stand me in good stead, as the cosmic joker had decided that I would have to handle 'illnesses' with various labels.

Remembering Patrick's visual case studies gave me the confidence to carry on. In the first year I was on the phone to him on innumerable occasions for advice and reassurance as I found myself thrown in at the deep end without any real warning. My son, a shiatsu practitioner, joined me for a year in mid '96 and helped me enormously in that initial period. I also consulted my daughter, who was a pillar of strength when I felt unsure, though she did not work with me at that time. So I had a wonderful support system when I needed it most.

Interestingly, when I first got the Luminator it was plugged into the electricity supply and turned on 24 hours a day, 7 days a week, 365 days a year. Then in 1998 I moved it to another room. When I turned it on, something was not right. One of the little fan motors started making a rather disturbing sound (it sounded like a loose bearing), so I turned it off. Yet the Luminator continued to work. How did I find this out? The VRIC effect did not stop and the fuzzy pictures kept coming. From that day to this the Luminator has not been connected to any power source and yet continues to function and do what it does.

After the third quarter of 1997 I was pretty much on my own and had gained enough experience to be confident of the system and its phenomenal capabilities. A lot of new methods and variations were developed after that period. By then I had become thoroughly grounded, experienced and comfortable in the basic protocols, had learned to use them with efficiency and effectiveness and been rewarded with wonderful results.

There is really no aspect of the human that this system does not touch. The case studies or energy stories in the various chapters of this book have been selected with a view to demonstrating the depth, extent and scope of possibilities that exist within it. In every case the changes happened at many different levels. Quite simply, with this system the physical, mental, emotional and spiritual aspects of life can be explored and addressed as the need arises – with a degree of precision, specificity, depth, simplicity and directness unavailable anywhere else today.

Milestones

There were many important milestones on my journey of discovery and the methods discovered and systematized as a result are now part and parcel of the methods used every day at 3S. My clients were the agency through which I was taught. Every one of them came with a gift for me. Yes, they wanted something too, of course, and I was enabled to help them in ways I could never have believed possible. Some incidents stick clearly in my mind even after these many years. They were the significant milestones that helped me to understand more of what was going on with my clients.

One of my most striking memories is of a client in her fifties who showed me photos of herself at times in her life when she was happy and at times when she was acutely unhappy and wanted me to image her with these photos. I had not thought of doing that before. When I imaged her holding the various photos I was amazed at how her VRIC image fragmented, even though some of the photos that she was holding had been taken more than 45 years ago. While I knew in theory, from my psychoanalysis days, about the vast unconscious and its unseen and awesome power over the personality, here it was revealed in a photo. The past and the present were one, and the hidden pain of the past could be seen in the fragmented image of my client in the present.

Many years ago I had walked away from conventional psychotherapy as I had no interest in talking endlessly about the same problem without a real resolution in sight. The wonder of this system was that I did not have to discuss in gory detail what had happened in the past. Bringing the hidden trauma into form through words was not necessary or relevant. Using Biolumanetics techniques one could neutralize the pain where it existed in the being and see through a photo that the job was done. No guesswork was involved, no digging and delving into dysfunction, just an incredible and precise enhancement of function. And the client could participate fully in the process and literally see their fragmented self made whole again.

This particular breakthrough was incredibly helpful when it came to imaging children and teenagers who perhaps did not know why they were troubled or did not have the ability or the willingness to express what was troubling them.

A striking example comes to mind. He was seven years old and his mother told me that he had had a hard time when he was 17 months old and his little brother was born. When I imaged him holding his own photo at age 17 months his image fragmented, but the boy himself would not have been able to remember or explain his past difficulties. People often talk glibly about going to the 'root cause' of the 'problem' when actually it is almost impossible to do so unless one has access to VRIC.

Another time, when a client in his thirties held a photo of himself at the age of two he was perfectly clear and yet when he held a photo of himself at the age of three his image fragmented. I asked his father, who was present, whether he could offer any insights into this occurrence and after a moment's thought he remembered that his son had gone to school at three and had found it difficult to adjust to the new environment after the loving and protected environment of his home. The important point to note here is that whether the father had remembered the challenging event or circumstance or not did not really matter. The bodymind system of the client was truthful and unequivocal about the problem and equally rigorous about what it needed to resolve that particular challenge.

This technique was taken a huge step further when I decided to image people with photos of themselves as babies, as close to birth as possible. This was my way of trying to get to the so-called root cause of the suffering, at least in this lifetime. This came from the insight that the birth process can be traumatic for the baby and if the mother has been unhappy or unwell during pregnancy this will also have an impact on the child. Though it happened before birth, the effect could be seen in the here and now. Most importantly of all, it could be neutralized, thus stopping it from wreaking havoc in the present.

It is important to understand the difference between the process of neutralizing as done through Biolumanetics and the process of suppression as used in orthodox medicine. The orthodox system seeks to address the symptom as directly as possible without understanding the depth and complexity of the process underlying the disturbance, whereas in Biolumanetics we are asking the Super Intelligence at the centre of the individual's bodymind system what will help it to restore balance and neutrality and then giving it what it needs and not what we think it needs. One system assumes it knows better than the bodymind and seeks to bend it to its will whereas the other knows that the bodymind is doing whatever it is for a reason, though one may not ever find out the exact reason because of the complexity involved and the multiple factors that may be responsible. So it simply asks that individual's system what it needs for resolution. The system which created the discord knows exactly what will discreate it, so it comes up with the exact solution for a successful resolution. There is no guesswork and no force involved except the force of extreme intelligence and gentleness.

These processes of clearing and neutralizing the effects of the past are used with every client, no matter whether their stated challenge is physiological or psychological, and work incredibly well across the board. However, my central intention and interest when I engage with a client is not only the 'cure' of the 'illness' from which they may have come to seek relief but also their happiness, the fulfilment of their dreams and their recognition of the reason for their life's journey. The healing has to be at all levels, and though it doesn't happen in a straight-line manner, all at the same time, over and over again I have had the privilege, the pleasure, the joy and gratification of seeing an individual wake up and assume control of their lives in ways they had never attempted before. I have seen their courage awaken, their relationships blossom, their creativity flower and their lives become more than they had ever dreamed of. As one of my clients said, 'I got a lot more than I bargained for and a lot more than I paid for.' Another one said, 'Before I came here I thought my life was OK. I would not have dreamed that it could be so different.'

It is seeing these 'miracles' happen before my eyes that has kept me involved, captivated and captive all these years in a manner I would never have thought possible for me. So in the end I am using the system to access the hidden potential of the infinite human, which is what I wanted to do when I first came across it, and along the way the cosmic joker has taught me the true nature of wellness and illness.

Derek

This was one of my earlier cases and I learned many striking lessons from it. See what you make of it.

I had known Derek for a few years. I liked him. He was an amiable, charming and pleasant man. We were not close friends in the sense that we met infrequently, but it was a pleasant association and he had been to my place a few times for a meal. We phoned each other occasionally to keep in touch.

At the end of 1996 I found out through a mutual acquaintance that he was very ill and had 'MS'. I was sorry to hear this and phoned him to say hello. I told him about Biolumanetics and offered to help, though I could give no guarantees.

Derek was very happy to take up my offer, as the prognosis he had been given was quite dire. He already trusted me, as I had supported him with counselling through some very difficult times when his life had fallen apart due to a very destructive relationship. He had been wiped out financially and emotionally at that time and had become gravely ill. Derek had never been the complaining sort, though. In fact he was always quite undemanding and very positive in his outlook.

At the time I was still relatively inexperienced as far as Biolumanetics went and I had never treated anyone with 'MS'. The only thing I was sure of was that the treatment could not harm Derek.

The following interview was recorded in February 2002, five years after Derek had been to 3S for treatment. In the interview he gave me details that he had not mentioned at the time. He had not told me, for example, that he had lost the sight of one eye or that he had been unable to walk for a while. All this was news to me and in a way I was glad he had not told me when he had first come to see me, as it had helped me to remain optimistic.

This is an abridged version of our phone interview:

Thrity: I am going to take you back to the time when you came here to 3S. Can you tell me when you were diagnosed with 'MS' and about the process you went through in order for the doctors to come to that diagnosis?

Derek: That was approximately nine years ago. I went to the doctor first of all because there seemed to be something wrong with my balance and my co-ordination in reaching for things. I was sent to the Royal Free Hospital at Hampstead and they took lots of blood samples and did a lumbar puncture. They sat me in a very dark room with lots of lights flashing and I had to keep pressing buttons when I saw the lights, to check my vision. Then I went back to the doctor and he said, 'It's MS.' He had originally thought I had had a stroke, because I was talking in quite a slurred way. In fact people at work had wondered whether I'd been drinking, because I sounded as though I was drunk. My mouth also seemed to be down to one side and that's why the doctor initially thought it was a stroke. But then he said it was MS and that was that.

Thrity: When you were in that state, did they do anything? Could they do anything?

Derek: The doctor said to me there really wasn't anything he could recommend. There were beta blockers, but he did not like the thought of those. He did say that because I was older I wouldn't get it anywhere as badly as somebody younger. But nevertheless it was a real shock to me.

Thrity: At that point you were working only 15 hours a week – you couldn't work full time?

Derek: No.

Thrity: What happened if you worked full time? Did you try to work full time?

Derek: I did, but I just used to get so tired. I couldn't even pick up two coffee cups without dropping one of them. I was in a terrible condition. I suppose it was the MS feeding on me or the thought of it feeding on me.

Thrity: What was the time span between this happening and your previous relationship, which was a very difficult one for you?

Derek: Uh, two years.

Thrity: It happened two years later?

Derek: Yes, but while I was in that relationship I did lose the sight of my left eye completely. I had to go to Moorfields Hospital to have all sorts of tests done, and looking back over my records, the doctors thought that maybe that was the beginning of it.

Thrity: That was a particularly stressful time in your life.

Derek: Totally. And stress was the one thing that always made me feel worse.

Thrity: Yes. And at that time you were counselling the unemployed – not an easy thing to do. It was a very stressful job.

Derek: I used to be terrified!

Thrity: I just want to establish a history so that when I write it all down it will be complete and accurate.

Derek: Yes.

Thrity: How long was it before you came to see me after your diagnosis? Roughly?

Derek: Two or three years.

Thrity: In those two or three years had anything deteriorated or were things just the same?

Derek: I had deteriorated.

Thrity: In what way?

Derek: I'd reach out for something and completely miss it. I'd walk into doorways instead of going through the door.

Thrity: Why? Because you couldn't see?

Derek: No, because I would just lose my balance. I was also unaware of things, my vision wasn't so good and one particular time I couldn't walk properly for two weeks. I just could not walk.

Thrity: What do you mean? You had to lie in bed?

Derek: No, I didn't lie in bed, but when I was walking I would drag my leg behind me. It was horrendous. I couldn't drive, because I physically couldn't lift my foot onto the brake. I had no control over the whole of the left side of my body. It just seemed to shut down on me. Then of course you phoned me and told me what you were into and I came to your house and there was [the Luminator] buzzing in the corner. You got me to stand between two plants and took some Polaroid pictures of me, which were quite weird really.

Thrity: I also gave you [a Lumanetic frequency pad].

Derek: Yes, I put it on my chest and it calmed me amazingly.

Thrity: What were the changes that happened for you?

Derek: Through [Biolumanetics] and through talking to you I felt better almost immediately. I felt a sense of wellbeing. On the next visit, when you took the photographs I was in focus.

Thrity: What was happening to you at the physical level?

Derek: I had a wonderful sense of wellbeing.

Thrity: And your balance and your eyesight?

Derek: Were absolutely fine.

Thrity: What, within just a couple of sessions?

Derek: Yes. People I spoke to said, 'It's amazing, I can't believe you are the same person. What's happened?'

Thrity: Right. Your sense of balance, what happened with that?

Derek: My balance was fine.

Thrity: Do you remember that instance when you were going to lose your job and you came and you had a very fuzzy photograph and I asked you what was the matter and you told me you were going to be made redundant again? I asked you how you felt and you told me you felt very stressed. It was showing in the photograph. Do you remember that? That was a very important photograph for you. After that we sat down and I said, 'How do you feel about losing the job?' and you told me you felt very anxious. I then asked how your partner felt about it and you said she was very anxious. I just laughed and said, 'That makes two anxious people! Very beneficial for both.' [Gentle humour makes people realize a situation is not as serious as it may appear and there is another, less fearful viewpoint.] Then we discussed various options and I reminded you of your many talents, your resilient and optimistic nature, that if you could have one job there was no reason why you could not get another and we discussed a whole series of things that you were good at and that you could do. At the end of that you felt that you could do whatever you needed to do and your whole mindset had changed.

Derek: I felt very positive, yes.

Thrity: Yes, and then we took another photograph of you holding nothing and you had become coherent. Do you remember that?

Derek: I do.

Thrity: That was, I think, a moment of realization.

Derek: I believe so. Yes, I realized I could be what I wanted to be and that I wasn't tied to that one thing that I was putting so much importance on.

Thrity: And after losing the job that was causing you stress, you did manage to get another job fairly rapidly, didn't you?

Derek: Yes.

Thrity: Was it a better job or a worse job?

Derek: Oh, a totally better job. A complete notch up.
(It was much more enjoyable and brought him much more money, which enabled him to move to a nicer flat.)

Thrity: Right. After that, were you working full time?

Derek: Yes, I was working full time without any problems at all and doing longer hours than even full time. I would be up at half-past five in the morning and leaving at a quarter to six to arrive at the office by seven o'clock and getting back at almost about seven o'clock. I was doing a long day.

Thrity: You were OK with that?

Derek: I was tired, but anybody would be tired.

Thrity: You were not exhausted, your voice was not slurred, you were not losing your balance or any of those things, and your eyesight was OK too?

Derek: Everything was fine.

I had forgotten to ask Derek a very important question. So I phoned him back and asked him:

Thrity: Do you remember when you first came I asked you whether you were prepared to consider the possibility that you did not have MS. Do you remember that?

Derek: I do indeed.

Thrity: What did you feel when I said that?

Derek: I felt confused. After undergoing the lumbar puncture and having the doctor say to me so categorically that I had MS, it was difficult to accept, I suppose. It would be for anyone.

Thrity: Absolutely. I am not in any way doubting that. But did you change your mind about that? Later when I asked you if you had MS, you categorically said, 'No, I do not.' Do you remember that?

Derek: I do.

Diagnosis

When Derek had come to me with his categorical 'diagnosis', he had 'known' the 'prognosis' of his 'illness' – it was 'incurable' and 'progressive'. It was a no-hope, no-win situation, there was nothing to look forward to, and his life and his body were likely to fulfil his fearful expectation. In Biolumanetics we can see that thought creates form. To break the mindset and reverse the process of fear to one of hope was the starting point for me. It was a vital key to Derek's participation in his own healing. I have to say at this juncture that it was not the only key, but it was a very important one.

At the time I asked him, 'What does it mean to have MS? What are the physical markers for your illness?'

He told me about his failing eyesight, his loss of balance, his walking into doors, his extreme exhaustion and his inability to work for more than 15 hours a week.

Then I asked, 'So, if all these markers were to disappear, would you have MS?'

He said, not with any belief or conviction, that if they disappeared, then he would not have MS. At that point his belief in the doctor's diagnosis was greater – very justifiably and reasonably – than his knowledge of my healing discipline or of the magic that lay locked in his own bodymind system. He had come along to try something as a last resort, but a large part of him was convinced that there really was no hope.

My views on the subject of diagnosis are radical. I know from my experience of working with Biolumanetics that 'illness' is an energetic phenomenon. How can one ever 'diagnose' a flowing sea of information that is the human body? How can one 'cure' a flow of ever-changing dynamic complexity? The language does not compute. It does not make sense.

With a standard diagnosis there is little or no understanding of the complex multi-factoral nature of the 'causes' of 'illness'. There is little or no understanding of the interconnected nature of the human bodymind system. Making a diagnosis on the one hand confirms to you that something is wrong, but today there is increasing evidence that knowing what is wrong does not necessarily mean that you or a practitioner knows how to put it right. Side effects, symptom shifts, the recurrence of a condition in an even more severe form or the downright worsening of it, as well as the current increase in iatrogenic illness (illness as a direct result of treatment), show the clear gap between the laudable intention and the less than perfect reality.

Knowing how to put symptoms right or effect cures is neither simple nor easy – and does not follow in a simple linear way. The two processes are separate and non-linear or unpredictable. While I totally accept that symptoms and suffering are real and not only in the mind or the imagination of the client – after all, Derek's symptoms were not imaginary – the model of understanding from which a diagnosis comes has to be considered an incomplete and therefore inaccurate model.

The flaw in understanding arises from viewing the body as a static, mechanical, chemical entity or object rather than a dynamic flowing process. I would concede that it would be halfway reasonable for Derek's doctor to say to him, 'It appears you have the symptoms of MS at one level and we do not know much about MS. I would go and explore other avenues of stress management and see if you can be helped,' but in fact there was no qualification of any sort in the statement that was actually given to him. That was absolute. Furthermore, there was no understanding of Derek's gentle character or the challenging relationship that had precipitated the chaos in his system that had ended in the symptoms of the severe illness that could so easily have destroyed his life. There was no enquiry into what made his life tick or gave it meaning. There was no understanding of Derek the loving, feeling human. He was simply a collection of symptoms that added up to the drastic fearful acronym 'MS'. The various tests at the physical level, the so-called hard evidence, were convincing and yet so incomplete – a small part of a very large picture that was mistaken for the whole and resulted in a 'sentence' of disease and death.

The fault, if any, does not lie with doctors. Most of them are sincere, devoted and caring, but they are using a model of understanding that is fatally flawed because of its incompleteness.

So, in short, is there anything to be gained by a diagnosis? There are pros and cons and I have to say the answer lies in the phrase 'It depends.'

I was at a seminar of energy practitioners, all eager to learn. After the demos and the explanations, it was question time. The person handling the questions was a Russian doctor who was also a physicist and an energy-medicine practitioner. Quiet, thoughtful, softly spoken and in my view very knowledgeable, Dr Michael Teppone was impressive. His response to every question started with the phrase 'It depends.' I smiled and thought, 'A man after my own heart.' In that one phrase lay a whole way of perceiving reality, a philosophy, an attitude and an approach to the universe that came from a deep understanding of the dynamic flow, vast complexity and infinite variability that exist at the vibrational level – a world of probabilities and possibilities but not of simplistic certainties. The seemingly fixed reality of the physical level, with its seeming certainties and definite and 'right' course of action with predictable positive results, is far from being an actuality.

Coming back to the benefits of an accurate diagnosis, the best that can be said about it is that it can give a detailed and in-depth picture of a very, very small part of a complex whole. It is useful as a starting point, a pointer, provided it is made within the framework of a much larger understanding. Tests can be useful to assess change, provided the tester is trained to look for more than the obvious, and a diagnosis can be useful in a crisis or emergency situation in providing a very short-term plan for the management of critical illness. However, with the insights gained through working with Biolumanetics and my exploration of the new non-invasive but potent technologies, I would venture to say that in a few short years, when we really begin to harness the power of subtle energy, expand our understanding of the extraordinary human bodymind system and cease to view it primarily as a physical, mechanical, chemical entity, then the present systems will be seen to be primitive, crude and obsolete. They will be simply a part of human history, the process of exploration, another step on the way to understanding ourselves.

In the meantime, who is responsible and who is to blame for the current state of affairs? Everyone and no one. All of us. That means you and I and the whole of society. It is simply part and parcel of the process of evolution. All of us have contributed, knowingly and unknowingly, to what is. It is so easy to point fingers and assign blame when we do not get exactly what we want – health or cures or whatever. But to effect real change, the understanding of the whole body of humanity has to change. As that happens, the new systems will seamlessly come into their own and a new, gentle, effective and potent paradigm of health, wellness and super function will become the order of the day. That day is not far into the future. It has to start with you and me making different choices now. You and I are the movers and shakers and every great change has to start with one human daring to be different.

So, getting back to my friend Derek, you have to ask yourself, did he or didn't he have MS?

Memorable Moments

As well as Derek's case, there were many other memorable moments along the way. Here are a few more...

This incident happened at the beginning of 1996, in the very early days of my practice. A couple had come from South Africa to visit. He was a trance medium in his forties and she was an astrologer and healer in her early fifties. They had come to see a demonstration of the aura camera I had been working with, with a view to purchasing one for themselves. I thought it would be a matter of interest to them to know about the Luminator and Biolumanetics. As a courtesy, I offered them a VRIC assessment to demonstrate the system. I did not know anything about them and took no case history. I simply harmonized their energy as a couple and came up with a particular Lumanetic cream for the man to carry. He went off with it and I thought no more about it.

They came back a couple of days later. They seemed quite excited. The wife picked up a colour leaflet from my coffee table and asked him, 'What is this colour?' He replied, 'Red.' Then she asked him the same question while pointing to something green. He recognized the colour as green. I was a bit mystified and waited for them to tell me what it was about.

He told me that he had been diagnosed as colour-blind when he was four years old. His father was an opthalmologist. But now, for 'no apparent reason' that he could fathom, he had suddenly recovered the use of his colour vision.

I was amazed and excited, as I knew one of the components of the Lumanetic cream was an energetic light enhancer which was supposed to energize the pineal and was known to improve eyesight. I knew the theory, but had never experienced anything like it.

To gain confirmation that I was on the right track, I phoned Patrick, told him what had happened and asked if it was possible. His laconic answer took my breath away: 'It happens very often.'

The couple moved house shortly afterwards and I lost touch with them. I would love to know whether the improvements held.

He was a 15-year-old. He was in a boarding school. His skin sallow with pimples, he was very unhappy and closed-down. His problem was bedwetting, which was causing him great mortification, shame and unhappiness.

After two VRIC assessments his bedwetting stopped, never to return. I could hardly recognize the delighted, happy and grateful boy, bright and full of confidence, who announced quite triumphantly that he was absolutely fine. Carrying two Lumanetic energy-information creams in his pockets was all it took.

I can still see the happiness in that young man's face and it fills me with delight, gratitude and wonder.

DL was in his fifties, very kind and generous, and had been diagnosed as dysphasic (I hasten to say not by me). He certainly could repeat himself a lot and someone had rather unkindly described him as a bore. He was actually well read, very well informed on all holistic matters and had experienced many different therapies.

After undergoing the coherence enhancement with Biolumanetics, he fell in love with a young therapist and showed me, ever so shyly, some lyrical poetry he had written about her. There was nothing dysphasic or boring about those fluent, beautiful and tender poems. I remember being touched by the tender feeling heart that lay hidden behind a slightly clumsy exterior.

Electromagnetic Stress – Health Time Bomb of the 21st Century

Today we live in electromagnetic environments that can be very unhealthy for us. Televisions, mobile phones and computers, despite all their benefits, are health time bombs. Excessive use of them can be very damaging. There are few real solutions when the body becomes 'allergic' to all things electronic or electrical, but one of my clients taught me that Biolumanetics is one of them.

SG was 29 when she came to 3S. Rather surprisingly, it was her mother who rang me from the north of England to make the appointment. SG lived only 15 minutes away from me in London, but she was unable to use a phone – not just a mobile phone, but any phone at all. Her mother sounded desperately worried; her daughter had been ill for ten years. She was in the middle of having a course of treatment that had already cost upwards of £6,000 in the last few months and there had been no improvement in her condition. She was also seeing an osteopath and an acupuncturist for pain control for previous injuries.

SG duly arrived for the appointment. Quite diminutive, with a bright smiling face and cheerful manner, she did not give the impression of being seriously ill. But as I got to know her, I could only admire the pluck and courage with which this young woman faced her life, which was extremely challenged at many levels. Her innate resilience was readily apparent from day one. Whatever her suffering, she was not a whinger or whiner and did not exhibit any self-pity. It was very impressive.

During the first assessment she described her condition:

'I have had a very long string of health problems and emotional problems as well. I have had glandular fever since last June. Actually, I have had glandular fever on and off for over ten years. I felt a little bit better in July and went back to work, but after two months I felt really unwell. My glands get sore – they are sore now – and I get feverish and I have still got a high number of anti-bodies in my blood. I have had anti-viral drugs, IV treatment, every-thing, but nothing has worked. Underlying it, I have endometriosis and I also have a lot of sports injuries, which occurred ten years ago. About a year before I originally got glandular fever, I damaged my knee and ankle really badly and I have chronic tendonitis, which is very painful, as a result. Then in June of last year I could not use my mobile phone at all – it coincided with the recurrence of my glandular fever – and by Christmas time I was using the cordless phone a lot, but before I knew it, I could not use any phone. In March I went back to work, but by April everything electrical had started affecting me. Whenever I was near an electrical appliance I would feel dizzy and my face would go numb. Now it happens with everything – TV, radio, everything. Even listening to a CD is not possible.'

SG had developed hypersensitivity to all things electrical. She agreed that her whole system was in chaos and that she was in a downward spiral of frightening proportions, but her sensitivity to electrical things was what most concerned her: 'It comes out of nowhere. One day I will be fine with the radio and the next day it is gone.'

Only half-jokingly, I said, 'Falling apart at 29!'

SG laughed and agreed that she was indeed falling apart.

At the second assessment, she explained:

'I came to see you on a Tuesday. The week following was awful. I was tired as I hadn't been before, because, touch wood, glandular tiredness is not something I have had. I had awful pains in my kidneys and I felt really fagged out. Then in weeks three and four I was with my parents and I was doing pretty well, actually. My glandular fever had always been up and down anyway, but I was definitely noticing a difference in my sensitivities. Up until then I had not been able to listen to the radio or go near a TV without feeling dizzy or feeling numbness in my face, but then I discovered that I could listen to the radio with no problem, although I did not overdo it, and walking into a room where the TV was on did not affect me, but then round about the end of week four, it wasn't so good. I don't know if it was because I had overdone things or because I had done quite a lot physically, but my glands fired up. Maybe it was combination of getting excited and doing too much and maybe the gap of over five and a half weeks between treatments was too much. For four weeks, though, I was doing really well. I was really amazed, especially about the CD player and the radio, as they are normally such a problem.

I can tell you one more thing: I had chronic tendonitis before and now it is nearly gone. My osteopath, to whom I have been going twice a week, said all the crystals in my foot have now gone, so I am only left with the original injury. Oh, and another thing – I have not had to take any painkillers for my knee or my ankle or

WHY I HONOUR VRIC ABOVE ALL
PRECISION – SPECIFICITY – ACCURACY

In the two VRIC images opposite you will notice that the client is holding something in her hand. She is holding Lumanetic frequency-energy-information vials each containing a different frequency. Each vial contains 'nothing' except distilled water at the physical level, yet the different invisible energetic information that each one contains can be SEEN to have a dramatically different effect on the client.
No guesswork required to know which one is the precise solution for this client.

just in general. And I can sleep. Before I came here, my insomnia was chronic to the point where sometimes I could not sleep for two nights.'

I told her that the sleep and the pain had been helped due to the Lumanetic frequency pad. SG remarked that the one night she had not slept was the night when she had not worn the pad.

So what did we do for SG that brought about such remarkable results? We stabilized and strengthened her field with Lumanetic energy creams applied to various receptor points under the eyes and between the toes, plus a Lumanetic frequency pad on her solar plexus area. Not a single physical molecule of any medicinal substance was in any of the energetic non-substances used to create coherence for her, but the results were 'almost too good to be true'.

CHAPTER 8

THE HUMAN ENERGY FIELD
THE HEALING FIELD, THE KILLING FIELD

In the discipline that is Biolumanetics we do get some truly incredible results. Why and how is it possible to treat serious physical illness in the body without taking any tablets, injections or remedies, in fact nothing remotely physical, since all the Lumanetics are simply vibrational informational non-substances? If you took them to a laboratory and asked for them to be analyzed, you would find nothing except plain water or cream. 'Is this a placebo effect?' I hear you thinking. 'It sounds like patent and blatant nonsense, most unbelievable, a bit of voodoo, perhaps.' The puzzle is actually solved quite simply if we understand the fundamental truth that we have an energy field and that in Biolumanetics we treat the body by treating the field. We 'talk' to the field in the language of light and information, which is the language it understands.

A lot of people have no idea that they have an energy field. A few people have heard of the aura, but most scientists and doctors, at least in the West, completely pooh-pooh the idea. Scientists who do know of it take great care to call it something other than the plain unvarnished term – terms like 'endogenous field' sound better than 'auric field' or 'aura'. This prejudicial approach is in line with the approach that refuses to accept the efficacy of homoeopathy, even though it has been around for 200 years and is the treatment of choice of millions. The prejudice stems from the limited belief that if something cannot be 'measured' or seen under a microscope, it does not exist. Unfortunately, because of this, very little research has been done in this field (no pun intended)

So what is this energy field? Why is it important?

The Light-Energy-Information Matrix

The human energy field is the master light-energy-information matrix that holds the master keys to the physical system. It is a healing field if you can learn and use its secrets or it is a killing field if you don't. In Biolumanetics our primary purpose is to create coherence in the field. We have found that when this is done, the physical body reorganizes and changes as a result of this new information.

The solid flesh-and-blood body exists because of this invisible field and not the other way around, as is generally supposed. It is not that the body emits an aura but that the field is primary and the body is secondary in the causal chain. The field, and the information within it, creates your body, which is just a denser field of fluctuating energy. This light-energy-information field interpenetrates and interacts with every single atom, cell and molecule simultaneously and continuously. Think of yourself as a field of light and information or a configuration of energy and you will be close to understanding what your body is made of.

This electromagnetic energy field holds all the information about every single experience that the body-mind-soul has ever had. This is held in encoded form and until the key is available to decode that information, it remains inaccessible. Unfortunately, it still has the power to create chaos in the body and elsewhere.

Light is the electromagnetic carrier wave that holds this encoded information. The field is a transceiver of information (it receives, records, registers, holds and transmits information) on a continuous and changing basis as you interact with the universe via your thoughts, feelings, memories and experiences. Addressing the field level directly is a quick, effective and elegant way to create change in the body and much more.

The field also holds the key to the memory of disease, which is why I call it the 'killing field'. The reason why diseases recur is because the memory of them remains in the field. Over a certain period (some say one year, others seven years) every single atom in the physical body is replaced. The skeleton renews itself every three months, the skin is new every month, we have a new liver every six weeks and a new stomach lining every five days, so how and why is it that the same peptic ulcer persists for more than five days? Where is the information held which keeps the body producing the deadly acid? In our experience with Biolumanetics we would concur with Val Hunt, the great researcher at UCLA, when she says this information is held in the field – and it has to be addressed, resolved and neutralized at that level for lasting and effective healing to take place. If this is not acknowledged and addressed, this invisible, silent information will continue to create havoc and the body will pay the price of that ignorance.

While many systems work with the human energy field, including hands-on healers and body workers, Valerie Hunt with her system and Harry Oldfield with his PIP scan and electrocrystal therapy, only Biolumanetics has the quality of total precision and specificity made possible by VRIC. This is for one vital reason: no system other than Biolumanetics has a simple, single, bottom-line objective parameter of the whole – the light emission as evidenced through VRIC. With VRIC imaging one can see exactly which frequency or combination of frequencies will create coherence for the whole human system in an objective and verifiable manner in the form of a clear or fuzzy photograph. The other systems are also highly effective, but because there is a degree of inter-pretation required and as the perception of the practitioner is a necessary part of the whole process, the results will be variable. This is inescapable, as wherever there is perception there is distortion to a greater or lesser extent, depending on the quality of coherence of the perceiver. We can never be zero or neutral. None of us can – we are creatures of our own field and subject to its information.

Valerie Hunt found out some interesting facts about this field. Though it appears invisible to the human eye normally (aura readers can and do see it), it emits a signal that can be picked up by telemetry instruments if one is looking for it. Of course, if you do not acknowledge its existence, then you won't look for it. Val Hunt did look for it. She would place probes on various parts of the body and measure the vibrations that were being emitted by that body. These vibrations correlated with various colours. Valerie Hunt found that the vibrations of the physical body and its parameters ranged from 2–3 cps (cycles per second) to 250 cps. That appears to be as far as they go. The signals from the human energy field, however, though very faint, or low in amplitude, start at 450–500 cps and can go up to an astounding 1000,000 cps. I do not know whether this upper limit is dictated by the limit of the measuring instrument. My guess is that there is no real upper limit. This is what my work in Biolumanetics would indicate. However, at the moment this is only speculation on my part.

Certainly your light field is totally unique, much more unique than your signature, and contains your energy signature, which is the sum total of all that you are at any given moment, including all that you have ever been. It is your calling card and defines you to the universe and other people before you open your mouth and say a single word. The field is your first point of contact with the universe. It is constantly reading information and factoring it in and deciding for you what and how you will interact with the universe. All sensory perception is filtered and made available to you through the field. Everything that you see, hear, touch, smell or taste is permitted entry only if it passes through this primary, unique, personal and distorted filter.

The key to physical health and vitality, to emotional health and loving relationships, the key to your passion and to finding and achieving your soul's purpose, is a coherent and vibrant energy field. How is the following for a new equation?

Coherent energy field = a coherent life

To take an example:

Phil S was 32 when he came to 3S. He had suffered with 'psoriasis' since the age of four. He was also dyslexic, by his own account.

Phil was quite shy and not overly confident. He never got angry with anyone except himself. He was vegetarian and had been brought up in a family where meditation was practised. He was an artist. He taught art at a girls' school for a living. Phil was essentially a very gentle soul. It would be hard to imagine him doing anything wild or unethical. Well-spoken, well-mannered and very undemanding, he was someone it would be impossible to not like.

Phil was the youngest of four children. His parents had divorced when he was four. He was on good terms with both parents and had been brought up by his mother.

Phil was 'treated' using Biolumanetics to create coherence in the energy field, the Monocrom light-colour dome to open up his emotional range and a special music programme for his 'dyslexia'. *(For more information on the Monocrom light-colour dome, see page 285.)*

After five sessions Phil's 'psoriasis' and 'dyslexia' had disappeared and he was much more confident in himself as a teacher. Initially, he had found handling the emotional dramas of the senior girls quite challenging. His anxiety had rested in the solar plexus area, which affected his digestion. This was addressed by placing a Lumanetic pad on his solar plexus. As his anxiety abated, his confidence grew proportionally.

Phil stopped coming after that and I did not hear from him until he came back just over a year later. His psoriasis, which had disappeared for a whole year, was back, though it was not as severe as before. Since he had last come we had discovered some new techniques and I knew they would be very relevant for him. I asked him to bring photos of himself when he was four years old, which was when his psoriasis had started. Sure enough, when we did the VRIC imaging with Phil holding photographs of himself at four years old, his image fragmented when he held the photo in his right hand, which is the male side. We neutralized the emotional charge held in his field from that critical time in his life with the appropriate Lumanetic frequencies.

That session was a turning point for him. After that his psoriasis almost completely disappeared and a new Phil started emerging from the chrysalis. Later I asked him if his paintings had changed since he first came to 3S and lit up when he told me that he had started to include people in them for the first time. He was also reading a lot more and was enjoying that. (So where did his dyslexia go?) He was also much more confident dealing with women and a nice sense of humour was emerging. He was much more in charge of his life, was in the process of buying his first house and was planning for his future. He even acknowledged to me that he 'felt furious' when he saw someone behaving badly.

As he gained more untrammelled access to a greater emotional range, his paintings and his life became even more vibrant. In early 2007, many years after he came to 3S, I discovered that he was now married with two children and completely free from the psoriasis that had troubled him since he was four years old.

III

BIOLUMANETICS AND THE NEW SCIENCES

'As soon as questions of will or decision or reason or choice of action arise, human science is at a loss.'
Noam Chomsky

'We are bits of stellar material that got cold by accident, bits of a star gone wrong.'
Arthur Eddington

CHAPTER 9

CHAOS THEORY AND BIOLUMANETICS

WHERE EXTREME SIMPLICITY AND INFINITE COMPLEXITY MEET

When I read *Chaos* by James Gleick I was delighted. I did not understand all of it by any means and I had to make a special effort to understand its specialist vocabulary – the 'perturbations', the 'periodicity', the 'scaling', the 'bifurcations', the 'strange attractors', etc. – used to describe the various observations of this new science that came into its own only in the 1970s and '80s, but 'chaos theory' had the quality of a revelation. It did not fit any of the old paradigms. It was and was not mathematics and it was and was not physics in the sense that its insights did not fit in with the prevailing views of either mathematicians or physicists at that time. It was truly pioneering stuff.

This new level of knowledge only came into its own with the computer age. Computers have the power to crunch vast amounts of complex mathematical data and in doing so can reveal exquisitely orderly underlying patterns never before seen by human eyes. This bears a striking resemblance to VRIC, where the phenomenon of the parallel universe can actually be seen. And, as already mentioned, sight is the sense we use the most and believe the most.

The insights of chaos theory were music to my ears. For me, this theory buried forever the mechanical, linear, 'very logical' and very absurd view of the world. It showed that the linear view was logical at one level yet limited and inaccurate when it came to understanding nature, which is in essence non-linear. One could use the old laws to make machines, but nature is not a machine.

In a strange kind of way, chaos theorists found that they could begin to understand the awesome depth and extent of complexity and the order therein. With their computers they could visually reproduce fractals, Koch curves and Lorenz attractors – the beautiful patterns that reveal the simplicity and order that underlie the complexity of the processes of nature. But they could not, in real terms, in the physical reality, duplicate any of these results, however small and tightly controlled the conditions of the experiment. They could never succeed in making them predictable. So while on the one hand they understood how they happened, they also realized they could not make them happen. Nature could not be reduced to mathematics and calculations. Essentially nature is mystery. It is unknowable, and certainly not controllable. In essence chaos is the science of the unpredictable, the non-linear, the science of complexity. It is, as its name implies, the science of disorder – a seeming contradiction in terms. I call it the science of paradox, where two opposite and seemingly irreconcilable realities co-exist side by side at the same time.

As I see it, the fundamental insight of chaos theory is that disorder has order underlying it, though it does not appear to be so. So order and disorder are simply different states of order. Another insight is that complex dynamical systems are essentially unpredictable or unknowable and yet paradoxically utter simplicity and infinite complexity exist side by side in the same system.

It was also interesting that using chaos theory scientists started to understand and use the concept of multi-dimensionality, though not in the way I understand multi-dimensionality.

Another very important insight that has come from this new science is the so-called butterfly effect, which says that a butterfly flapping its wings in one part of the world (in effect an extremely small input of energy) can create a tornado on the opposite side of the world (can result in a very large effect) far away from the initial 'perturbation'. For me this remarkable insight also reveals that nature is an interconnected web and that everything impacts on everything else and has an effect on the whole. This is of course happening on a continuous basis and obviously applies to the human bodymind system, but is not really acknowledged or used in biology or allopathic medicine. (This statement is not made without consideration.)

One can infer from these insights that if there were one simple verifiable reproducible parameter that held the master key to the infinite complexity of a whole dynamic system, then using that information and working with that parameter one could influence the entire complexity that comprised that system – a sort of butterfly effect in reverse. If a small input or 'perturbation' could result in a huge effect multiplied unpredictably and exponentially, then it would be possible, with the right informational energetic input, to create huge change which was coherent and global.

From the research cited in *Chaos*, which takes us well into the late 1990s, there does not appear to be any success in this endeavour, most certainly not as far as humans go. Humans are, after all, the most complex, non-linear dynamic system by far, especially when you factor in the subjective universe of their feelings, their attitudes and their will, let alone the impossible complexity that is the physical body and the connection between these two infinitely complex aspects.

So far the only way we have had to understand nature and living systems is to study them at the level of complexity. In my view this can be useful at one level, but only to a very small degree. This approach can never be totally successful. No matter how far, wide or deep one digs or delves using the most sophisticated measurement and treatment tools of physical reality, one will only find more complexity – and more and more, into infinity. It is an open road, a road leading everywhere and nowhere. Following it is interesting and absorbing, yes, and real understanding always seems tantalizingly close, yet it remains elusive and will always remain that way. Neither the greatest supercomputer nor the most powerful electron microscope can ever hope to understand the workings of a single human brain weighing all of three pounds, let alone the flowing sea of information that is each human being.

However, now consider the staggering notion that while success in this respect has eluded the cleverest minds on Earth, despite all the billions spent on research, a single universal parameter to create coherent global change in the infinitely complex human has been found and has been present on the Earth plane since 1978, when the Luminator was invented. It is understandable that this master parameter – the light waveform-photon emission of lifeforms as seen through VRIC imaging – was not discovered until then. Until the altered magnetic environment revealed the quantum universe of the human being, it was impossible to scientifically assess the whole and therefore to use this simple key in any meaningful way to create coherent change for the whole. But with the advent of the Luminator and VRIC imaging, creating coherence for each person is a possibility for the first time in known human history.

Quantum Coherence, Visual Coherence and Supercoherence
Becoming the Living Laser

Quantum Coherence

In recent years frontier scientists who were dissatisfied with the reductionist mechanistic approach to understanding the human started to explore the phenomenon called quantum coherence. The quantum coherence model is an attempt to understand whether some kind of coherence is implicated in how the extreme complexity of the bodymind system functions as a co-ordinated unit.

An irreducible and essential quality of coherence is something called a 'phase relationship'. In the laser, as we know, the peaks and the troughs of the wave have to match exactly, or be 'in phase', for the exponential laser effect to happen. This is a delicate affair and can be easily disrupted, as the waves have to be in exact alignment. This obviously requires extreme precision. The conjecture in the quantum coherence model is that there is some kind of phase relationship involved in the bodymind system, an interconnected communication system that informs each cell, atom and molecule what to do on a continuous basis.

This is a kind of coherence that involves a degree of precision of a much higher and more complex order than the simpler man-made laser. To quote Mae-Wan Ho, a scientist I admire greatly:

> 'A quantum coherent state is a pure state – a state of oneness – that has the property of factorizability ... The ideal quantum coherent state involving the whole system is a global attractor to which the system tends to return when it is perturbed, but as the system is always open, it will invariably be taken away from the totally coherent state ... The more the actions taken are at odds with the coherence of the system, the more time and entropy are generated and the more the system ages.'

In simpler terms, and in my understanding, this is how the process works. The energetic impulse at the sub-atomic, quantum or source level is continuously influenced by and responsive to the thoughts, emotions and consciousness of the individual. If this input is coherent, then this orderliness is communicated to all the cells of that organism instantaneously and globally and the whole vibrates in sympathetic resonance in response and creates order at every level – a whole mighty orchestra of 50 trillion cells playing in perfect tune with each other. It also returns to the same coherent state, creating a never-ending cycle of orderly energetic behaviour. If, however, the energy of our thoughts, feelings and actions is not in phase or is misaligned with our own nature, then the process of quantum coherence is jeopardized and incoherence, disease and dysfunction follow.

Quantum coherence is in essence a state of oneness or unity in diversity. As Mae-Wan Ho says:

'So it is that we perceive ourselves as a singular "I" intuitively, despite the extremely diverse multiplicity of tissues, cells and molecules constituting our being. Quantum coherence entails a plurality that is singular, a multiplicity that is a unity.'

In other words we could call it oneness.

Herbert Fröhlich, a German professor of super-state physics at the University of Liverpool, was one of the first people to come up with the theory that the state of quantum coherence was actually present in living systems. It had already been observed in other areas. A simple explanation of superconductivity and superconductors is necessary here (quote taken from www.physicscentral.com):

'Metals are good conductors of electricity. That is, they have very low electrical resistance, but this resistance is not zero. A voltage difference is still required to generate the current in the metal, and the metal heats up while the current is flowing. The electrical resistance of an object depends on its temperature and declines slowly as the temperature falls. However, when certain metals are cooled to temperatures close to absolute zero, something strange happens. The metal in this state loses all electrical resistance and the current will flow indefinitely, even in the absence of any applied voltage.'

This effect is called 'superconductivity' and the materials are called 'low-temperature superconductors'. It seems that superconductivity is a quantum coherent state and is also a super-efficient use of energy, as in effect one is getting an output of energy without any input. In other words, one is creating free energy.

So what can this coherence accomplish? Fröhlich emphasized the lossless transmission of energy from one mode to another. This form of coherence is related to the principles underlying the laser, though lasers do not operate at temperatures close to absolute zero. It was not, however, generally thought to exist in lifeforms – who also do not operate at temperatures close to absolute zero. Nevertheless, this 'biology of effortless action', as Mae-Wan Ho calls it, or 'biology of extreme intelligence', as I would also term it, is obviously a very desirable state, and if one knew what would initiate this process and then maintain it we would have superb health and an unending flow of vital energy at our command. Again, however, while the theory is there and is valid, up to now there has been no way of assessing quantum coherence in real objective terms and therefore of initiating or enhancing it for humans or complex lifeforms.

To make a whole orchestra of 50 trillion cells play in tune and create a perfect symphony, there has to be a conductor who knows the whole score and then has to communicate this complex information to the various players so that they play in concert and do not create a cacophony. To date no conventional science – in fact I would go further and say no science – has discovered the master conductor and it is sometimes referred to as the 'ghost in the machine'. Mae-Wan Ho came close, very close, to solving the riddle, but before VRIC and the Luminator there was no way of accessing this master conductor, no way to engage in dialogue with this awesome Intelligence. One could observe the process and marvel, but that was all. Now we have the means to engage directly with this process.

Visual Coherence

The visual coherence process as observed through VRIC imaging in the field of the Luminator is the process of observing quantum coherence in action. It is the same process that is objectified for a complex lifeform in the only real laboratory: life. VRIC imaging not only enables us to assess the state of coherence of a whole lifeform with extreme accuracy, precision and objectivity, but the Biolumanetics methodologies actually re-establish and enhance quantum coherence – or rather what I call 'supercoherence' – in a system that has lost its ability to maintain order and has descended into the chaos of dis-ease, dysfunction or despair.

When order is restored through re-establishing coherence at the quantum energetic level with laser precision and total customization for each individual, the bodymind system not only throws off the toxicity of illness but actually reconfigures the whole energy system to behave in a more efficient and intelligent way than was previously possible. You are dialoguing directly with the master conductor of the orchestra and initiating order at the alpha-omega-alpha level of your being – the central point, the beginning and end point, from where everything is initiated and to which everything returns in a never-ending cycle.

Again, light is implicated in this whole process (remember Fritz-Albert Popp's work). It is the carrier of information, and the information that it carries to and from all your cells will determine whether your system remains healthy, vibrant and well or degenerates into dysfunction and disease.

Super-efficient use of the primary resource of which you are made gives you the possibility of becoming an energy superconductor. Very little loss of energy means lots more coherent energy is available to use for creativity, rejuvenation and sheer vibrant health. So you engage in the process of becoming a human energy laser. That is the radical possibility that emerges out of this process.

Supercoherence

The title of this book is *Supercoherence*. This is a new term I wish to introduce to differentiate this process from any other process or parameter on

Earth at the present time. It is quantum coherence plus something more.

When I encountered the idea of quantum coherence, the primary question for me as a non-scientist was what lay behind the initial impulse of order at the quantum level of expression of any given lifeform. What factors energized the quantum impulse of energy-information to embark on a coherent course and create quantum coherence and the creation of global and vast order or to go towards incoherence or chaos?

The study, practice and experience of Biolumanetics and VRIC imaging tell me that intention, perception and emotion are the key players in this process of creating order at the quantum level – and at every level. The conscious level, i.e. of the personality, the unconscious and subconscious level, i.e. the hidden agenda of the imprint, and the superconscious level, i.e. the level of the soul, also have a direct input in this process. What happens at the gross physical, cellular, molecular and genetic levels happens as a direct consequence of something more fundamental and important and much further up the causal chain.

Supercoherence and VRIC make it abundantly clear that the language of the soul and the language of the cells is the same, the body is singing the song of the soul and the state of consciousness has a direct and immediate effect on the body. This is not surmise or speculation any more. It is not something that can be ignored simply because there is no way to factor this profound and powerful yet unquantifiable information in any 'meaningful' and 'acceptable' way to 'good' 'evidence-based' science. The Luminator and VRIC imaging have provided that way.

Up to now, in the interests of 'objectivity', mainstream science forgot, dismissed and unwisely chose not to factor in their equations the most essential parts of the human – attitudes, heroism, generosity, a sense of humour, determination, creativity, passion and a sense of purpose. It reduced them, and itself, as a consequence, to the limited understanding of so-called 'facts', figures and statistics. It confined itself to the study and understanding of the infinitely complex processes of cells and molecules and genes, forgetting there was a feeling, intentional, emotional, conscious and above all unique human being attached to those processes. So science lost its humanity and became 'objective', misguided and incomplete all at the same time.

With VRIC, however, for the first time it is possible to factor in this essential subjective level and science can come home and become human, truly intelligent and learn to acknowledge, in its own 'objective' terms, that which it has hitherto ignored. It can become a science of wholeness, of infinite possibility instead of simplistic certainty, of the subjective, of the *now*, and of the truth, which was its original intent.

So supercoherence, as evidenced through VRIC imaging, is a new parameter of wholeness and function. It is a process that anyone can engage in and it is a new and radical paradigm based on a new and more complete understanding of the extraordinary and magnificent human. This enables all of us to assume our rightful place in the universe.

CHAPTER 11

THE RADICAL IMPLICATIONS OF THE LUMINATOR AND VRIC IMAGING
THE INTERCONNECTED UNIVERSE

In 1997 I sent an article on Biolumanetics to my friends in Scotland who published an alternative magazine. I also sent some pictures of a VRIC assessment of a family. I thought they would be delighted and amazed. However, when the article appeared in print, these most extraordinary pictures had been reduced to a minuscule size.

I was puzzled and slightly annoyed. I am very fond of Ian and Ronnie, the publishers, so I phoned Ian and asked him why they had reduced the size of the pictures to the point of losing their impact. He was a bit embarrassed at first, then conceded that the plants in the photos were fuzzy and because that was 'not possible', they had put in the photos to please me but had reduced them to something insignificant so they would not look foolish in publishing them.

In a sense, if they had discussed it with me, it might have been better. As it was, I understood why their reality had been so shaken. The cosmic joker had been having a field day when it produced the VRIC phenomenon and the fuzzy plants are disconcerting, to say the least. When I first saw my own image and the plants beside me fragment when I went to Michigan all those years ago, I remember the feeling of disbelief, followed by awe and wonder as the implications began to dawn on me. This was reinforced over the following days when my daughter and I saw the hundreds of other images that had all fragmented the same way. One part of me was awestruck with wonder and the other part kept thinking, 'This cannot be real. This cannot be happening.'

The conclusion, however, was inescapable: everything was connected – me, the plants and, even more disconcertingly, the 'inanimate' painting on the wall! Even the plant pot became fuzzy when I became fuzzy. I had an impact on everything and therefore everything had an impact on me. There was no 'if', 'but' or 'maybe'. I was inextricably interlinked with the All That Is.

In fact, taken a step further, all of us are part of That and only That. The connection is through light, which is the master carrier wave of this interconnected information system. With VRIC, for the first time we can see this in the five-sensory reality and can become more responsible for ourselves, instead of thinking, 'I'm all right, Jack, and to hell with you.' It is a wake-up call, not some abstract theory or pious preachment. In clear visible terms it shows that you and the world around you are continuously, invisibly – now visibly – impacted by your thoughts and actions, and that you in turn impact the world around you. What goes around comes around, and not in some faraway Neverland, but now, at the speed of light. It also shows that you are a significant member of the universe and that you count. It shows that every choice you make counts and that you always have a choice.

But the most important insight, which has been confirmed over the years through the observation of this incredible phenomenon, is that the universe responds to emotion. My emotions are felt by this feeling Intelligence that speaks and responds in the language of light. It is a feeling universe and I realize that it cares, listens and responds.

The Luminator: Into the Fifth Dimension

Examining the implications of the Luminator tells me that it is a tool of the fifth dimension that has found its way into this material third dimension. On that level it looks very ordinary – a long rectangular box with two air vents. Inside the box are two little fans run by electricity, one at the top and the other at the bottom. In between these two fans are two Perspex barrels containing Perspex rings resonating with mysterious information. But from the third-dimensional box and fans suddenly we are catapulted into the fifth-dimensional world of invisible information. When air passes through these liquid informational rings, it acquires completely different characteristics and an altered magnetic field is created out of 'nothing' by 'nothing' except information. No fancy electronics are required and not even electricity.

It is impossibly mind-bending to try and figure out how air passing through rings of liquid information, with no visible power source, can create an altered magnetic field which creates a coherent light field and as a result a hole in the third dimension of space-time. Nevertheless, this permits us, through VRIC imaging, to get a glimpse into the sub-atomic reality of the fifth dimension, where the world of thoughts, feelings and intentions is seen to be as, if not more, real than the physical dimension. With the Luminator, the veil between the dimensions is lifted to allow us to see the reality of both dimensions at the same time, and the multi-dimensional reality is seen to be the reality that is. As Deepak Chopra said so eloquently, we 'penetrate the mask of matter'. With VRIC every one of us can know and experience that in an intensely personal way. We can understand that we are both physical and energy beings – neither one nor the other, but both.

The light field of the Earth, as already mentioned, is incoherent. It is light going in many directions, with no recognizable order. The light field around the Earth is obviously vast. Ask yourself how can this little pocket of ordered coherent light that is the field of the Luminator hold its own in the midst of the impossibly large unordered light field of the Earth? How can coherent light, with its highly organized nature, be so effortlessly instituted, maintained and expanded without any physical input of power, simply the power of information?

Think of the implications of this: the tiniest amount of a higher order of information effortlessly prevails over unimaginably vast amounts of disorder. Organization is the law of the universe. All that is unorganized 'wishes' to be organized and, given the opportunity, will do so. Humans are subject to this law at every level. Coherence is the law of laws, and coherent light, as evidenced through VRIC, is the visible manifestation of that most fundamental order.

I have always wondered what Einstein would have thought about the Luminator and VRIC. When he became aware of the quantum universe and its dynamic fluctuating nature, its uncertainty and its seeming randomness, he knew there was something fundamental that he had not figured out when he said, 'God does not play dice with the universe.' He wanted to know what the invariants were, the unchanging or immutable laws that held the universe together. The supercoherence process as evidenced through VRIC imaging shows clearly that they are love, light and superconsciousness. These are as relevant and real as gravity, electromagnetism and all the other laws of the 'physics of dead matter' as the great scientist Dr Mae-Wan Ho calls the old paradigm view. It is a living, feeling, interactive, responsive universe. Einstein's intuition was right indeed.

But until the Luminator came along there was no objective way of knowing or proving this.

IV

The Power of Emotion

'As none can see the wind but in its effects on the trees,
neither can we see the emotions but in their effects on the face
and body.'
Nathaniel LeTonnerre

'The feeling is often the deeper truth, the opinion the more
superficial one.'
Augustus William Hare and Julius Charles Hare

'Perhaps everything terrible is in its deepest being something
helpless that wants help from us.'
Rainer Maria Rilke

CHAPTER 12

EMOTIONAL COHERENCE
AND SUPERCOHERENCE
UNDERSTANDING THE IMPORTANCE
OF EMOTIONAL ENERGY

One of the most important and yet poorly utilized energy resources is emotional energy. It is at once the ace in the hole and the joker in the pack as far as core vitality, function and coherence are concerned.

Today it is widely recognized that stress is a killer. It causes depression, illness and dysfunction. Industry and society lose billions because of it. Stress is caused by the inability of the organism to adapt to a particular set of circumstances. The factors that bring this about are different for each individual. It may or may not be possible to change certain factors that seem out of our control. However, the one factor that is almost always a key component in any stressful situation is the loss of emotional coherence.

Emotional energy, like any other resource, can be squandered, misused, overused or even simply stuck and unused. Unfortunately there is seldom any training to help people manage this most basic and potentially creative or even explosive resource. How we feel from moment to moment is essentially a matter of how we choose to respond to our perceived or felt experience. But the more energy we have tied up in self-conscious reactivity to other people or circumstances, to our own discomfort, to physical distress, to the pressures of work and the demands of family, the less free energy and attention we have available for any creative purpose.

The most common misuse of emotional energy is simply to throw it off or waste it rather than conduct it and let it regenerate. This applies equally to the rituals of anxiety, worry, anger or even overwhelming grief.

Whether we are locked in conflict with a colleague, suffer the incompetence of subordinates or the oppression or anger of superiors, the outcome is always the same: a reduction in free energy and attention and a loss of vitality and coherence. In this respect the microcosm always reflects the macrocosm and vice versa. The vitality of the individual corresponds directly to the vitality of the group and the vitality of the group mirrors the vitality of society.

Emotional energy has power beyond imagining and vast amounts of it are unavailable for useful work when it is diverted, distorted and blocked because of the painful experiences of our past and the belief systems that perpetuate them and hold us in bondage in the present. Unfortunately, the deep unconscious realms and the field in which these non-verbal experiences and the accompanying potent charges that vitiate our vitality are held are not easily accessed. So they do not yield readily to counselling, psychotherapy or visualization or affirmations. They also continue to create havoc unless they are neutralized.

At 3S we have found that in every single instance without exception emotional energy is a major causal factor in the loss of function, no matter what the challenge or the circumstance. Emotional energy is the key to wellness and the key to illness. Ability, capability and training to use this master resource with coherence make the difference between wellness and illness, between function and dysfunction, between success and failure.

Emotional coherence is the master key to super health and super function and a direct way to access supercoherence. So the end game and goal of all the methods we use to restore coherence are to retrieve, recover, reorganize and realign emotional energy.

Assessing and Restoring Emotional Coherence using VRIC

G was by temperament very amenable. She was cheerful, friendly, very pretty and liked to take care of people. She was adopted and she had a close friend she regarded as a sister who was temperamentally very different. She was very troubled and had a long history of destructive and tempestuous behaviour. G had always compensated for this and had smoothed over the various messes her 'sister' had got herself into over the years. However, this longstanding pattern was not benefiting G in any way and she did not know how to resolve it. She did not feel capable of letting her 'sister' face up to the consequences of her outrageous behaviour. She feared she would have no one to turn to and somehow wanted to protect her.

The latest drama had taken a toll on G. Her 'sister's' son had been getting married and G had travelled up to Scotland for the wedding. Everybody had been there – the bride and her family, the groom and G and all the guests – but the groom's mother had decided, for no particular reason, that the most dramatic entrance was no entrance at all: she had decided not to attend her son's wedding. And she had done so without warning anyone. G had had to step into the breach and pacify everyone. Despite the high drama, the wedding had been celebrated. But now her 'nephew', who had been distraught and then very angry, never wanted to see his mother again, the bride's parents were not impressed and G was left feeling totally drained by all of it.

VRIC IMAGING – ASSESSING EMOTIONAL COHERENCE
THE IMPACT OF EMOTIONS ON THE BODYMIND

'I feel drained' with 'sister's' photo after emotional drama.
Very incoherent.

Holding 'sister's' photo + 3 Lumanetic frequency vials.
Energetic challenge neutralised – coherence re-established.

I imaged G with a photo of her 'sister'. She became totally incoherent with it and looked the way she felt: fragmented. For the first time she could see what she was doing to her energy body. Her image showed her her own suffering in graphic detail.

The interesting thing was that the 'sister's' image also became incoherent. This showed G that no one in that incoherent energy dynamic was benefiting. G was very insightful about others but not very perceptive about her own needs, so it was a shock to her system to see that her constant rescue of her 'sister' was actually non-beneficial to both. This was a moment of truth and it sank in. G knew she could not rescue her 'sister' – she had to sort out her life by herself. As long as G continued to smooth over her messes, she would have no real motivation to do so and would not acquire the necessary skills or strength. The most helpful thing G could do for her 'sister' was to tell her politely and softly that she could *not* help her, because she did not know how to, and that she should get professional help. That might sound harsh and callous to start with, but would actually be the most helpful for both of them.

G agreed. She knew she had to do things differently from before. She could see it. No amount of counselling could have done what those photos did.

We resolved the incoherence by choosing the relevant Lumanetic frequencies and re-imaged G holding them with the photo of her 'sister'. This time the image was clear. Emotional coherence had been re-established in G's energy field. The issue had been cleared at the energetic level and as G could see this, she was most relieved.

A couple of days later she reported that she was feeling much stronger and was back on good form.

At her next visit I asked her how things were going with her 'sister'. G had made great strides and had started to change her response when her 'sister' phoned with her dramas, becoming less and less interested in helping and rescuing her. A non-nourishing emotionally destructive pattern of many years' standing (G is 38 and her 'sister' is older by a few years) had been substantially modified in one session.

I imaged G again with her 'sister' to assess the progress and see for real how the relationship had changed for G The challenge was still present, but it was significantly less than the last time. Looking at the image showed her that she had made progress, but that she had some way to go. No third party was involved here, just total precision and honesty from her higher self.

This time the challenge was resolved the same way as before, but with different Lumanetic frequencies. G's energy system was being strengthened and made more resilient every time an energetic challenge was resolved in this precise manner and as a result she has since become much stronger emotionally. Though she is still always kind, she is also becoming skilled at setting her boundaries very politely. As a result her energy levels are much better and she has time to do things that she enjoys. Her periods, which would disappear for months when she was under stress, have for the first time in her life become as regular as clockwork. Her PMS has disappeared; her digestion, which was not good, has improved; her sleeping patterns, which were extremely erratic, have become regular; and her career has taken off (see VRIC images, page 120).

The Conquest of Fear and Biolumanetics

I was driving down from Edinburgh to Chesterfield with a friend. It was late at night, around midnight. The motorway was clear but unlit and it was raining. I was driving around 70 miles per hour. In the back seat was an unsecured 17" computer monitor, plus the whole computer.

Suddenly, without warning, the car skidded and went out of control. It veered to the left, then like a drunk veered to the right, veered to the left again, then careened to the right and hit the central reservation sideways. At that point I was able to bring it to a halt.

I had observed this process happen as if in slow motion and had felt totally unperturbed by it. I had not felt panicked and had instinctively done all the right things. The damage to the car was minimal. When I stopped the car, my friend was shaking and panicky from shock. To my surprise I realized that my solar plexus was totally steady and calm. I could not believe it. I realized that I had not felt any fear during the whole incident and had been totally in control. This was convincing proof to me of how strong my energy 'body' had become as a result of Biolumanetics. My reaction was in striking contrast to a similar accident I had had many years ago, when my car had gone out of control and crashed into a shop window. I had been in shock then and unable to really take it in. I am not normally either panicky or particularly fearful, but this incident on the motorway was a very clear demonstration of a very unordinary response to extreme circumstances.

It does seem that the Biolumanetics process of strengthening the energy field somehow clears fear from the energy system. To take another example, I used to be absolutely terrified of spiders. All rationality deserted me when I looked at one, and when I saw its many legs moving in my direction I would be seized with unreasoning terror and would run away as fast as I could. When I had young children and my daughter was also terrified of spiders, I had to overcome my terror and would kill them. But after the Luminator came into my life, I found I was no longer afraid of them. The terror had been replaced by tenderness, much to my surprise. Now I would not dream of killing spiders. When I find them, I take them very gently in a dustpan and put them out of the house. I have also learned to admire immensely the consummate skill with which these little master engineers build their exquisitely intricate, perfectly proportioned webs floating in space. This huge shift has happened without any conscious effort on my part and I am grateful for it.

Some more dramatic incidents come to mind:

Lily was very fearful when she first came to 3S. Her breathing would become shallow and she would panic and hyperventilate when she was stressed. And it did not take much to stress her. She was very sensitive, a very good artist and extremely pretty. But her fear was overwhelming. Her voice, in contrast to her vibrant sense of colour, was a dull and colourless monotone and reflected her lack of confidence.

All that changed after a while. The deeply ingrained fear of many years disappeared and Lily's life at all levels began to reflect this fearlessness.

One day she arrived late. She had been always on time before and so I asked her if she was OK. She told me she had just been mugged by a huge man on the train. I was concerned and asked her how she was feeling after that nasty and frightening experience.

Even with the progress she had already made, I was surprised when she told me how angry she had been. She said that that if she could have, she would have jumped off the train and collared him. While she was telling me this, her voice was strong and confident. This was not a Lily I was familiar with. I smiled at the thought of this young woman chasing a huge man and was glad that she had not been foolhardy. I asked her what she would have done if this had happened a few months before she started Biolumanetics and she said she would have collapsed, started crying and probably called her mother or her partner.

It is interesting to note that Lily did not have to think about her response. Her instinctive response had changed radically as her energy system had been made coherent. Her system had to be strong for it to have the ability to make that response, though. No matter how much you want to, if your bodymind system is not functioning at optimum, you will not get the result you desire. *You are only as strong as your weakest point.*

Emma lives in a rural area. Her house is 'surrounded by fields and rabbits' and there are no people within easy calling distance. Her husband's work takes him away for weeks at a time and before she came to 3S, whenever she was on her own she would frequently stay awake all night. In fact her original reason for coming to 3S was chronic insomnia. At that time she had not slept for several weeks and was totally exhausted and unable to function with her characteristic dynamism.

After using Lumanetics for a few months, Emma was pretty coherent. Her erratic sleeping patterns had disappeared and she was sleeping well, even when her husband was away. She had also been given two CDs with psycho-acoustic music to use, which helped.

One night when Emma's husband was away, at four o'clock in the morning suddenly the security lights around the house lit up. That woke Emma, who was quite nervous. She got up and looked out of the window. There was a car there that she did not recognize. While a part of her was worried about who was in the car and she considered the possibility that it might be someone with malicious intent, she acted with remarkable presence of mind. She phoned a friend, told him what was happening and asked him to come round.

The friend phoned the police and then phoned her back. She had nothing to worry about – it was a police car and they were looking for someone. That was all. The mystery was solved.

Emma phoned me the next morning to tell me the story. What had amazed her was how little fear she had felt. What was even more amazing was that she had been able to fall asleep immediately afterwards and sleep through till the morning. Her system had been able to find a balance point; no recovery time had been needed even after that rather traumatic incident.

S was a Japanese client. He was very sensitive and could not handle emotional confrontation and came to see me before a very difficult meeting with someone. He was dreading it, as he had already seen how the other person could behave and how verbally aggressive he could be, and he knew that what he had to say to him was going to displease him. The situation was that S had come all the way from Japan for a job interview in England and the company had requested the interview and had paid for the trip. It was understood that he would take the job. However, the terms he was being offered were not good enough and S wanted to refuse, but he did not know quite how to do so. He was dithering.

After the discussion with me he was clear about exactly what he wanted and knew that all he had to do was ask for it. That was all. He said the company would never agree to these terms, but I asked him to be clear about his own bottom line and said that was all he needed to do. He could not know what another person would do; he could only know what he needed to do. He was given two Lumanetic creams to carry to keep his logical and emotional side in perfect balance and to give him the energetic strength to deal with whatever he was presented with.

At the meeting he actually asked quite calmly for what he wanted, instead of accepting what was on offer. His worst fears were then confirmed when the other person went totally out of control and started shouting and creating a drama.

Under normal circumstances S would not have known what to do. But now his response was a calm 'I cannot talk to you while you are like this. Can I see your boss, please?'

S was extremely pleased that he had felt strong and calm under attack and had been able to handle the situation with such aplomb. It would never be the same for him again when it came to a confrontation. Simply carrying two little frequency creams containing nothing except information had kept his energy rock-solid and with that there was no fear to be felt.

Impossible? S swears by it!

Tim was 34 years old. He found his father very domineering and had never been able to stand up to him. He felt angry, bitter and resentful, but was totally unable to speak his mind or voice his needs. Whatever he said was brushed aside.

Tim had also had 'epilepsy' since the age of one and his life was ruled, constricted and bounded by his fear of the unpredictable nature of his illness. He was afraid to lose the support of his father because of his illness. He said he had no life and was desperate.

At the end of the very first session with Biolumanetics he was given a frequency cream to carry on his person amongst other Lumanetic tools to create coherence in his energy field. In his own words:

'Before I could not talk to my dad, I was too scared to say anything to him, but since I started wearing [the Lumanetic frequency

cream] I have been standing up for myself and telling him what's what. I have told him, "The way you are carrying on, every day that goes by I am losing respect for you and there will come a time when I am not going to have any respect for you at all and then you will lose me entirely!"'

Tim's dad was uncharacteristically quiet when he heard that and actually thought about what his son had said and took it on board to some extent.

How did Tim find the courage to speak up for himself for the first time in 34 years? Carrying a little pot of cream with an energy signature seems an improbable and unreasonable answer – or does it?

Incidentally, in the month that he had been carrying it he had not had a single epileptic fit and the severe stammering that he had had since he was five years old had almost disappeared.

As Tim learned to trust me and realized that I did not judge him, he opened up and told me how his stammering had affected his life. I had never really thought about what it meant to have a stammer, but now I was let into another world – on one level quite funny in a black sort of way and yet also very poignant. Tim said:

'You don't know what it is to stammer. It makes you a liar. I know when I am going to stammer, so if, for example, I am trying to tell my mother I am going to Jo's place and I feel I am going to stammer the word "Jo", I say "Bill" instead. If I am at a pub with friends and I want a whisky, if I am going to stammer the word "whisky", I will ask for a beer instead, even though I don't like beer.'

Recently he had been on a flight. A pretty woman had been sitting next to him and they had started chatting. When the stewardess had come around offering teas and coffees, Tim had got flustered. He did not like tea and liked coffee, but thought he would stammer the word 'coffee' so he asked for tea instead.

I listened with amazement. Tim told me that he had done many things to try and overcome his stammer and had succeeded for short periods but then regressed. It was time to try something new. By this time his stammer was nowhere as bad as it had been when he first came, so I knew he would succeed. I said, 'If you like coffee, you should have coffee. If you like whisky, you should have whisky.' I suggested that the next time he wanted coffee or whisky, he should just go ahead and ask for what he wanted and if he stammered the words, it was perfectly OK, he would still have what he wanted rather than something he disliked. I told him he could never be sure until he said the word whether it would come out as a stammered word. In any case, if someone was stupid or unkind enough to laugh, it was a reflection on them rather than on him and he should take no notice of them. He did not become any less good or intelligent when he stammered.

Tim took this on board and when he was faced with the same dilemma – tea or coffee – on his next flight down from Ireland to London, this time he chose coffee. He triumphantly reported that he hadn't stammered at all and it would be coffee all the way from now on!

He was smiling, confident and empowered, and I was delighted. He had conquered his stammer instead of his stammer controlling his life.

Love, Chaos and Coherence

Mary had come for her appointment straight from the airport, where she had just seen her husband off on a long business trip. She was glum and patently unhappy. I had not seen her like this before.

Mary adored her husband and they had a very loving relationship, but his work took him away for weeks at a time. Mary recognized the necessity of the business trips and was very conscious of the need for each marriage partner to have the freedom to create their destiny without emotional manipulation, but that understanding did not stop a part of her from feeling bereft whenever she was away from her loved one.

She was normally upbeat, very caring, very considerate of people's feelings (almost too much at times), very capable and honest, passionate about her work and her life and very heart-centred – altogether a very nice person. But the day she came to see me she admitted she had lost it. She felt that nothing would make her smile again. She also said she felt like that every time her husband left on one of his trips. She could not sleep for several nights afterwards and would become tired and try to suppress her feelings by working hard, which was good for her work but not particularly good for her body or mind. She said it was really good for her to have come to see me when she was at her worst and I agreed with that sentiment. I knew Mary to be a conscious and aware person. This was her cycle of suffering and the time had come to address it in real terms. She did not need sympathy but resolution.

The VRIC imaging revealed she was out of coherence. The image that appeared was of a sad creature, slouched and fragmented. Mary was not given to self-pity. When she saw her image she remarked, 'I look like Mother Dolores, or the Mother of Sorrows.' She had no wish to be that. She understood the world of energy and that being radiant and coherent was not only beneficial for her but for all who interacted with her.

She told me she had always been a sad child, but did not know why. Her family had been a loving family, so where had her sadness come from? The secret was buried in her cellular memory and in her encoded field. We made no attempt whatsoever to dig and delve for it. That wasn't necessary. To neutralize that secret message, a new more nourishing and beneficial message, more in line with her conscious beliefs and aspirations, was needed in her field.

She was asked to hold the relevant Lumanetic energy vials for creating coherence and to affirm verbally, 'I am whole, complete and perfect in my own right,' and a photo was taken. The image was coherent: Mary looked her radiant self once more.

When she saw the image she was both relieved and delighted. Her field had accepted this new information and henceforth it would be easier for her to remain what she wanted to be – a radiant and loving person. Now her love for her husband would not be tainted with suffering and her relationship would not be needy and fearful but a non-needy one based on delight and intimacy, which is what she had always wanted.

She left looking and feeling very different from how she had been just a couple of hours before. When we spoke the next day, she told me that she had felt fine ever since, had had a good night's sleep and was raring to go back to work.

Love can create incoherence.

SD was a beautiful blonde. She was married with two girls. I had been seeing her and her daughters and they were doing well. One day she said she wanted to see me alone. By now she trusted me and obviously wanted to share a confidence. She told me that she had fallen in love with her husband's best friend and had plunged into a secret affair with him. She had been dissatisfied with her marriage for a while. There was nothing she could pinpoint specifically, but somewhere along the line she had fallen out of love with her husband. She felt terribly guilty about the affair but did not want to stop seeing her lover. The affair was not a casual one – both parties had fallen deeply in love – but she did not want her children to suffer and did not want to deceive her husband. She was in a terrible bind and terribly unhappy.

I did not presume to judge the rights and wrongs of the situation but asked her to bring photos of both men and of her two daughters. The imaging would tell her more than I could.

Next time she brought the photos, and when she imaged with her husband, she fragmented, whereas with her lover she was totally coherent. When she saw the images, though, she said she did not want to hurt the children by leaving their father, even if she was unhappy with him. I asked her if her lover liked the girls and she said they got along very well with him and liked him a lot. I asked her to hold the photos of both the girls and her lover and she was coherent, as were the girls and the lover. There was no problem as far as they were concerned – VRIC images cannot lie.

When faced with this, SD knew that something had to be done to resolve the situation. I told her that she needed to come clean with her husband, that she had to take her courage in her hands and tell him the truth.

She decided to follow my advice. Her husband was initially devastated, but at least they were talking frankly and honestly again after a long period of non-communication. He said he did not want the marriage to end and would do whatever he could to make her happy. Her friends and her mother thought she was mad to be contemplating leaving him – there was nothing wrong with him, he hadn't done her any harm, and why wasn't she thinking of her children? So what if she wasn't particularly happy?

She phoned me to tell me that as a result she had decided to make a go of it with her husband and not see her lover again. What did I think? I told her whatever she did was OK and she could count on my support, but that she had decided to sacrifice herself for her children. I also thought, though I did not say this to her, that she had let go of her dreams for her own life and happiness and that in doing so she would not be happy and in the long run neither would her husband. In my view compromises of this sort often do not work. Joy does, but here the joy would be gone.

SD and her husband stayed together and sold their house and moved into another one, but a few months later they decided to divorce amicably. I had known this was likely from the imaging, for now I could see that SD had found the courage to be true to herself. She left her husband and made a commitment to her lover; her children supported her through it very well and arrangements were made for their father to have full access to them. Her mother accepted her decision to find her own happiness and a short while later her husband became involved in a new relationship and everyone was happier than they had been in a long while.

In my view, it is our birthright to be happy. Compromises and silent unhappiness exist in some long-term relationships, but this loss of hope and intimacy and the resulting anger, disaffection or sadness, even stoically borne, do long-term damage to everyone involved and perpetuate the cycle of suffering. When the radiance that shines from us when we are happy gets dulled, it is not only a loss to us but to society as a whole. But one person declaring their desire and their intention to be happy and affirming it through their actions gives us all hope of finding happiness ourselves. Most of all, it teaches children by example that it is right for them to learn to be happy.

A qualification is necessary here. I am not an advocate of casual sex or licentiousness, though I do not presume to judge it. However, I do believe that sacrifices and emotional pain are neither particularly virtuous nor helpful. A clean separation is definitely preferable to years of mindless suffering, which does not benefit anyone in that dynamic.

Managing Anger with Biolumanetics

M was 16 years old. He was the eldest child in a large orthodox religious family. He was referred to 3S because he was prone to fits of uncontrolled and unpredictable rage. He was very bright, gregarious and extrovert and was at a boarding school, but he was losing friends as a result of his unpredictable and moody behaviour. He did not like himself when he was angry, but he had no control over that part of himself. He also slept a lot and was not doing well at his studies, considering his obvious intelligence. He was very articulate and very keen to make a good impression. He had a difficult relationship with both parents and could be quite demanding and manipulative with them. He only trusted his grandfather and preferred to stay with him in the holidays.

Using Biolumanetics and VRIC imaging we established coherence. M was given two energy-information creams to use under his eyebrows, one for the right eyebrow and a different one for the left eyebrow. When I asked him how he felt at the next assessment he told me he felt 'calm inside'. His tutor confirmed that the change was readily evident: M was much more amenable, his energy levels were better and he was more focused on his work.

M was progressing apace, to everyone's relief and delight, including his own, when suddenly I got a call from his father. He said M had had a severe relapse. He had had a violent outburst and had hit his sister. He admitted that M's sister had indeed provoked him, but said, 'He did not have to hit her so hard.'

Why had this happened when M had been doing so well? I was a bit taken aback and was not at all sure why he had lost control. However, at the end of the conversation his father said, 'By the way, those creams you gave M to apply under his eyebrows, M has finished one of them, so he has been using the other one on its own. Is that OK?'

The puzzle was solved. Applying only the one cream had made M totally incoherent and that was the reason for the lapse. I told his father that actually it was not all right for M to have used the single cream when he needed to use both. It was OK to avoid both, but it was not OK to use one on its own.

When M came to see me a couple of days later, he did not mention the incident to me. I assumed he was ashamed of his lapse and wanted me to think well of him. I did not tell him that his father had spoken to me, considering the strained nature of that relationship, but eventually I did manage to get the story out of him.

I imaged him holding the offending cream and sure enough his VRIC image became totally incoherent. This was a great relief to M and he understood why he had lapsed so badly. It also demonstrated to him the power and the precision of the process and that it could not be messed around with. Needless to say, he never did that again. He was also taught several ways of handling anger, how to understand himself better and what to do when he felt out of control.

Again, it is impossible to believe the effect of a tiny dab of cream under an eyebrow, but such is the power of the frequency universe.

Over the years I have used Biolumanetics with many youngsters who have been troubled and emotionally out of balance. So many 'dysfunctional' young adults appear impossible to deal with or talk to. They might not be able to explain why they feel the way they do, let alone know what to do with the powerful energy that surges through their body and mind. Their behaviour might be angry, disruptive and out of control as a result. I wonder how many of them could lead productive and happy lives if this simple, profound and powerful process was available to them. It is disconcerting at one level – and very hopeful at another – to think that the difference between a functional and a dysfunctional life can be something as simple as a cream under an eyebrow.

From Crisis to Joy

AW came to me completely distraught. He was 32 years old and had been adopted. He was very bright and had a very clear mind, but had never found it possible to be happy. He did not have much of an opinion of his adoptive parents and definitely disliked his younger half-brother, who had, in his words, 'totally ruined' his life.

In his search for happiness he had done a phenomenal amount of inner work, tried various personal-development methods and attempted to explore the deep self in some unconventional ways, all to no avail. He also had made a huge effort to contact his biological mother and she had met him once and then decided to have no more contact with him. He did not know his biological father and wanted to connect with him, but had met a brick wall.

Suddenly, out of the blue, he had received a call from his adoptive mother, who had told him that she had some news about his father. Without any preparation or warning, she had told him the dreadful truth: that she had found out that his mother had been raped and he was the result of that unfortunate event.

He told me all of this while weeping and bemoaning his fate and saying he thought he was 'devil spawn' and less than nothing. He was also absolutely furious with his adoptive mother for giving him the news in that insensitive way and called her some really unpleasant names.

I liked AW enormously. Tall, dark and dour, but bright, intense, conscientious, capable and very vulnerable, I could see he was in deep trouble. I asked him mildly, 'Did you ask your mother – the adoptive one – to find out about your biological father?'

He admitted he had. So she had done this at his behest and now the truth was more than he could bear and of course he wanted to shoot the messenger. His adoptive mother had been insensitive, there was no doubt about that, but now the worst was known and he could start the process of coming to terms with it and integrating it into his life.

I reminded him he was strong, capable and resilient and had managed to live independently in a foreign country. (He had been born and raised on another continent.) I also told him that he had the absolute strength and capacity to handle whatever the universe put on his plate. I reassured him that he was not diminished in any way by the circumstances of his birth; in fact he was a good person and was in no way responsible for what his father had done. I advised him not to go into blame, shame and all the wasteful ways of clinging to the past, as this would not serve to create the bright future that was his entitlement and his responsibility. I also held him gently and he allowed himself to be held. Just as the mind is reassured through words, the body has to feel the reassurance to integrate it. AW became calm.

I imaged him with his mothers (biological and adoptive) and a photo of the Divine Mother that a friend had given me, and cleared his field using Lumanetic frequencies. He left with the customary frequency vial on his wrist. The photographs as usual did their magic and he could see the healing of his fragmented self and the healing of his mothers.

He phoned me a few days later to tell me that after the assessment he had 'hit the ceiling' – his way of saying he was on top of the world – and was beginning to feel the joy that was in his system but that he had had no access to before. I was delighted.

A few days after the assessment his adoptive mother came to visit from abroad. AW met her and was able to talk to her and weep his sorrow and share his pain. His anger had disappeared. The circle of healing was complete.

AW is now learning to love and trust more than he ever has before and I daresay life will meet him and give him what he seeks most, which is love.

Healing beyond Time

CP was an old friend. She was her mid-seventies, had a bright open mind, described herself as a 'subversive', was adventurous, had great *joie de vivre* and was deeply spiritual. Along with a few others, she had initiated and completed two major projects some years ago in the field of our mutual interests. However, to me she was the prime mover, as the others had long since disappeared. At the time of these projects she had had a very challenging relationship with a particular member of the team. This had caused huge distress at the time and CP had become very ill. She had since done a phenomenal amount of work on understanding and forgiving both herself and her protagonist, but she conceded that there was still a residue of negative feeling when she thought of that person. She described it thus: 'Although over the years I have analyzed our relationship and my feelings and done what I could to clear the feelings she brought up in me, forgiving her and wishing her well, nevertheless I sense a pressure on my auric field that is aggressive and oppressive.'

I knew the huge trauma she had undergone at the time, so I offered her an assessment, as I know the residue of that emotional charge would probably still be there and that it would not be to her benefit.

CP was game for the adventure. She duly came with a photo of her former protagonist and two images were taken, one with her holding it in her right hand and one with her holding it in her left hand. She was amazed to see her image fragment when she held the photo in her right hand. Though that challenge had happened many years ago and she had done all that inner work, a part of her was still suffering and she could see it for herself. The feeling self never lies and it was asking for help.

We duly followed the supercoherence protocols for clearing her field of this challenge and came up with the Lumanetic frequency combination that would re-establish coherence and bring resolution at this deep and previously inaccessible level of her being. She went home with a frequency vial strapped to her right wrist. I generally advise people to wear these vials for 15 days.

This is an excerpt from an account she sent me of her subsequent experience:

'I had no idea what I might expect in the days that followed, but that first night I woke with an overwhelming sense of fear approaching me from behind like a giant tsunami wave accompanied by a "hooshing" sound. I found myself instinctively bowing over to the ground, knowing that I would not be swept away as long as

I held to the ground of my being, which I knew to be divine. The weight of the water pounded down on me, but I knew that I was anchored in the divine and indeed was totally divine. I realized that what I had experienced was part of my being – within me rather than outside me. Both the fear and the surviving of it were part of what I was essentially.

I have always known that perfect love casts out fear.
Part of my lesson in this lifetime is coping with powerful women who can be very threatening. Sometimes their power masks their fear and sometimes it is a measure of their insensitivity.
However, this experience of fear rising to a crescendo but then having to fall away, leaving me exhausted but triumphantly free, was new for me.

In the two weeks that followed I began to balance up and to realize that there was a Part 2 – that I needed to let go the attraction/ fascination of that whole experience. I needed detachment and that too has come. Now not only has the aggressive pressure on my auric field gone but I can think about the woman as I might anyone else, detached from the way things were and from the fascination with the process by which this came about. I marvel at the subtlety of the knowledge and healing that lies within these processes with our superconscious. I am so grateful for having benefited from them personally.'

Peace, detachment and strength – all of this from wearing a little vial containing a few drops of water with information. Would you call this magic?

A couple of months later CP happened to meet her protagonist and felt completely serene, neutral and totally unaffected in a manner she had not experienced before. She described it as 'like meeting someone new – there was no charge'.

Clearing the Stigma of Past Failure

The subject was his early sixties. He had come to 3S to find out why he was unable to succeed at his chosen task. He wished to empower children and their parents and his vision was global. He was a trained coach and had done various self-development and motivational workshops, including a fire walk with a well-known motivational guru. He had created an extensive website, authored an ebook on his chosen subject and put in endless hours trying various ideas to get his project off the ground. Now he was writing to everybody he could think of who could help him. However, he was getting nowhere fast and the proverbial brick wall was right in his face. Could I help him?

We began the process of getting to know each other. He told me about his life, his family, his two failed marriages, his conflict with his sister, whom he was taking to court, and about another business he had been involved in which had failed many years back. He had a resilient nature and was persistent and willing to try new methods to achieve his goals. He had not brought too many photos from his past, but he talked me through them, explaining why each one was significant.

During the second session I was struck by a particular photograph of him at the time when his previous business had failed. I asked what that had been like for him. He confessed to a sense of failure, a loss of self-esteem, a fear of financial ruin and the effects of all of that on his family – huge unresolved pain covered over by a veneer of positive thinking and seeming self-confidence.

I imaged him with that photograph. Sure enough, his VRIC image fragmented. He could see that the pain of that time was still present and his denial mechanisms weren't working. The message of failure was very potent and present in his field despite his positive attitude at the conscious level.

We neutralized the charge using Biolumanetics methods and I gave him the relevant frequencies to wear. This process was repeated over four sessions using the same photo and was fascinating to observe, as one could see with total precision to what extent the trauma and its effects had been truly neutralized. On the fifth session when he was imaged with that particular photograph there was no charge there and the photo was clear. He was gratified and relieved to see this for himself.

To help him recover more coherent energy, I addressed the issue of his conflicted life and suggested rather strongly that when that much energy was being expended in conflict and occupying so much of his head space, he could not very well expect to have the energy for new ideas and the energetic means to implement them. I told him it did not matter who was right or wrong, in the case of his quarrel with his sister the only person who would get rich would be the lawyer. Did he even know how much it was going to cost in monetary terms? Not a very sensible strategy for someone who had limited resources.

He took on board all the points made without too much cavil. I admired that trait. I was also impressed by how quickly and sincerely he tried to implement the various suggestions that were made. He may still have some way to go, but with his persistence and tenacity and the belief he has in his vision I am sure he will find a way to make it happen now that his field has been cleared of the stigma of failure.

VRIC IMAGING – RE-ESTABLISHING EMOTIONAL COHERENCE
CLEARING THE STIGMA OF FAILURE FROM THE ENERGY FIELD
MEETING THE HIDDEN SABOTEUR WITHIN

Holding photo of self at time of business
failure many years back – incoherent.

Holding photo of self at time of business failure
+ incoherent baseline VRIC image with the relevant
Lumanetic frequency vials neutralises hidden energy
challenge and creates coherence.

143

From Despair and Depression to Stardom and Excellence

AM could not keep the smile off his face. He sat down and still could not stop smiling. It was infectious and I was grinning delightedly at him in return. I waited for him to tell me why he was so happy.

A few months ago (six sessions back), when this 36-year-old man had walked through my door, persuaded by his partner, another of my clients, the picture had been very different. Then he had looked extremely tense and unhappy and had found it almost impossible to return my smile of greeting. A tight body had been matched by a tight smile. With his intense deep blue eyes, AM had been very good looking, but very unhappy.

In that first session he had described himself as a failure. He was deeply depressed and had been offered medication, but had refused it. He did not know where to turn and in his own words felt 'desperate'. He felt that coming to me was a 'last resort'. There was nowhere left to go.

He was actually a fine martial artist. He had been to China to study his chosen art and had put a lot of time, effort and money into it. By his own account he was very skilled at it. He was also an aspiring actor. That was what he wanted to do more than anything else. He was well educated and well spoken, but whenever he went for an audition, he could not go through with it. He desperately needed a show reel, but again and again he would book the studio and then something would prevent him from going through with the recording. The same thing had happened when he had gone to Los Angeles – he had talked to people in the industry and had got them interested, but had not been able to get past this inner block that prevented him from following through. One could be tempted to say, 'What a load of nonsense. He should pull himself together,' but it was unfortunately not as simple as that. He was constantly being stymied not by an external enemy but by a part of himself that was stronger than all his positive qualities.

We looked at other areas of his life. He had been badly injured at one time and he had had a difficult relationship with his father that had affected him a lot. He badly wanted to trust, but found it almost impossible. He described an experience with a martial arts teacher. The teacher, who was skilled at martial arts but in his arrogance and high-handedness had forgotten to be a decent human, had been owed money by a man and had been having difficulty collecting it. He had asked AM and a few other students to go with him to the airport, abduct the man and strong-arm him into returning the money. AM had been his right-hand man, but had wanted no part of it, so had made a lame excuse and left. The abduction had gone ahead anyway but had gone horribly wrong and the man had died as a result. The teacher had gone to jail, as had all of the students who had accompanied him. AM had escaped by the skin of his teeth.

It was becoming clear that AM had great difficulty with the important men in his life. So the male frequency was restored using Biolumanetics methods. AM was given a Lumanetic frequency pad to put on his solar plexus (he admitted to feeling his tension in his gut) and was asked to treat himself with monochromatic light in the Monocrom light-colour dome using colours that he enjoyed. At the end of the session he was beaming.

In subsequent sessions we cleared his energy field, using photos of him in hospital with his injuries and with his father and addressing other issues.

As he began to experience real beneficial changes in his mind and body, his depression started lifting and he started to see the light at the end of the tunnel. By now he trusted me and I gave him one suggestion as to what to do. He was still extremely fragile emotionally and could revert to pessimism and blaming himself if he did not fulfil his high expectations. I told him that if he felt the slightest positive impulse to do something, he should act on it instantly. I told him the impulse would come from nowhere and would last for only a very short while and it would be easy to not do anything about it. But he was not to give himself time to talk himself out of whatever it was, just to do it.

AM now had the key to the locked door of his dreams. What happened was amazing beyond belief. By synchronicity, chance, fate, destiny, call it what you will, soon after the assessment, he heard of a martial arts film producer who was about to start a project. He actually could not believe what he did next: he found out the man's address and went and knocked on his door. He was on the point of running away, but did not. The door opened and he found he could talk to the man and that he was very interested in what he had to offer. Destiny could now smile on this earnest, intense, talented man and allow him to live his dream.

Nothing could stop him now. He went from strength to strength. From having no work and no hope and no show reel, he was offered, with no effort at all, parts in four films, plus the job of fight director on a couple of the films, and became so busy that he did not have the time to eat or rest. On the day he came to see me, beaming from ear to ear, he had been offered one of the leading parts in an important film. He thanked me sincerely and said, 'I know I could not have done it without you. I remember you telling me it would happen with ease and grace.'

I know he will do very well, yet how easily it could have gone the other way. To top it all, he does not yet have an agent and in that field it is almost impossible to get work without an agent.

From despair and dysfunction to miracles and stardom in a few months – that is the power of supercoherence. That is the power that lies locked in all of us.

VRIC Imaging – Past and Present Are One
Assessing and Neutralising Past Trauma in the Bodymind

Client had a serious motorcycle accident ten years back.
Holding a photo of himself in hospital at that time makes him incoherent
ten years later. His bodymind system is still feeling the effects of the trauma.

Client holding photo shows past trauma cleared and neutralised with Lumanetic frequency
pad + 4 flower essences. Clean slate energetically after ten years.

148

BIOLUMANETICS AND VRIC IMAGING – CLEARING PAST PATTERNING
BREAKING THE CYCLE OF SUFFERING
STARTING WITH A CLEAN SLATE

Holding photo of parents when mother was pregnant with him – incoherent.

Holding same photo with the relevant Lumanetic frequency vial neutralises the energetic challenge which client has had before he was born – coherence achieved.

VRIC Imaging – Assessing Emotional Coherence
What Is Our Image of Our Body and Ourself
How Do I feel about Me? Science of the Feeling Self

My beautiful friend SA as she really is.

How SA feels about her surgical scar
and herself. 'I feel ugly.'
Lumanetic energy cream applied on scar
brought up this disempowered image.

These images were shocking for the client and made a very real impact, made her understand in real terms some of her patterns and behaviour, where she could not acknowledge herself for any of her many gifts and achievements.

Feeling compassion for herself became possible for the first time in her life.

ASSESSING THE TRUTH OF RELATIONSHIP WITH VRIC IMAGING
LOVE AND CHAOS – HOW DO I REALLY FEEL ABOUT THIS RELATIONSHIP?

Holding photo of self with partner – RH – male side - incoherent.

Holding photo of self with partner – LH – female side - incoherent.

Client had fallen madly in love with a charming, charismatic, exciting but erratic, troubled and untrustworthy man. A turbulent affair ensued, which lasted for four years. She knew it was not beneficial for her to continue, but could not give up – hoping against hope and waiting for him to change. She knew she was behaving in a manner that was not in her best interest – but could not walk away. Her health and career suffered and life was not fun a lot of the time – but there was this irresistible pull.

After a series of sessions, this final one (with the shocking photos above) showed her how this relationship impacted her and helped her to let go. She was in conscious control of her destiny again. She has regained her vitality, her career has taken off and her creativity and confidence which had disappeared are back.

VRIC Imaging – The Effect of Sound on the Human Energy Field
Sounds that Hurt – Sounds that Heal

'I feel like I have been battered.'
Notice the right side of face appears swollen – incoherent.

Post-five-minute session on the Monochord
music-sound table – coherent.

G was almost forty minutes late for her appointment. G is very considerate and is almost never late for her appointment. This was unusual. I waited for her to tell me why. She looked a bit harried. She had had a verbal fracas with her partner who was now her ex-partner. I took a VRIC image to see how she was. In the image the right side (the male side) of her face looked like it had been slugged and appeared swollen. She had one look at the image and exclaimed 'That is exactly how I feel, battered.' She had been battered by words and had not been touched physically, but at some level this battering had registered and was plainly visible. Unkind words and verbal aggression can impact the energy field and the bodymind as a consequence. Sound has a powerful effect on the field and the physical level. Harmonious sounds and loving words evoke feelings of pleasure while dissonant sounds and hurtful aggressive words can create feelings of disquiet and other unpleasant feelings which then have a direct impact on the physical level. To neutralise this sonic battering was simple. GC was put on the Monochord table and her whole body floated on the ocean of gentle rolling sounds for five minutes. When she got off the table she was smiling and her normal happy self. The next VRIC image taken after the monochord session revealed she was coherent.

VRIC IMAGING
THE SUPERCOHERENCE SELF-EMPOWERMENT

Base photo showing disempowered and
fragmented self – incoherent.

Making statement, 'It is okay for me to be strong and a woman,'
holding Lumanetic female frequency tube on LH – female side.

Nouri has been in a bad marriage for a very long time. She has stuck it out for a variety of 'reasons' financial and 'for the sake of the children' and the result is that she gets very angry, very depressed and disempowered. Often she is on the verge of taking anti-depressants but does not wish to go that way. She comes in looking exhausted, dragging her feet, unable to smile despite her sweet temperament. The latest onslaught has taken its toll.

The base line image shows her how she really feels, completely disintegrated. After the assessment and the coaching she is asked to hold the female Lumanetic frequency in her left (female) hand to strengthen her female side which has been battered and asked to affirm that 'It is okay to be strong and a woman.' The result speaks for itself.

She goes out the door looking and feeling completely different from the way she came in just a couple of hours back.

LIFTING THE HEAVY WEIGHT OF HIDDEN SUFFERING
FREEDOM TO BE TRULY HAPPY REGAINED

Holding photo (right) in
LH female side – incoherent.

Holding photo (right) LH with Lumanetic frequency vials – coherent.

Photo of self at ten years in the
garden of her home in the UK
soon after the traumatic loss of
her father. Uprooted from
Kenya where she was born and
raised and brought to live in
the UK. Father died within
days after the move.

TP was beautiful, youthful, extremely bright, highly qualified and very highly regarded in
her profession, capable, conscientious, deeply feeling, authentic, genuine and sincere and
ecologically aware. She was well travelled, had lived on several continents – one of those
humans I regard as universals – and had a very broad outlook and a sweet and winning personality. I had always liked and admired her and regarded her as exceptional. I was a bit surprised when she wanted to come and see me.

She told me she was in trouble, was finding it very hard to be happy and, despite everything
she had done, her life did not make sense at a deep emotional level to her. She was not satisfied with this state of affairs. She did not know what her next step was – though she knew
what she didn't want, she didn't quite know what would make her truly rapturously happy.
There was an edge of despair and desperation in her voice, but no self-pity. She knew she
needed help and was sure it was not psychotherapy that she needed.

She came from a close and happy family and had warm relationships with her mother and
siblings. She had been born and brought up in Africa and had happy memories of her childhood there. Her father was of Indian origin and her mother was Scottish. At the age of 10
she had moved with her family to the UK. Within two weeks of the move her father had
died, leaving her mother with five children, the youngest only two years old. The shock and
trauma would affect everyone in that family in a variety of ways.

For her first assessment she brought loads of photos of herself and her family and we did
the imaging and established coherence.

The images in this book are from her second visit. She is holding a photo of herself at home
in England at the age of 10, after her father had died. In the photo she appears to be smiling, but it is patently not a happy time for this little girl. Her VRIC image shows the
extreme suffering of that time is still present with her now. Looking at it, she can understand
what a load she has been carrying without her conscious knowledge and why she finds it so
difficult to be happy. The next photo shows the emotional charge neutralized with Lumanetics.
Looking at it, she feels the wonder of the freedom to be happy again .

SUPERCOHERENCE AND THE UNDERSTANDING HEART

Baseline image with parents after the death of mother –
incoherent.

With same image making the affirmation
'I love and accept them just as they are' – coherence.

Client lost her mother a few months ago. Client is a bright heart-centred woman. She loves both her parents dearly but does not always approve of them. She had gone to visit with her father recently and asked him how he was. She got an unexpected reply, which shocked her deeply. He said he was 'better than ever'. She could not believe he could be as unfeeling as that. This was very hard for her to accept.

During the assessment we discussed the possibility that different people cope with loss in different ways; his way was as always to bury himself in his work.

At the end of the assessment I asked her to make a simple affirmation of acceptance of them both. I knew this would make her coherent. The head had understood and analysed what was wrong, why it had happened etc., but the end result was incoherence for all. The heart simply accepted them and herself with no conditions. The result was coherence for all. She left much happier and at peace than when she came in.

CHAPTER 13

CHALLENGING CONDITIONS

REALM OF 'MIRACLES'?

The next four case studies serve to illustrate the speed, power and effectiveness of the system under extreme conditions.

Healing a Fractured Life

L was 50 when she came to 3S. She had been a very fine jazz composer and a professional musician who had had a successful international concert career until her 'MS' finally put a stop to it. She was also an aspiring author and had almost finished her autobiography when she first came to 3S. She had been diagnosed as suffering from 'MS' 15 years before.

She came at the suggestion of her carer and therapist, Jane. She had visited 3S and been impressed with the Biolumanetics process. She felt that it was more advanced than anything else she had seen and she wanted L to try it, even though L had been told when she had been diagnosed that there was no cure, in fact no treatment for the disease in medical terms.

At the time I had decided to take a four-month sabbatical to write a book about my work and had stopped taking on any new clients, so I was not willing to take on L at that time. I thought, given the serious nature of her illness, I could not possibly do her justice and it would be highly inappropriate to take her on. At best I could see her regularly for less than two months and then I would only be seeing clients over one weekend every five weeks. So I told Jane to bring L back after that. But Jane would not give up, so eventually I accepted L as a client under those conditions. I have to say I was uncomfortable about my decision.

My worst fears were confirmed when I first met L and saw a sorry figure in a wheelchair. She had been brought by taxi from central London and the long journey had been exhausting for her. She could not hold her neck up. She was tall and weighed all of six stone. She was incontinent, having to go the toilet every 30 minutes during the day. At night she was up every hour to empty her bladder and had no proper sleep or rest. She had bedsores, had great difficulty evacuating her bowels and had not had a period in several years. Her voice was slurred and her speech was incoherent. She did not talk much and would scream like a terrorized child when she wanted to go to the toilet. She was in a downward spiral of frightening proportions. I had never handled anybody in that condition before. I felt quite cross with Jane for having persuaded me to take her on. I honestly could not see what I could do to help her. However, she was here and I had promised, so, with serious misgivings on my part, we started the process of creating coherence in her bio-light-energy-information field.

I have to confess that when I was faced with L, I forgot for a moment that we do not define disease at 3S, forgot the extraordinary nature of the Intelligence that is always present in each being, no matter what 'state' they appear to be in, and forgot that a person is not ever their 'symptoms' but always more, much more. I also forgot that I was only the enabler and it was not my knowledge that was crucial, but the Intelligence in L's bodymind system that would do the healing and be allowed to 'speak' through the process of VRIC imaging. The power was not mine, but neither at one level was the responsibility.

With the exception of a couple of homoepathic remedies and flower essences on a couple of occasions only Lumanetics were used to create coherence.

What happened for L was amazing beyond belief. Generally she came every four or five weeks. Within a short while changes began to happen in her body. She started eating properly and put on a stone and a half in weight. She started regaining her bladder control too. After a few sessions she only needed to empty her bladder four times a day. She slept all night with full bladder control and did not need to use incontinence pads any more. The bedsores disappeared with the external application of the Lumanetic drops. Bowel evacuation became regular and easy, thanks to the Lumanetic transceiver pads. Her voice strengthened enormously and her speech was no longer slurred, but clear and strong. Her menstruation resumed, which delighted her. (I am not sure I would feel the same if mine came back!) She also told me that previously she used to suffer from premenstrual syndrome, but that was no longer the case.

When we talked initially about her relationship with her mother, she said quite vehemently that she hated her. She had not met her for many years. No counselling was used at any time regarding this issue. It is pointless to tell someone, especially someone as ill as L was, that it is not right to feel whatever they feel, and endless analyzing and preaching can be sanctimonious and counterproductive. On the other hand, I knew that this relationship would have to heal for L's body to heal. We started the process of reorganizing her energetic relationship with her mother at the field level using VRIC imaging and Lumanetic frequencies and her mother's photograph. As the emotional charge that was held in the energy body was neutralized in her energy field, something astonishing happened: her mother came to visit her out of the blue. The relationship, which had been non-existent for years, was re-established. An old friend, who had known L for many years, could hardly believe that this relationship had healed so suddenly without any effort. We have observed such things happening many times with this process and this is the aspect of the work that gives me the greatest pleasure and satisfaction.

In Biolumanetics we know that our relationship with our respective parents has a bearing on the side of the body that is physically challenged. We regard the right as the male side, connected to our father relationship, and the left side as being the female side, connected to our relationship with our mother. This applies to both males and females. This is not generally known, but over the years I have encountered many cases which bear this out. L's left side, her mother's side, was far worse than the right. Her left leg was completely useless and there were many more physical challenges on the left side of her body than on her right.

Sometimes high drama takes place in assessments. One day we were addressing L's left side by getting her to hold some Lumanetic frequency vials, in this case only in her left hand, when suddenly she announced rather dramatically that she couldn't see. Jane asked her, just to make sure, 'Can you see anything at all?' L said she couldn't see anything at all. I was nonplussed, to say the least.

A couple of minutes later we asked her whether her eyesight had returned. This time she said, with great vehemence, *'No, I have MS.'*

There were three of us apart from L in the room, and recalling the incident later, all of us felt the words had been spoken by someone other than L – one could call it a sub-personality. Up until now L had never said to me, 'I have MS,' so it felt as if a part of her that wanted to hang on to the disease had emerged. The interesting thing was that her VRIC image holding the vials was clear and coherent, so those were the frequencies she was given to take home with her. A small bottle containing the liquid which contained the energy signatures in those offending vials was strapped to the pulse point on her left wrist.

After three to four days Jane phoned me to report the strangest occurrence. Previously L's left side, arms and legs had been noticeably different in tone and colour from the right. The right side was a normal warm flesh tone whereas the left side edged towards a bluish tinge, probably due to a difference in the circulation. Suddenly the two sides had become more even in hue and the left side had lost its bluish tinge. There was also a bit of feeling in the left leg. L could feel pain in her extremities, whereas she had not been able to feel anything previously. And all this from putting a vial containing water (with energy and information) on her left wrist.

After this, L started having healing dreams in which she saw herself walking again. I consider this the turning point in her journey to healing. Some months earlier I had asked her to confirm what I had initially intuited about her feelings of hopelessness and despair, and she had admitted that she had wanted to die. But now I knew that she really wanted to live. I found the dreams of great significance. L's unconscious was now on her side, creating healing instead of havoc.

Around this time there was a rather funny incident. Jane lived with L. One night she suddenly woke up to hear her saying, 'I am desperate, I am desperate!' She asked her whether she was desperate to go to the toilet. 'No,' said L, 'I am desperate for my legs to work.' This was very heartening.

Early on I had asked L about music. Did she listen to any? Jane had said that L had told her she now hated music. I could understand why. Music had been her life, both the composing and the playing. Neither had been possible for some time; her hands did not have the strength. But after a while I received a call from Jane to say that L had asked to play the piano and had started to compose music again.

On another note I have to say there was an additional indispensable ingredient without which I do not think L would have done as well as she did. That magic ingredient was Jane. Jane treated L like a sister and loved her and looked after her with unfailing patience, good humour and kindness, better than any friend or family could and well beyond the call of duty. She was an angel for L. While I know that L benefited phenomenally from Biolumanetics, I honestly think that the results would not have been anywhere near as good without Jane's love and devotion. Someone up there or in here was looking after L when Jane came into her life.

Unfortunately, L stopped coming at the end of 2002 when Jane went for a holiday abroad. For various reasons Jane did not or was not allowed to go back to her and the connection was broken.

I learned an enormous amount with L and from her. I also learned that I must not write anybody off as untreatable, no matter what the 'symptoms' or definitions or diagnosis. This case gave me a degree of confidence in the awesome power of two incredible systems – the Supreme Intelligence that resides in each of us and the incredible system that is Biolumanetics, which permits me to communicate with this extreme Intelligence with such elegance, simplicity and precision.

The Power of Self-forgiveness and a Little Miracle
The anguished voice was desperately calling for help over the

phone. The woman told me her story of misfortune and her subsequent descent into the hell of suicidal depression, total dysfunction and nine Valiums a day. I felt sympathy, but was not sure I could help. It was obvious she had no money and certainly could not afford my services, but the fact that she still was looking for help and an indefinable something in her voice made me decide that I would see her.

When she came to my door, she looked unwashed and was simply crying uncontrollably. I ushered her into the Luminator room and she sat down. In between bouts of weeping she told me her story.

At one level it was pitiful. Four years back she had had an affair with a married man and had become pregnant by him. He had made her have an abortion and then had a baby with his wife. This event had been more than she could bear. She could not stop lactating and hadn't for four years. She had also developed polyps in her uterus that caused her to bleed excessively. Simultaneously she had descended into a mental hell from which there was no let-up, and her life, her job and everything had disintegrated and fallen about her ears. But now, through this horror and haze, something in her said she wanted her life back. She told me that she had always worked before and wanted to work again. On the other hand, she told me she couldn't see – there were clouds in front of her eyes – and she could not hear because of the tinnitus that was driving her mad. To top it all, a few months back, a man had broken into her house and raped her while she was asleep. She was not eating properly, her house was in total chaos with dirty dishes everywhere and she could not find the motivation to clean it or herself. Yet she told me she had been houseproud when she had been well.

She actually had no idea what I did and had been referred via some practitioners who ran a telephone helpline and had seen my work.

I did not insult her intelligence and tell her everything would be all right, but listened to her with full attention and no emotional input on my part. More tears at this point would not help anyone.

I imaged her and she was out of coherence. She was still weeping at this point and her lower lip would not stop trembling. As a course of action emerged as a result of the imaging, I knew what would bring resolution at that level. As I applied the Lumanetic frequency cream under her left eyebrow, her photograph cleared, as I knew it would. But I can still recall my own amazement at the speed of her response. As soon as the cream touched her skin, her crying stopped as if someone had turned off a tap. She calmed down and I put her into the Monocrom light-colour dome for two to three minutes, took her out and sent her home. I told her I would see her every 15 days.

By her second visit she was no longer crying uncontrollably. I followed the same protocol, established coherence through the imaging and put her into the dome for another three minutes.

By her third visit, something had perceptibly changed in her. A weak smile was attempting to come through like watery sunshine after a cloudburst. She confided that she had come to the centre by bus. I asked her how long it had been since she had been on a bus. It had been four years.

By her fifth visit I could not recognize the woman who came through the door. No hangdog expression, no self-pity, she was wearing a smart soft peach-coloured skirt and was smiling. She had not come by bus today, she had driven, something she had not attempted since an accident some time before. Not only was she obviously not in crisis, she was on her way to healing. I wonder if she saw my jaw drop at her transformation.

Now the real work could begin as far as I was concerned. Up until now we had not discussed self-responsibility and self-accountability, as it would have been totally inappropriate and counterproductive. When a person is absorbed in such a deep level of suffering they cannot be reached by words, however wise and well-meant they may be. They have to be brought out of crisis before they can begin to take responsibility for their own healing. But now deep-seated guilt at aborting her unborn child and unresolved anger at herself and her then lover had to be addressed and resolved through an act of conscious forgiveness for her transgression.

We started gently. By now she knew me well and trusted both me and the process. I asked her how she felt about aborting the unborn child and she came back immediately and said she felt like a murderer. I asked her if she would do it again. She said there was no way she would repeat it. So she had become wiser through the experience. She could agree with that. Also, she knew that given the circumstances of that time she had done the best she could, even though it had not appeared that way after the deed was done. If she could have done it differently she would have done, but she had not, so she could not.

I explained that staying in the disposition of pain and punishment on the one hand while trying to get her life back on the other was not likely to be easy. She had to give herself permission to let herself off the hook of her suffering, as it was not serving anyone, certainly not herself. She accepted this advice and asked what she should do.

I gave her a simple ceremony to perform. I asked her to find a photograph of herself as she had been four years ago, put some flowers and a lighted candle in front of it and tell that person in the photograph that she forgave her. I told her it would be OK to cry. If the tears came, she was simply to let them come. But she had to say the words and hear herself say them. She agreed to do this.

The next time she came she had a story for me. She had been out walking and had seen a briefcase lying on the road. She had picked it up, opened it and found the card of the man it belonged to. It also contained papers and an empty wallet. She had phoned the man and he had thanked her sincerely for the retrieval of the case. He had also asked her if he could pay her in some way in return for her kindness. She had declined – she had not acted in the expectation of any return – but the man had sent her a gift anyway. Out of all possible things in the world, it had been a candle.

The significance of this had not been lost on her. She said it was as if a bit of magic had happened and that she had been told that God wanted her to do the ceremony.

On another level it was my pleasure to observe that this woman who was completely out of it just a few weeks ago, with her house and life in chaos, was now reaching out for life in this proactive manner and the universe was aligning with her intent in this truly magical way.

By now she was only on four Valiums a day and desperately wanted to reduce her intake further. I told her she should do it very gradually over a few months.

I stopped seeing her then as she was out of crisis. She started to see a counsellor, which made the break less difficult.

A few months later she wanted to see me again. She was not in an emotional crisis; her images were coherent. Her polyps were still there and she had become more anaemic because of the constant bleeding, but she was emotionally stable. She had decided to have the polyps removed surgically and she could understand and accept her situation from a calm and hopeful space. Though she was not yet happy, she now had the real possibility of claiming her life back.

I would like to clarify that I am not judgemental about the rights and wrongs of abortion. I believe it is up to the person(s) concerned and it is none of my business.

Beyond Psychotherapy with Biolumanetics

M was 19 years old. His rabbi rang and asked if I could help him. He was going back to NYC in six weeks to be married. He had lost his mother when he was very young and his stepmother did not care for him. He was a good boy, but very troubled.

I wondered why the rabbi had waited until there were only six weeks to go. Last-minute panic? Trying to keep too many balls in the air? His own personal stress? Anyway, that was the situation. I told him I did not know what I could do given the short time frame, but I was willing to try.

The rabbi duly arrived with M. M walked in, head down, gaze averted, and walked past me as if I was not there. Not a promising start.

We went into the Luminator room for the imaging. M would not talk to me directly, addressing any questions he had to the rabbi. He was obviously highly intelligent at the intellectual level and totally unintelligent at the emotional level, to the point of being completely dissociated. He could not relate to anyone – he simply did not have the know-how. He was happy with his books and studies and basically wanted to be left alone. I could not help but wonder at the wisdom of marrying this child to any girl – my imagination did not stretch that far. His photos showed him to be incoherent and when the rabbi was imaged with him he became incoherent too. The rabbi had obviously tried everything and was at his wits' end.

I put the relevant Lumanetic frequency cream at M's feet and his photo cleared. He came to see me a total of three times in the six weeks and the transformation was plain for all to see. When he came into the house the second time, I was taken aback when he said hello to me and readily engaged in direct discussion. He admitted he felt calmer inside and altogether better in himself. I observed that he had begun to relate from an emotional level instead of retreating to the safety of the intellectual level. The rabbi had noticed the changes too.

I was still not sure that it was wise for this child to be married and I said so to the rabbi, but was told that it was not possible to delay the marriage. So off he went to NYC and was married.

Several months later I received a phone call. M was coming to the UK for a visit and wanted to come and see me. I was delighted. This time he came with a mate who had previously been his mentor at college in the UK. I asked him how he was and what it was like to be married. It was nothing heavy, just a pleasant enquiry, but I cannot forget what he said to me in reply: 'Please can you just help me without my having to talk about it?' I told him it was perfectly OK for him not to talk. The images would tell the story far more accurately than he could. We finished the session and I gave him a Lumanetic energy cream to carry on his person. He also had ten minutes in the Monocrom light-colour dome. Within a minute of coming out, it was plain that some emotional knot had loosened in him. It was gratifying to see this bright, animated and obviously happy young man leave to go back to his life.

A few days later his mate phoned me. M had phoned him from NYC and asked him to thank me. In his words, 'I feel like a new man.'

Let us examine what was done and more importantly what was not done to achieve this result. There was no analysis of any sort at any time in the whole process – no discussion of the lost mother, the 'wicked' stepmother, what was wrong, what he would do to make it right, no counselling or coaching of any sort. No attention was given at any time to dysfunction – acknowledgement, yes;

attention, no. The child that was this young man would not have wanted or been able to engage effectively at that level.

To ask someone what is wrong is not always useful. A lot of people, especially young ones, get tongue-tied and cannot explain the pain and turbulence of their feelings in a meaningful way. Words on their own, in my view, are simply not adequate to resolve issues that lie buried deep within the psyche. But in this case, carrying one little frequency cream and sitting in monochromatic light for a few minutes did the job.

Seeing Yourself in a New Light

RW came on the recommendation of someone who was running an obsessive-compulsive disorder support group. When he phoned and made the appointment he did not tell me much about himself or his condition and by then I did not remember anything much about OCD or clinical depression or the psychiatric scene, despite my earlier studies in psychoanalysis.

When he appeared at my door, my son, who was helping me at the time, took one look at him and told me not to touch him with a barge pole, as he looked very disturbed. He also looked heavily drugged, and he was.

My response was slightly different. Yes, he did look disturbed, but he had found his way to me. Since I do not advertise, as I want the flow (of my life or clients) to be natural and not forced in any way, I believe that if people find their way to me, then there is a reason for it, perhaps hidden, that is useful to both them and me.

RW said he had come because he wanted to ask some questions in front of the Luminator. I asked him what they were. He told me his life was hell and there was the possibility that he might have brain surgery. He wanted to ascertain whether this would be beneficial or not. So he asked the question and was imaged. It turned out it would be OK for him to have brain surgery. Then he asked me if he could ask another question. Something in the way he said it made me ask him what the second question was. He wanted to know whether it would be OK for him to commit suicide. I told him point-blank that he could not ask that question. Then I decided to assess his coherence using VRIC. Sure enough, he was incoherent. No surprise there. But as I went to apply a trace of cream to his eyebrow to create coherence, he backed away from me with terror in his face. I immediately moved away from him and assured him he did not have to do anything he did not wish to do.

A few days later he phoned and asked if he could come and see me again. I was quite blunt with him and asked what he wanted to see me for, as if he did not want to undergo the process there was nothing I could do for him. He said he had changed his mind now, so I agreed to see him.

He came and finally, with great trepidation and after asking umpteen questions about the contents of the Lumanetic cream, actually underwent the process and of course his VRIC image cleared.

He was in his late thirties at the time, 38 to be exact, and it transpired that he lived in a psychiatric institution and had been there for many years. He had had psychiatric problems since early childhood and had been in institutions of various degrees of restriction in his unhappy life. He had had all the help that was possible under the system and his condition, by his own description, had been termed 'intransigent' because of its long-standing nature. He had been severely depressed for years, had had many psychotic episodes by his own confession, had mutilated himself and had threatened suicide many times. Being severely obsessive-compulsive made any kind of productive life impossible, as the anxiety of just touching anything was unbearable. He was in hell and there did not seem any way out. And yet at another level, despite the severity of his dysfunction, he was highly intelligent, articulate and insightful – a curious combination of contradictions. I decided to see him on a regular basis, partly out of compassion, partly out of curiosity, in the interests of research. As he had very little money, I agreed to see him if he paid for his photos. I felt it was important for him to participate in some way in his own healing.

Though RW was intelligent and articulate, he was also highly manipulative and could be very argumentative, contradictory and full of self-pity. According to him, he wanted to help himself but his dysfunction prevented him from doing so. His life was not worth living, he could not enjoy any of the things normal people did and he felt that life had dealt him a very wicked and unfair deal. It was a constant litany of complaint. I treated him as I would any other client and did not sympathize or align with his dysfunction. He would try and manipulate me and say he felt like jumping under a train or that he could use the scissors in my stationery tray to hurt himself or me and then he would wait to see my reaction. I would simply tell him that if he did kill himself, he would still have his own unfinished business to clear and would not be free of his suffering. It did not perturb me, as all of us have to leave our body at some point.

When RW saw that I neither reacted nor panicked when he said such things and that I was not to be manipulated, he stopped trying to do so. But he would still complain to me about his psychiatrists and how they were of no use and had not been able to help him, and how the talking therapies were useless as well and what a waste of time the drugs were. I told him that his doctors had given him all the help that was possible in their model of understanding and that he had plenty to be grateful for.

I showed him how to start the process of making changes in tiny increments. I remember one analogy that really struck a chord with him: I told him how a drop of water could wear away a stone if it dripped on it long enough. How hard the stone and how soft the water, and yet the effect was sure. And then I said that every thought, every intention, every little effort was like that drop of water, and though the stone of his dysfunction might appear to be the same, it was slowly wearing away as every single thought, action and intention had an impact.

I also taught RW some simple relaxation exercises and showed him how to contain his dysfunctional side, to compartmentalize it and still carry on the healing. I showed him how to neutralize the negative messages that had taken over his thoughts and to consciously think the opposite. If a negative message could not be got rid of, its impact could still be minimized by a message that was equal but opposite.

RW would never acknowledge that anything had improved in his life. In fact he would phone at any time and the conversation would always start with: 'I am very depressed.' I would tell him, 'R, tell me something new. I don't want to know how depressed you are – I already know that.'

No one else had ever shown RW that he was anything but completely dysfunctional. Everyone had given up on him and patronized him. As I did neither of those things, I suppose I was a lifeline for him. Whenever he needed a pep talk he would phone me.

For quite a while he kept saying nothing was improving, but he still kept coming to see me. One particular session was very dramatic and it proved to be the turning point for him.

RW had been convinced by what everyone had told him, that he would never improve and that he would never be able to survive independently. His past history was clear evidence of that. Whenever he had tried, it had ended in disaster. Yet in the incoherent environment of a psychiatric institution it was unlikely that he was ever going to become functional anyway. I knew that he was coherent now and that he could probably hold his own, but there was no way that he would believe that. In this pivotal session he made two statements: one was that it was OK to live independently and the other that it was beneficial to live in a supervised environment (an institution). Two VRIC images were taken. They clearly indicated that it was OK for him to live independently.

RW took one look at them and protested vehemently, 'I don't feel like that!'

I told him, 'Yes, I know you don't *feel* like that, but there is a part of you that is much smarter and that *thinks* differently.'

RW protested mightily, but he could not easily gainsay the message of the coherent VRIC images. He could see himself, literally in a new light, for the first time in his life, instead of the way his psychiatrist or his mother or his carers saw him, and in fact how he saw himself. He went away looking thoughtful.

Some months later, he actually moved into a semi-independent environment for the first time in his life. He was terribly apprehensive and very anxious, but he survived. A few months after that he moved to a completely independent environment. This was unprecedented. He had exceeded everyone's expectations, most of all his own. I was delighted. He told me later that those VRIC images had been the single most important factor in the momentous decision of trying to reclaim his life.

Over a year after I stopped seeing RW I got a phone call from him. He had called to wish me a happy new year. We chatted for a while. Yes, he was still depressed. I asked him if he had managed to stay independent. Yes, despite all the anxiety, depression and dysfunction, he had managed to stay independent.

I have to say that made my day and it was a wonderful gift from the universe, a truly auspicious start to my year. All the time and effort had been worth it.

VRIC IMAGING – CONSULTING THE 7TH SENSE
EXAMINING OPTIONS – THE STATEMENT METHOD
ROBERT DECIDES HIS DESTINY

Beneficial to move to an independent
environment – coherent.

Beneficial to remain in a supervised
environment – incoherent.

CHAPTER 14

VRIC AND THE ARTFUL SCIENCE OF SUCCESSFUL RELATIONSHIPS
HARMONY, INDEPENDENCE, AUTHENTICITY, INTIMACY, DELIGHT

Until now you have seen what the Luminator and VRIC can do for the individual. While that is extremely impressive, it is a very small part of the capability of this system. The really mind-blowing aspect of it is its capacity to assess the coherence of relationships.

Everything is relationship; everything and everyone exists within the context of relationship. Our primary relationship is with the self, the internal environment and the creative Super Intelligence, and the nature of this relationship then extends to the external environment and the cosmos and, most importantly of all, to the people in our lives – our parents, our families, our friends, our professional associates… The list is endless. We are not isolated, nor are we islands.

Even loving relationships can be stressful, as we all know. Each person seeks to have their own needs fulfilled while (it is to be hoped) being mindful of meeting the needs of the other(s). This is not an easy business and often results in stresses and strains, the loss of intimacy and trust, disappointment and the loss of hope as the other cannot or will not change as we want them to. Unpleasant dynamics can develop and the continued, increasing and accumulating strain can result in the breakdown of the relationship or manifest in physical or mental illness. At best it may lead to a resigned acceptance, a kind of peace which is not real peace.

Family Assessments

At 3S we often call the whole family for an assessment. This may sound absurd – the objections range from 'Why should I go to the doctor when it's you who's sick?' to 'It's your problem, not mine. You fix it. I don't have the time.' However, when I first started I wouldn't agree to see clients if their family refused to participate in the process. Today, as I know a lot more about the capabilities of the system, I do not insist on it. In fact, at times it is more effective to see the different protagonists individually, as some of the most important and deeply-felt emotions may not be able to be addressed when others are present because of fear of one sort or another.

Using VRIC we are able to establish the truth about the state of a relationship at the energetic level, rather than trying to assess what is happening by what people say. This prevents a lot of difficulties from arising. When problems have to be openly defined, each person involved will have their own very different understanding of them and their 'cause' and all sorts of hidden or not-so-hidden agendas come into play. Blame, guilt, anger, fear of loss, loyalty and not wanting to hurt another can result in a complex puzzle in which clarity, objectivity and fairness can be hard to find. It is also possible for the practitioner to become inadvertently entangled in the dynamic, due to their own personal bias, no matter how neutral they may seek to be. If, say, I as a woman have had a hard time with men all my life, it will be difficult for me to remain unbiased towards a man who seems to be acting very unpleasantly towards his partner, and vice versa.

As already mentioned, when I was in my twenties I studied psycho-analysis for many years and then turned away from it. Today I believe very strongly that analyzing problems endlessly not only does not work, it is actually counterproductive. What does it matter who did what to whom and when? What good does going over and over the same sorry sagas again and again do? If energy follows attention, which it does, focusing attention on problems cannot help to solve them and may even amplify and perpetuate them. I also believe that words alone, however wise, well-meaning, insightful, helpful or comforting, are not enough. Deep long-standing pain and the resulting non-nourishing patterns of thought and behaviour are not easily modified or washed away with words. Something more is required to repair the psyche, the self and the body that hold these hurts in the cellular memory and in the field.

How we address this is very simple. We have each person stand on their own and we take a photo of them in the field of the Luminator. Then we have the family stand together and take another photo. If there are children, they are included. The photos show clearly when a relationship is in trouble, as the image of one party or other will lose coherence. As people see this silent witness to the truth of their relationship and its effect on them, words are not needed. Each picture is worth a thousand words. The images reflect the unbiased truth from that place of truth within each person. The games are over.

People often ask, 'Who is the problem, the person who becomes incoherent or the other one(s)?' I have to say no one is the problem and everyone is the problem. The problem is the energy dynamic.

ASSESSING THE COHERENCE OF RELATIONSHIPS
WIN–WIN FOR ALL
STRENGTH – HARMONY – AUTONOMY – AUTHENTICITY

Baseline VRIC Image shows both persons
energetically challenged – incoherent.

Both persons wearing Lumanetic frequency pads creates
coherence for both. Energetic harmony established.

VRIC Imaging – The Artful Science of Relationship
Examining the Truth and Nature of Relationships

VRIC images of a conflicted business relationship.
Disturbing as they are, it helped both parties to see the extent of the conflict.
The business relationship dissolved, though not immediately.

The Energy Story

We find that in every family there is an energy story. We observe it as soon as they come in the door. Who is in charge? Who is angry with whom? Who has taken a back seat? Who is the controller? Who is seeking attention? Who has given up and resigned themselves to the situation? What is each person's role in that whole dynamic? This view is not taken to judge or score points or take sides, as we know in this system that either everybody wins or everybody loses.

Once we have seen the 'problem', what can we do about it? We address it in two ways. First of all, we use Lumanetics to create coherence for the whole dynamic. This means asking people to hold various Lumanetic remedies until VRIC imaging shows that all of them are clear and therefore coherent. Sometimes both partners in a couple need a Lumanetic frequency and sometimes only one person in a whole family needs one to make the whole family coherent.

It was the mother who initiated the session. Her 17-year-old son was causing her a lot of worry. He had a very important exam in a few weeks and he just wasn't studying. She was extremely anxious about this, as the result of this exam could have a serious impact on his future – it could determine whether he gained admission to university or not. No matter how much she tried, though, she was getting nowhere with him. He was becoming quite antagonistic and she was at her wits' end.

The woman was in her second marriage and she came with her husband, her younger son by her second marriage, her older son (the one who had the exam) and her daughter by the first marriage. She was very much in charge and deeply concerned and caring, but wanting control – a very familiar scenario, I have done it myself.

She spoke for everyone, and though she could not see it, the others did not like it. Her older son was especially angry, as young men can be when their adulthood is not acknowledged by their mother.

The imaging was very revealing for all of them. When the whole family was imaged with the mother, her image became totally fuzzy, and everyone else, who had imaged clear before, became fuzzy too. Now everyone, including her, could see the effect she was having on the whole family. She obviously loved her family and meant well by them, but the end result was not beneficial to anyone. No amount of counselling or reasoning could have achieved what this one photograph told her. It was a moment of realization.

The wonderful thing about this system is that not only do you see the 'problem', you actually resolve it at the level at which it exists, and all parties in the interaction – the clients and the practitioner – can see through the imaging that it has been cleared. In this particular case I gave the mother a Lumanetic frequency pad to place on her thymus area and re-imaged the whole family. Everyone was clear and everyone could see that.

After this first step there was an important second step. For the dynamic to change between the mother and the older son, both had to change. I follow a simple rule that says that the problem belongs to the person who has the bother. That person has the greatest incentive to change. In this case it was the mother. As we started the process of establishing emotional coherence, I told her that I understood her fear for her son's future, but her actions were having the opposite effect of what she desired. They were not benefiting her and her son was so angry that he would not talk to her. In fact, the more she nagged, the less he studied. It was an impasse and no one was happy. My simple and blunt instructions to her were:

'Don't talk to your son except to call him for dinner.' This would break the deadlock in two ways and would benefit everyone. Without his mother's nagging, this young man would have to take responsibility for himself and would not spend his time, effort and energy reacting and resisting the 'control' of his mother. To him I said, 'Your mother cares for you and is nagging you because she loves you, though she is not doing a very good job of showing it at the moment. Don't cut off your nose to spite your face. Study for your future because you want to and not to please or displease your mother.' He understood this and felt understood.

I also told the mother privately what was likely to happen, which was that when she stopped nagging her son he would not believe that she had really changed and would test her resolve by pushing her boundaries until he realized that the change was for real. Then and only then would there emerge the beginnings of a healthy, happy and healed relationship.

She phoned me a week later. She confessed that she had thought there was no way that she could follow the instructions I had given her about not talking to her son, but after the first 24 hours she found she could not get angry any more and her anxiety had lessened. The Lumanetic frequency pad had seen to that. Her son had done exactly what I had predicted and tried hard to press her buttons, but contrary to her normal pattern and to her own expectations she had remained calm. She and her son subsequently wrote and thanked me for my help in healing their relationship.

Long-standing non-nourishing patterns of fear and anxiety are very hard to modify, except when we use energetic tools that can address the unconscious levels where the patterning needs to be neutralized or replaced with a more nourishing pattern. Love, unfortunately, can create incoherence and disharmony, as we will fear for our loved ones and want them to be safe and happy. But from that laudable desire it is easy to go down the slippery slope to trying to control people for their own good.

Incoherence can also come about when a person sacrifices their own needs for what they perceive as the greater good. I remember one family in particular. They came to me in the early years, but my memory of them is vivid after all this time.

The family came from an orthodox religious background. Both parents were in their mid-twenties and there were five children ranging in age from about seven years to six months.

The young father was the one in trouble. He was a grocer and was working with his father in the family business, but was suffering from panic attacks that were extremely severe and very embarrassing. Initially he was very resistant to bringing his family with him and his justifiable objection was reflected in his question: 'Why should I bring them when I am the one who is sick?' For the first couple of assessments he would only come with his wife and his baby daughter. Finally one day I told him I needed to see the whole family. Again I met with resistance. I said, 'When I tell you how to run your grocery shop, then you can tell me how to do my job.' This was very blunt and matched his blunt ways. He immediately agreed to bring his whole family.

I won't describe their assessment in detail, but will share with you the aspect of it that really surprised and shook me: I imaged each of the parents on their own and the father imaged clear and the mother imaged fuzzy. She had not complained of any illness or challenge and yet the pictures told a different story. Then I imaged the father with the children. Everyone was clear. Next I imaged the mother with the children. Everyone fragmented. You should have seen the surprise on everyone's face, including mine.

What was to be made of this? The mother was a very good mother, but she was putting herself last. She was taking care of everyone but herself. Under normal circumstances if I had told her that she needed to look after her own needs, she would have disregarded what I said, but when she saw the effect she was having on her children, the message went straight home. She could see that when she was well her children would thrive and when she was not they would not. She was not to sacrifice herself but to look after herself in the interests of her family.

In that assessment she was also the one who was helped with the Lumanetics. When we re-imaged her holding an energetic solution with the children, everyone was coherent. This also gave her husband the opportunity to see that his wife, for all her protestations of being well, was the one who needed help.

His panic attacks, incidentally, disappeared after his very first assessment.

This was a case of someone needing to do more for themselves, but sometimes someone may need to do a little more for the family:

The clients were a young Indian family who were close friends of mine. The family unit was comprised of the parents and three children. The father, of whom I was extremely fond, was kind-hearted and generous to a fault. Apart from having a full-time job he was always busy doing good works, had a very good social conscience and had done a lot of self-development work, but – and this is a big but – he did not help out at home. His wife also had a full-time job and managed the house and the children pretty much by herself. She never protested and I always referred to her as a goddess and sometimes asked the pair of them, only half-jokingly, why she put up with him.

When I imaged her with the children, everyone fragmented. I then asked him to stand in with the family and re-imaged them. Everyone became coherent. Because he is very dear to me, I could tell him bluntly what I thought it meant – that he had to participate more actively if he wanted to do well by his family and that his uncomplaining wife needed some help. I told him that the family unit was incomplete without him. Though he was not best pleased at the time and did protest, the message went home because of the images. Today he does a lot more at home and I consider him a wonderful family man as well as a wonderful human being.

In this next case, the healing took place between father and son:

CC was 27 years old when he came to 3S. He was suffering from clinical depression and had been on anti-depressant medication for some months. Shoulders drooping with loss of hope and vitality, his face dulled with sadness, his eyes lacking sparkle, his physical appearance very clearly reflected his unhappiness.

He was sharing a house with several others, was not eating properly and was smoking quite heavily. He was working at a mundane job and studying for a degree at the same time. He was an artist, a musician, highly intelligent, articulate and passionate about the things he believed in. He had a strong sense of fair play and justice and a slight contempt for the conventional lifestyle of a secure job, mortgage, marriage and family. His older brother had followed that route and been successful in conventional terms, but although CC got along well with him, he wanted something very different for himself. He had not been to an alternative practitioner of any sort before he came to 3S and had come along semi-willingly, persuaded by his paternal aunt, to whom he was close.

CC's father had left when he was three years old and he had been brought up by his mother. His father had maintained contact and had always contributed financially, but there had been no contact between the two parents. It was actually his father who brought him to 3S. He seemed to care a lot for his son. I did not sense the same degree of feeling from the son for the father, however. There was no animosity, but no closeness. I could see CC had shut down on his feelings towards his father. Perhaps there was guilt on the father's part for having abandoned his child at such a tender age; perhaps there were anger and hurt on the son's side for the same reason. Huge emotional issues, unexamined, unaddressed, unspoken and therefore unresolved, had some bearing on the present unhappy state of this young man.

He was treated using a combination of Biolumanetics, the Monocrom light-colour dome and the Monochord sound table. The Biolumanetics process was used to create visual coherence in the energy field and the Monocrom light-colour dome and the Monochord sound table were used to enable the bodymind system to remember the joy it had forgotten.

This young man who had lost his creativity and forgotten to smile came out of the dome beaming. It was a joy to behold. When he was imaged afterwards, his shoulders were no longer slouched or drooping and his posture was noticeably more positive. He was given four Lumanetic creams to take home with him. They were to be applied twice a day on certain points on the body.

On his second visit, 16 days later, he came very willingly, again with his father. We started the session with Biolumanetics and the imaging. When father and son stood together in a particular configuration, both became incoherent. There was an energetic challenge between the two. It is so easy and tempting to assign blame and some people may think the father was to blame here for having 'abandoned' his child at such a tender age, but it was not as simple as that. The father told me, 'If I hadn't left the marriage when I did, I think I would have died.' Both had suffered and were still suffering. So using VRIC and Lumanetics we harmonized the energetic challenge in the relationship. Even after all these years it never ceases to amaze me that is possible to see, assess and address this subjective emotional level in this totally objective way and to see the beneficial changes that ensue.

CC and I then talked of anger and how he managed it. Did he feel angry? What made him angry? What did he do when he was angry? Was it OK to feel angry? I told him how powerful emotions, if not acknowledged and understood, would create havoc in the bodymind and could cause illness and dysfunction of one sort or another. It was important, I explained, to own one's feelings. One could try to suppress them, but because they were part of one, they had nowhere to go and would make their presence felt in other, unpleasant ways. I told him all he had to do was look at his feelings. He could do it safely. He did not have to talk about them, or act them out or analyze or rationalize them in any way.

This was his first lesson in self-understanding. He was very receptive and participated intelligently in the discussion. We did not discuss the past at all, or his relationship with his parents. His father was not present at that time, but sitting outside in the waiting room.

I also asked CC if he was prepared to consider the possibility of reducing or giving up his medication at some point. He said he needed it to be functional, he had exams coming and the medication helped him to cope. I did not press the point. All I wanted to do was plant a seed.

This time he was given a Lumanetic frequency pad to cover his solar plexus, some energy creams and some drops to take orally.

By his third visit, a month later, there had been a huge improvement. He felt a lot better, his smoking had reduced substantially without any effort on his part, he was eating better, was just generally much more together and felt much happier. The imaging session showed him to be coherent; however, he still needed the frequency pad on his solar plexus.

He loved music, so he was given another session on the Monochord table, which he thoroughly enjoyed, followed by another session in the Monocrom light-colour dome.

On the first three visits he brought his anti-depressant medication along to be imaged, but on his fourth visit he came without it. I asked him about it. He said he hadn't brought it because he had forgotten to – and then added he had not taken it for a while because he had been feeling fine without it. Just a couple of months before he had said he could not do without it, and now the need for it had effortlessly disappeared. I have to say I was delighted. He was not only not in crisis any more but he was in charge of his life and his creativity was flowing again. This was a totally different young man.

In the last session of the series, CC checked out very well. He could hold his coherence, his gut was calm and the stress was simply not there. This was apparent in the imaging and was corroborated by CC himself.

He passed his exams with flying colours and has not been on medication since. He also has a much warmer and closer relationship with his father now, by his father's account and to his father's gratification.

ENTERING THE
TRUTH ZONE

*'Your life is the instrument with which you experiment
with truth.'*
Thich Nhat Hanh

'We don't know a millionth of one percent about anything.'
Thomas Edison

*'Common sense is the collection of prejudices acquired
by age 18.'*
Albert Einstein

CHAPTER 15

BRIDGING THE GAP

WISDOM AND SUPER FUNCTION IN THE TWENTY-FIRST CENTURY

We have now seen some of the extraordinary nature and power of Biolumanetics. Over the years, however, as I have explained this, certain objections have arisen again and again. People simply have no frame of reference for it, so there is a very real gap in understanding. An explanation is often met by a disconcerting wall of incomprehension, sometimes followed by denial, sometimes by overt or covert hostility. There is no easy way to bridge this gap, because the only way we can really know anything is to participate in it and try it, especially when it is something new. However, in this chapter I would like to clarify some of the issues that have been raised.

It is at once beautiful and very challenging that the Luminator is new, revolutionary and radically different. It is the equivalent of introducing a villager with a bullock cart to a supersonic jet. If the villager has only ever experienced travel in a bullock cart, it is inconceivable for them to imagine the possibility of flying through the air at many hundreds of miles per hour. The mind has to make that leap into the totally 'impossible' and most times will find itself unable to do so.

I have learned through breaking my head against that wall that the 'impossible' really does not exist. Today, if and when I choose to use the word, which is rarely, I always qualify it – that something *appears* to be impossible *for now*. Just to say that something is impossible because you have not experienced it, read about it or seen it and no 'expert' has told you about it is not good enough. Neither is putting your faith solely in 'experts'. When the radically new comes, it can come from anywhere, unexpectedly and without warning. The revolutionary is the way forward for the evolution and the expansion of human knowledge. The energetic nature of the universe is constant renewal and creativity. There is no lack of newness in the universe – there is endless creativity, the like of which we absolutely have no concept.

So many people have fixed opinions and aren't open to anything that might challenge them. I can say that I was that fool not so long ago. I had all kinds of opinions about all kinds of things about which I actually knew very little. My saving grace is that I have now learned to love the new and if I hear of something that is new I make a point of going and exploring it and hold off forming an opinion until I have done that.

Standard Objections

There are some objections to Biolumanetics that have been expressed so often that they have become almost standard. One tends to come from people in the vast field of what is termed 'personal development' and this is: 'But I can do this myself. After all, the power is within me.' To this my response is, 'Yes, in theory you can, but in practice that is often not the case.' I myself believe that at one level we are all totally extraordinary beings, but in practice let me ask you, how many times have you personally had the peak experience of absolute power and belief and joyous quiet confidence in your life, especially when challenges arise and the chips are down?

How is your life working out? I see people who have practised meditation for umpteen years, or chanting, or who have made affirmations or undertaken visualization or many other worthy practices. These are not immature people. They are sincere, genuine and well-intentioned, and their desire is authentic. Yet their lives are often falling apart on some level or other, perhaps their health or their professional and/or personal relationships, and they are experiencing a huge amount of suffering. When I say to them that there is an easy way and that easy way is coherence, the objection comes back, 'But I can do it by myself.' Yes, you can – you can go on riding the bullock cart and you will reach your desired goal, but it will take a lot longer and involve a lot more effort than if you take the supersonic plane. But the choice is always yours.

Does that mean I am denigrating and devaluing meditation, chanting and all the wisdom of the ages? Absolutely not. They are all beautiful practices to partake of and include in your search for happiness and function. I put before you another analogy. Let us take a beautiful musical instrument and an equally beautiful musical composition. What are your chances of getting a superb musical performance if the instrument is out of tune or, worse still, if a couple of strings are disconnected? Potentially it is possible, but it is unlikely. If you are the instrument and you are out of tune, all the meditation and the chanting have to be performed on a faulty instrument. Furthermore, if the instrument does not know it is faulty and thinks it is in perfect tune, this reduces even further the possibility of retuning it so that it can be played to its maximum potential.

The new processes of Biolumanetics do not take away from the old ones, *they simply have the power to enhance them exponentially*. The process of creating coherence in your energy field with the absolute precision of VRIC is tuning yourself to the absolute perfection that exists within you, perfection that your instrument has not experienced before. Please remember, precision equals perfection. And VRIC also gives you the opportunity to know when you are out of tune – there is no guesswork involved.

The other part of the objection often put forward here is that people *have* perfected themselves on their own – rishis, sages, gurus and prophets have all done it. That's fine, but, I ask you, how does that help you? Why are you still where you are? People have been following saints and sages, gurus and prophets for millennia – why are we still in the state of suffering that we are in? Why haven't we all become illuminated like the great ones we so admire, revere, venerate and worship? The dividing line is very thin between those great ones and the 'ordinary' suffering, aspiring human, yet the gap seems unbridgeable. The difference, I daresay, lies in the coherence of a person's energy field. Coherence gives you the possibility of becoming illuminated yourself, of becoming your own master teacher, by communicating directly with that other One who is you, through VRIC, where you talk to your higher self, with no intermediary.

The Traditionalist Argument

The other strong objections to Biolumanetics come from the traditionalist who is also a technophobe. The reasoning goes something like this: technology is somehow not pure, it takes away from the purity of the experience. While that can often be true, it can be easy to tar a new super-consciousness technology such as the Luminator with the brush of older technologies that bear no resemblance to it. This super technology actually establishes external objective parameters of perfection and function that are necessary but have never been present on Earth in living memory. With it, we can see what to aim for and what is possible in an objective verifiable manner that is without precedent in human history.

Today 'technology' has become a dirty word because of the heedless use of it. This is not to say that there is anything inherently wrong with technology *per se*. After all, a knife that can be used to cook a gourmet meal can also be used to kill someone. The fault lies not in the knife, but in its inappropriate use. After all, if there were no technology, we would still be living in caves. And while the great spiritual ones of the past did not use technology, there is nothing to say that they would not have, had it been available.

The point is that things have to be examined, evaluated and assessed on their own merits and with a degree of discernment. What we need is not more or less technology, but less prejudice and greater discernment. Fortunately, this grows exponentially when the human energy system is made coherent.

I have seen people who call themselves 'spiritual' have all kinds of categories and classifications of what is 'not spiritual'. Technology often is consigned to such a category. Ultimately, however, everything exists only by the grace of the Supreme Intelligence. Every single atom is the manifestation of that Intelligence – for it cannot be anything other – and that includes technology. If it is present on the Earth plane now it is here for a reason. Let us not fear technology but learn to use it mindfully, with clear intent, and to accept it as a gift, for everything is a gift.

To the traditionalist I would simply say, 'Look at the new. Not all the wisdom of the ages was disclosed thousands of years ago.' The universe is constantly renewing itself and wisdom can and must be found in the modern age too. We have to discover it in the now and in the context of our own lives. While the essence of wisdom may remain the same as it always has, new insights are constantly being brought to light through the new scientific disciplines of quantum theory, holographic theory, chaos theory and complexity theory and, of course, most immediately, the re-establishment of supercoherence in the human energy field through the Luminator and VRIC imaging.

CHAPTER 16

VRIC Imaging:
X-Ray/MRI of the Soul
Self-responsibility, Self-accountability,
Self-acceptance

When things go wrong in our lives, when disaster faces us in one form or another, whether it is the collapse of a long-term relationship, the loss of a job or the onset of a serious illness, there is a desperate need to find out why things went wrong. What happens most often is that we look outside ourselves for reasons why fate has dealt with us as harshly as it has. Whom do we blame? Whom do we call to account? Often we find ourselves thinking that if only our boss hadn't sacked us or our partner hadn't deserted us or the doctor had detected the illness before it got out of hand, in short if only someone else had behaved differently, then everything would have been fine. In the larger context we assign responsibility to and direct the accompanying rage and blame at the government, the police or some other authority or power figure. We feel thwarted and in some way cheated by the universe itself.

I have been in that place myself, so I know it very well. It is on one level comforting but on another level counterproductive. This mindset, which seems so plausible and persuasive, actually gives our power to whatever or whomever we 'know' has more power than we do and so makes it impossible for us to recover. Our hands are tied before we start. Then it becomes very hard to come to terms with the fearful realization that we actually have to redress the situation or the 'injustice', and the person who was the 'cause' of our pain may not want to, choose to or know how to make 'right' the 'wrong' that has been done to us.

I remember a client whose life was in a total mess at many different levels. Finances, relationships, health – everywhere she looked, her life was at crisis point. Running from pillar to post, she was trying every therapy she could think of, yet somehow the suffering and pain in her life would not ease. She kept asking, 'Why is this happening? Why is my life in this place? I am innocent.' She wanted to hang on to this feeling of innocence, she could not let go of it, and her life carried on crumbling about her. Why did she find it impossible to move from this helpless position to a more dynamic one from where, maybe, she could have retrieved some of what she had lost? The missing link was a non-acceptance of self-accountability and self-responsibility, with the accompanying sense of powerlessness, helplessness and hopelessness.

So, if you want to move on from your 'desperate' circumstances, you have to accept that you helped create them. The bitterest pill to swallow is the understanding that you have had some part to play in creating the mess that is your life. It may very well be, and most likely is, a very unconscious part, a very deeply hidden one, because had you known of it, you would have done things differently. The point is that you did not. You did what you did and the consequences, cataclysmic as they may have been, were assured. How does one break this chain of pain, dysfunction and victimhood?

In my view, it is not so easy to do. We do not want to face one vital and essential fact: that we are responsible. It is unpleasant and unpalatable. Over the years I have seen people squirm, wriggle, deny and go to absurd lengths to avoid accepting the slightest hint of self-responsibility. The barriers go up, the hackles rise, they become defensive, hyper-sensitive, fly into a rage or burst into tears the moment anyone suggests they had some part in the co-creation of their reality. We all do it. Our friends and close family cannot easily talk to us about it; they love us and they do not want to lose our friendship. Our parents, if they know the truth, would most likely not dare talk about it; they love us and want to protect us. They may worry for us and not be able to bear what they are seeing, but they don't know how to rectify it. Our enemies gloat with glee, because they knew what was coming. We need help desperately, but we become impossible to approach. The pain is too great, the shame is too great, the guilt is too great and the resulting emotional barriers are very difficult for anyone to get past.

There is, however, a part of us that knows our truth in gruesome and intimate detail. It is neutral, non-judgemental, yet exact and always accepts us just as we are. That part speaks to us in our VRIC images. In instance after instance I have felt the magic when realization dawns as someone looks at their own image and sees the truth of how they feel. If I appear fragmented, distorted and ugly, and I know I am responsible, I may have done it unwittingly, unknowingly, inadvertently, but I can take steps to repair this fragmented self.

In that moment of realization it is vitally important to understand that no blame be attached at any level. Blame is a waste of emotional energy. It carries a huge emotional charge and while one is engaged in the process of assigning blame either to another or to oneself, one is incapable of actually redressing the situation that is crying out to be handled. How comforting it is to blame and yet, on reflection, how stupid and counter-productive.

It is also important to understand that emotional energy is the life force of the universe. It is our most precious resource and it gets vitiated and distorted when it has to handle 'negative' emotions and the body-mind suffers as a direct consequence.

True Perception

What VRIC does is shatter the illusion in very dramatic visual terms, so that you cannot hide from the destructive part of yourself that insists on creating havoc in your life and then, when confronted, proceeds to hide behind a barricade of defensiveness, denial, anger and hurt or justification and rationalization. One can almost hear it saying, 'Who, me? I never did anything wrong! I did everything right. Everybody else is wrong and moreover my pain is your responsibility. If you do things differently, I will feel no pain.' VRIC permits us to see this fragmented self in graphic detail to see how our thoughts fragment our body, our mind and our life, and misalign us and our soul.

The key to self-responsibility and self-accountability is clear perception based on self-enquiry, with the resultant self-understanding and self-acceptance. Perception is the act of seeing combined with the understanding in personal terms of what it means to us. The distorted perception of our distorted emotions stems from fear of one sort or another, fear of our essential unworthiness. We guard this with our barriers and our defences. But it is not worth guarding; the pride, the arrogance, the lack of vulnerability are not worth preserving. It is much better to be open to this part of yourself and to bring it into the light and to look at it. We can then begin to understand why it defends what it defends. We come face to face with the part of ourselves that shows us our lack of self-love and our non-acceptance of ourselves. We can begin to understand and accept our pain and start the process of transforming this destructive and needy part of ourselves with tenderness and clarity.

When this happens, the barriers, defences, the fronts and façades melt away and we start to experience the depth of our pain and the depth of our love. As this process is consciously understood and engaged with, another aspect of ourselves emerges, fragile yet strong, tender and vulnerable, and it becomes easier to breathe and smile and we begin to taste freedom. This is the authentic self, which knows that it is loved and that it is powerful.

As a direct result of this work our emotional range broadens, widens and deepens beyond our wildest imagining. We are not precluded from feeling any more; the feelings are ours, we own them, understand them and accept them. They no longer overwhelm us. They are our friends, our guides, not our hidden enemies. We start to see the infinite nature of things and it becomes easier to act with appropriateness, discernment and refinement. That is a beautiful place to be.

VRIC is *seeing* our truth in all its ugliness and all its beauty. It permits us to understand and accept our less-than-perfect self without any criticism or judgement but with total clarity in a way that no other system on Earth has the possibility of doing. We see ourselves in all our nakedness and in all our glory all at the same time. VRIC, for me, is a tool of realization.

There are many tools of relief in this world – even an aspirin will give relief from a headache for some time – and there are many beneficial and helpful tools of resolution, many beautiful and effective healing disciplines and many extraordinary life-enhancing modalities such as modern light and sound treatments. There is, however, for me, only one objective tool of realization on this Earth plane and that is VRIC.

It has never been possible before to see how we appear to others or the impact we have on ourselves and on others through our thoughts, our attitudes and our intentions. No meditation, no mantras, no prayers, no chanting, no gurus or prophets, no NLP, no coaching, mentoring or counselling, no inspiring books or self-development workshops can make you see what you need to see to end the cycle of your suffering. They have to bypass the filters of your denial mechanisms and faulty perception. However much you may wish to comply, there is not and never has been an objective way of seeing whether you have achieved your aim. In effect you cannot see yourself. It has been impossible until now.

VRIC lays bare your defences and allows you to come face to face, with no intermediary, with the impeccable, intelligent and implacable part of yourself, your sovereign soul, so that you can surrender your pride, your shame, your guilt and your blame and lay them at the feet of the One. That One never judged you, it only allowed you to see what you did to yourself. It waited for you to come to the truth of yourself and it will wait for you forever, because it loves you, it never leaves you and it is *only* you.

When this realization permeates you and every cell of your wondrous bodymind starts to feel the comfort of its original pristine, intelligent state of true innocence, another level of your life opens for you, the like of which you may have never experienced. It is joyous, creative and productive.

Learning to See

He was in his late thirties, strikingly handsome, very well educated and well spoken, gentle and kind, yet doing a very mediocre and mundane job. He had a very close relationship with his mother and was not particularly close to his father. He still lived with his parents. I had met him at a personal-development seminar some time previously. When I started practising Biolumanetics, he found out what I was up to and was interested in experiencing it. I knew his mother as well, as she had done the same course, though at a different time. She was a hands-on healer, very soft-spoken woman but not very well herself, quite anxious and fearful, though very well-meaning.

When he told his mother that he was seeing me for Biolumanetics, she took exception and did not really approve. He reported her objections to me.

On the third or fourth session, he brought his mother along so she could see what we were doing. She came and was polite, but I knew she had reservations. She did not ask what I was doing; she sat there with her mind already made up.

When I was finishing the VRIC session and the man was holding the Lumanetic frequency vials that made him coherent, I asked his mother to stand next to him and imaged them together. He was still holding the Lumanetic vials that had made him coherent just a minute ago. The moment his mother stood next to him, his VRIC image became incoherent. This 38-year-old man could not hold his resonance, could not hold his coherence, when his mother's energy came into his field. He could not be his own person if she disapproved.

On the next visit, when he came on his own, we looked at that telling photograph and examined the implications of it. He had always insisted that he was quite independent and did whatever he wanted, but his photograph with his mother told a different story. He was still energetically tied to her apron strings, though he had not known it or had not wanted to know it. All she had to do was disapprove of something he did and he fell apart.

This was not happening at a conscious level; this was the story of his life. It was interesting that despite his good looks he had not been very successful in his relationships with women. Here he was faced with his weak point, his point of vulnerability, his destructive pattern, the chaos attractor that kept him tied to his mother.

A lot of men and women are tied in this way and have taken on their mother's or father's or their partner's suffering at some level or another. I have seen this in young and old. Age does not grant freedom; age has nothing to do with this level. To become your authentic self, those ties have to be cut and the relationship redefined.

However, they are not so easy to cut. When this man was faced with this realization, he stopped coming to me. However, I do know that he did leave home and buy a new house.

She was an extremely bright, very talented and very troubled teenager. At the time she came to see me she was recovering from anorexia, but had developed the unfortunate nervous habit of pulling her hair out, to the extent that she had to wear a cap to hide the bald patches. She had undergone all sorts of tests and was supposed to be dyslexic and dyspraxic. To quote from her tutor's letter to me:

'She was assessed by a clinical psychologist in 1995.
Although she had a good verbal reasoning score, her ability on
Arithmetic and Digit span, both of which tap into
short-term memory, was low.
An occupational therapist noted that she had certain dyslexic and
dyspraxic features. She had immature equilibrium reactions
affecting dynamic balancing and had difficulties with bilateral
integration, i.e. problems co-ordinating the two sides of the body
together in symmetrical and reciprocal actions.
She has been having remedial help from a perceptual therapist
for problems with spatial relations, visual discrimination, figure-
ground discrimination, visual closure and object recognition.'

I have to say I hate these labels; they mean nothing to me. This technical jargon describes dysfunction in detail, but has no real viable solutions.

I did know she could be very self-willed, dogmatic and

unbending when she chose to be or when challenged, yet she could be eminently thoughtful, insightful and caring at other times. She had a tremendous sense of justice, fairness and compassion, yet paradoxically at other times was very childish. She was a complex and very loveable character.

She loved money and was prepared to work very hard for it. She also drove herself mercilessly, living life to the full and burning the candle at as many ends as she possibly could, with no thought of respite or relaxation. In one particular session she informed me that she had taken a weekend job. I knew how full her schedule was, with extra tuition and exams around the corner, as well as a jewellery business and a hectic social life. From my standpoint, she was not being particularly sensible in the management of her key resource: her life-force. Her system was already buckling under the strain, as evidenced by her 'illness'. On the one hand she was trying to help herself by coming to see me and then perversely was undoing all the good work with the other hand.

Having been a very self-willed and opinionated teenager myself all those years ago, I knew I would have to step very carefully to get her to change her mind and choose a different course of action. I gently suggested that what she was doing might make her too tired and that her exams were more important in the long term than a temporary job. She wasn't having any of it. She told me point-blank that no matter what I said she was not going to change her mind. Here was a rebellious young adult telling me where to get off.

I did not take offence, but told her that it did not make any real difference to me what she did and there was no way that I was going to play the authoritarian adult who knew what was best for her. She should do what she thought was best, not what I said. That mollified her to some extent, but she still held to her point of view.

I admired her gumption and her determination to stand by what she believed, even while deploring her decision.

I knew what would break the deadlock. By now she had been to see me a few times and she trusted and liked me, but more than that she trusted the VRIC imaging and understood what it meant. She had insisted she was doing fine and was coping very well, but when we did the VRIC imaging her baseline image was very fragmented and incoherent.

I handed the photo to her without another word. She could now see what she was doing to herself.

A moment of realization, of becoming a self-responsible, self-accountable adult, had arrived for this highly intelligent young woman. She laughed and remarked, 'I can't fool Thrity as I used to fool my psychotherapists.'

For me, what was far more important was that she could not fool herself.

With the use of Lumanetics, her hair-pulling stopped, her anorexia disappeared and she started to enjoy her food. The memorable moment for me was when she told me she had actually fried an egg and eaten and enjoyed it. She passed her exams with flying colours, as I knew she would. (I take very little credit for her success in her studies, as she had private tuition in study skills from a very gifted and innovative tutor, my friend and client Sally Ann Olivier.)

CHAPTER 17

CLEARING YOUR FREQUENCY

CREATING COHERENT INTENT

Coming to Biolumanetics and the supercoherence process specifically, what exactly are we doing and why are we doing it? What is the rationale, the end game and the central intention or purpose?

As I understand it for myself, and I speak only for myself and for 3S, what we are seeking to do is to create authenticity – a life that is authentic and is centred on the understanding of the being as a soul. In very blunt terms, you did not come down to Earth in this physical form just to eat, drink, pay your mortgage, have a few children and die. That does not make much sense and I think it is a very limited view of what we really are and what we are here for.

I would say that the primary purpose of the Luminator, its *raison d'être*, is to make us understand in unequivocal terms that we are super-conscious beings. Yet, as we know, our lives do not show much evidence of that. So, going straight to the heart of the matter, what we are seeking to do with the Luminator is to clear our frequency.

Engaging with Life

In every moment we are interacting with the universe. The Superconscious

Intelligence that is the universe is reading our frequency and is responding to the information contained in that energy signature. Unfortunately, the universe has to read our desires, our hopes and our intentions through the colour of our distortion.

When we engage in the process of clearing our frequency what happens can only be described as magical. The deleterious effects of the past on the present drop away. Deeply ingrained conditioning and deeply rooted fears are neutralized at a very subtle level. As a result, protective barriers and façades become unnecessary. It becomes possible to deal with everyone with real love, care and consideration but without the need for approval or the need to pacify and pander to others because of the perceived weakness of our position.

Our struggle down the millennia has been to find our authenticity, and most of us, looking at our lives and human history, have certainly not done it. This system enables us to do so with ease and elegance.

The process of creating coherence is a way of discovering for yourself your soul's unique purpose and journey. When you do, you start to get in touch with your authentic self and discover what you came to Earth to do. You are now ready to engage in the real adventure that is your life. It will take you as far as you want to go and as deep as you want; it is not limited in its scope. The degree of clarity that emerges out of experiencing this process makes you understand that the limited, self-conscious view, the small view, the greedy, needy, fearful view, is not a true assessment of yourself. That disappears with no effort. Something else takes its place, something quite magnificent, which takes you to where you can be. But this only happens if your frequency is clear and coherent.

The way to your heaven is not paved with good intentions, it is paved with a coherent intention. What is the difference between a good intention and a coherent intention? A good intention is well-meaning, yet most of us know the truth of the saying that the road to hell is paved with good intentions. We may mean well, but despite that, very often we get results we do not like or want. In contrast, a coherent intent is an aligned intent. It has a power that is magnified many times over and is read very clearly by the Supercoherent Intelligence that is the universe.

In essence the supercoherence process is an alignment. It is, I would say, the highest alignment possible on Earth at the moment because of its objectivity and precision. It is an applications-based objective process, which makes it unique in human history. This makes it possible for ordinary people to participate in it and not be left out in the cold as they have been millennia upon millennia.

When this energetic alignment takes place, the conflict between logic and emotion, head and heart, and the resulting chaos and confusion melt away, to be replaced by a single focused intent which has the power, precision and potency of a laser or a superconductor. The energy is no longer conflicted, diffused, scattered or fragmented but clear, and effortless to use. The process, though precise and objective, is also totally non-linear and unpredictable. It is far more powerful than any linear process will ever be, in my view.

By the way, this can give some clue as to why affirmations, visualization and meditation, even when done sincerely, often do not work in the way we expect or want them to. We may blame ourselves for not 'doing it right' and try harder, only to meet with the same non-results, but it is important to understand that the unconscious mind is a million times more powerful than the conscious mind and the two may have very different agendas. When they do, you do not need to guess which one will win. How can you know when the intention of your unconscious mind is at odds with that of your conscious mind? This vital make-or-break information is the missing part of the jigsaw that has prevented us from fulfilling our unlimited potential. However, when the conscious and the unconscious align, as can be verified through VRIC imaging, then the superconductor principle kicks into action and miracles happen.

Aligning with the Universe

The process of clearing your frequency means that you have the energetic wherewithal to hold your frequency, to hold your own resonance and to know, feel and actualize your own power.

When your frequency configuration becomes more orderly or coherent, a process of alignment takes place at the energetic level, way beyond the boundaries of the five-sensory reality: the universe aligns with you. It has to; it is a completely lawful, effortless and impeccable process.

When this happens in real terms, as evidenced by VRIC, it means that the vast intelligence of the universe is now working with you and not against you. Then an almost overwhelming cascade of benefits you could never have dreamed of is showered on you – vast knowledge, new ideas and opportunities, radiant health, clear, harmonious and loving relationships. Supercoherence is the order of the universe and a coherent frequency signature is the key to the universe.

JC came to 3S because she wanted to mend her relationship with her daughter, who was in her twenties. She loved her daughter, but did not know how to handle her.

JC had been divorced for some years and though she had a steady job, she wanted change in her life, something to make it exciting and different. She had studied shiatsu and Reiki, but was not practising them. She had a pet bitch that she was very attached to. She was also in a hurry. She told me she was in the process of selling her house. She wanted to move somewhere different. She used to enjoy living where she was, but now her unimpeded view of open fields was gone because of new developments and it was not the same any more. She wanted a house with a view in a quiet location. She also wanted to move into it quickly.

We started the process of establishing coherence in her energy field. What transpired was at one level quite funny, though I don't think JC thought so at the time. Normally it takes several weeks to buy and sell houses in England, even with a firm buyer. But the cosmic joker was at work trying to fulfil JC's wish. Not only did she get a buyer, but the transaction was completed in record time and JC had to move out of her house over a weekend, without having found another one. She barely had time to pack. She put things in storage and as an emergency measure moved into a tiny house belonging to a friend of her son's who was working abroad. She thought she would now have the time to look for a suitable house.

Unfortunately it was not as simple as that. The home-owner came back from abroad and JC was confronted with the discomfort of sharing a small house with someone whose habits were very different from hers. Sharing a kitchen and television was bad enough, but what was worse was that the young man and her pet did not hit it off.

She tried to find another place to rent but was not successful and started feeling increasingly uncomfortable and unhappy. She was also looking at various houses to buy and finally made an offer on one of them, which was accepted. At that point it was not binding on either party.

JC then came for a VRIC assessment with the estate agent's blurb about the property. She wanted to image herself with it to check whether the house was right for her. I duly did the imaging and she became incoherent.

Now it was time to explore the dynamics of the process that had led her to make the decision to buy that house. I had known she would be incoherent with it, but did not tell her why until afterwards. I asked her if the house matched her needs as she had defined them – was it quiet and did it have a view? She said it did not fulfil either of her two requirements. So I asked her why she was making a sideways move and going through all the hassle and expense of buying somewhere that she knew was not to her liking. I knew she was actually running away from the discomfort of being in the house with the young man – she was making an important long-term decision from a position of discomfort which was temporary. If she were to make the change on that basis, she would soon find she was unhappy again. It was a very incoherent way to go about seeking what she wanted from life. No wonder her higher self showed her in no uncertain terms that her decision was not the right one for her.

She took the point and withdrew her offer for the house. I told her that it was quite likely that she would find a much more suitable one once she made the decision from a position of ease and grace rather than from a harried and uncomfortable place within herself.

JC was highly intelligent, while being very sensitive. She moved out from the young man's place and moved in with another friend. In a very short while she found a house that was entirely suitable and moved in. The house was bigger, better and had a better view than the previous one she had chosen and she was very happy with it. The imaging confirmed the appropriateness of her decision.

From a Conflicted Intent to a Coherent Intent

When this client first came to me she was around 33 years old. She had a warm, friendly personality and was intelligent, articulate and well-read. She had done a huge amount of personal-development work, including attending workshops and seminars and undertaking various transformative processes, and was very self-aware. She practised Reiki and meditated regularly.

Despite this, she had difficulty in her relationships with men.

She spoke longingly of having a decent man in her life and having children of her own. She had several good male friends who were either married or otherwise unavailable. She was also aware that she attracted the 'wrong' sort of male when it came to having a relationship of a more serious nature.

Here she describes her experience of the personal coherence process in which she chose to participate:

IL: I remember being very excited about coming here and seeing you for the first time. It was as if I had been drawn to you. When we decided to go with the therapy, it was to heal the relationship with my past. What came out during the session was that the blockage in my life was due to my issues with my father. That was obviously what it was – the imaging had shown that – yet I had a good relationship with my father. You said that it was the parent you were closer to who gave you the more difficult lessons, but because of the veil of love you couldn't really see it clearly. So I got the treatment and the solution [the relevant Lumanetic frequency cream on the left eyebrow] and I applied the stuff and the next day I was on a real high. In fact, I had been on a high ever since I had left this house [my house, where she had undergone the process]. The next day I was going to work and I remember talking to Jesus Christ straight, saying, 'Can you just help me to sell four pages of advertising space today?'

Thrity: How long does it usually take you to sell four pages of advertising space?

IL: It can be very hard work and can go on for a month or more. But by 11 o'clock I already sold two pages and before the end of the day I had sold four pages plus! That was fantastic confirmation of some sort and it seemed that my energy was really charged. Then two weeks later I had a nightmare that I had had many times in the past about my father's death. It had always been my great fear that he would die and I would not be there. [The subject is Polish and her family live in Poland. She lives in London.] When I had the dream, I vividly remember thinking that it was the part of him that had been related to the [emotional] issue that had died. That was what had gone. Three days later I called my mum and she said Dad had been to see the doctor on the very day of the night when I had had the dream, and that with new medication he felt good, just like a newborn. I knew there was a straight connection.

After that I went to a seminar. I wasn't going to stay on it, I just wanted to listen for a while, but the speaker was talking about commitment, so first of all I had to commit to being there, and then a lady started talking who had exactly same scenario as mine, the father thing. My issue was that I was so attached to my father that if I heard anybody even mentioning the word 'father', I would be flooded with tears, I was so emotional about it. It was something I just could not handle. At that seminar, though, I had no tears. I was so at peace I was able to engage with the woman's trauma without taking part in it. I was just sympathetic, just really cool about it. That was fantastic confirmation for me that things had changed.

Then I went to Poland to see my parents and I could clearly see that my relationship with my father was different. I was seeing him more as a friend, as a human being. I didn't have the kind of attachment and the desperation that were there before. I had done lots of meditation work on the issue before and I am sure that did something, but it wasn't even half as powerful as the treatment I got from you.

Thrity: How has your relationship to your mother changed? Did anything change in Poland?

IL: It was just better, it was more like loving friendliness and clearance. There was a lot of clarity between us. I told her about the treatment and said to her, 'I am so happy to have you as a mother.' I could see how that strengthened her, how important it was for her to hear it. It had a great impact. It also had an impact on my relationship with my brother, which had been terrible to say the least. In the past I had been very impatient with him because he was a little bit slow, but this time I found I had more of an understanding of him and more loving feelings towards him. So the whole experience was very different from my previous visit.

Thrity: When you asked your boss for a rise [which was after the treatment], what happened?

IL: Well, previously, whenever I thought about it, I just couldn't imagine how I would do it. Of course my relationship with my boss has changed recently. There was a time when he was really trying to humiliate me, but now he is a lot more lenient, a lot friendlier, and when I finally asked him for a pay rise I just felt so easy asking him about it. [She asked for more than she had originally intended and got it.] Yes, that was very powerful change.

Oh, another thing – the way I perceive men has changed as well. Now I can see that before I used to see men as a slightly different species. I had some very bad conditioning from my grandmother, who would never talk about men without making an initial derogatory statement like 'All men are rotten.' This reflected on my past relationships. Now I just see men very differently, perhaps more like friends.

I am also growing more and more fond of women. I am consciously discovering the beauty of the female race. My thoughts when meeting either a man or a woman are quite different from

THE CONFLICTED SELF AND THE SUPERCOHERENCE ALIGNMENT
CLOSING THE GAP BETWEEN THE INTENTION AND THE UNCONSCIOUS
HIDDEN REALITY – CREATING CONSCIOUS COHERENT INTENT

Verbally stating conscious desire and intent – incoherent.

Stating the opposite intent reveals unconscious intention at odds with conscious intent –
coherence. Which means that the client will not be able to achieve what she consciously
says she wants as her unconscious mind will oppose her. Remember, the unconscious is a
million times more powerful than the conscious mind.

Holding the correct Lumanetic frequency vial
and affirming what she consciously wants
neutralises the hidden challenge from her
unconscious and permits her the possibility of
making her conscious intent really happen.

what they were before.

There is definitely a change in me in that I am becoming more and more detached from things.

As her energy signature was cleared and her energy field made coherent, she attracted, and was attracted to, a completely different personality type. A few months later she met a wonderful Irishman, a healer, and is now married to him and has a baby boy.

Reconfiguring a whole life with a trace of cream on one eyebrow – impossible or miracle?

THE UNLIMITED HUMAN

'*Perhaps there is no such thing as a glittering mechanism in the centre of the Universe. Maybe we should think of the treasure that is waiting for us there in terms of magic rather than as a mechanism.*'
John Wheeler, physicist, at the Relativity Conference in Oxford, 1974

'*The most beautiful thing we can experience is the mysterious. It is the source of all true art and science.*'
Albert Einstein

'*When the doors of perception are cleansed, everything appears to man as it is – infinite.*'
William Blake

CHAPTER 18

KEYS TO PARADISE
ON EARTH
BEYOND RELIGION AND SCIENCE

When I studied psychoanalysis, my intention was to find out what made humans tick. At one level it was an interesting experience, I gained some valuable insights into why I functioned as I did, but on balance, after eight years, I chose to walk away from it. At the time I did not understand why I was leaving something I had spent so long doing, but I knew with certainty that it was definitely not what I wished to pursue. My heart simply was not in it.

Many years later, when the realties of the energetic world were revealed to me, I began to understand why I had walked away. In very simple terms it was a discipline which was founded on a model of understanding based on dysfunction. Classical psychotherapy and psychiatry describe dysfunction at great length and in great detail. Manias, syndromes, different types of depression, paranoia, schizophrenia – the list goes on and on. Is there something fatally flawed in this approach? In my view there is something very wrong in it. Describing something in endless detail and then giving it a long-winded name and in so doing coming to the fallacious assumption that we have understood it is not a particularly useful exercise. Then to compound our error we fit people into one of those little boxes and in so doing we categorize and condemn them according to their dysfunction.

In the description of dysfunction we forget one very important truth: analysis of dysfunction does not and cannot create function. In fact, in energetic terms, it is totally counterproductive. In simple terms it is known that energy follows attention. So whatever we focus our attention on will be given an energetic boost and will grow as a result. In essence when you are continuously analyzing dysfunction, you are never going to become functional.

All those years ago I wasn't aware of this, but I walked away from psychoanalysis because in very simple terms it did not make me happy. I had thought that through studying the subject I would find ways to be happier. Did I find what I was looking for? No, on balance I have to say that it did not fit my basic need.

I have a real disdain, distaste and repugnance for defining dysfunction. This is a controversial position and I have been involved in heated debates and discussions as to the necessity of defining dysfunction for many 'very good reasons'. After all, it is important to see the 'truth' and not deny it, so is this not an exercise in wishful thinking and denial, which will not serve the client? If we know what is 'wrong', then we have some chance of putting it right… So on and on the argument goes, but I am not buying into that position. The maximum I am prepared to concede is that if that is the truth, it is a very small part of the truth. It is not and never can be the whole truth of that being, because within each one there is at all times the possibility, the potential and the actual existence of super function.

Happiness is a simple basic need and the birthright of all humans, but when you look around you, you realize that we are not skilled at being happy. Why is this? And why are we so prone to the illnesses and the dysfunctions that we see in society as a whole and in humans as individuals?

The ills of society are simply the magnification and multiplication of the unhappiness of each one of us. The root cause, if you want to call it that, is our disconnection from who we truly are. For me, that is the reason why we suffer as we do, most inelegantly, most addictively. In general, we are addicted to our suffering because we haven't known anything else for as long as we can remember. Suffering is ingrained into our psyche, into our cellular memory and our energy field, and is what most of us are reconciled and resigned to.

We have forgotten some essential truths: that we are humans first, that we are children of this Earth second, and that if we are citizens at all, we are citizens of the universe. We are not defined by nationality. That may sound idealistic nonsense when in the very recent past we have seen Indians at war with Pakistanis, Israelis at war with Palestinians, the English at war with the Irish, and the US at war time and time again, the latest being in Afghanistan and Iraq. But what is the use of national boundaries and holy crusades and jihads when the only jihad and the only crusade that make sense are neutralizing the suffering within your own soul?

The suffering and forgetting occur because we do not recognize that the other, 'the enemy', is ourselves. There is no other; what you see out there is yourself. There is only you, the Superconscious Being, the centre of the universe. You are the centre of your own universe. Can there be six billion centres of six billion universes? Yes, and many more. I chose the figure of six billion because that is the number of humans on Earth now. In our forgetting of the Superconscious aspect of ourselves, we have created mayhem on Earth.

Similarly, there is no one holy land. Every atom in the universe and every grain of sand is every bit as holy as any other. It cannot be any other way, for every atom and every grain of sand is an expression of the wonder that is the Supreme Creative Intelligence that is this Conscious Universe.

The Human Spirit

There is a blood lust within the human psyche and every few years we give into this lust by going to war and when enough blood is shed and we have suffered enough, then that lust is slaked for a while until it rises again and the whole vicious sorry cycle is repeated again and again. So we seek by means of fear, force and control to control that which can never be controlled, which is the human spirit.

The human spirit is not limited. It has limitless capacity for creation. It has limitless capacity for spontaneity and joy, and yet most of us have forgotten that. We focus on the material and usually reserve the best in material terms for our family, forgetting the larger family of humanity to which we also belong. Essentially we are non-material beings come to experience a material reality. If we forget that and are beguiled into believing that the material reality is the only reality there is, then we will create hell on Earth, which is what we are doing at the present moment. We cannot take over the Earth, just as we can never take over another being, yet that is what political and business leaders often forget in dealings that are based on expediency at the cost of truth.

Many of us feel sadness and dismay at the state of the world, and feel powerless, too, as the powers that are aligned against us seem so mighty. We think, 'What can I, a single person, do? Can anything I do make any difference at all?'

I would say simply that you never were powerless and you are not powerless now. You have choice at all times. You have the freedom to make and live that choice that creates the possibility of heaven here on Earth. Do not walk away from it. The solutions are not as difficult to achieve as you think. You have at your command vital, indispensable and powerful forces – the forces of desire, intention and attention. Invisible, subtle and potent, these are the forces that create this world of form and matter, and influence it beyond your wildest imagining.

Scientists say that they have discovered the secrets encoded in the human genome and yet they also concede that they have discovered 3 per cent of what it does and the other 97 per cent remains unknown. So guess what we do in our exceptionally idiotic way? We call it 'junk' DNA. The Supreme Intelligence does not make junk; it has a purpose and use for everything. But what do you do with junk? You consign it to the rubbish heap, you dispose of it. How would you like to dispose of 97 per cent of your DNA? What would you find then? Human stupidity and human arrogance know no bounds when they lose the connection with the essential nature of the human spirit.

Beyond Religion

As far as religions go, we have made a mess there too. What started out as a simple seeking of an understanding of our sacred nature through love, compassion, mercy and justice, the attributes of the divine, has ended up in killing others simply because they call the Cosmic Intelligence by another name or worship it in a different language or through different rituals. Over the millennia we have unleashed more suffering, more chaos, more bloodshed and more injustice in the name of this awesome Intelligence than in almost any other cause. I can only wonder what this Cosmic Being feels and thinks as it observes what we do in its name. I do not know whether to laugh or to cry at the magnitude of human stupidity. The inquisitions and the crusades, the torture and the killings and burnings of people with a different belief system have left a deep, indelible and ugly shadow on human religious practice.

The keys to coherence, the keys to the kingdom of heaven or paradise on Earth, are not piety, duty or sanctimony and going to church, temple, synagogue or mosque, though that may be part of it. The Cosmic

Intelligence does not exist only in church, mosque, temple or synagogue, or in any man-made place of worship, as not a single atom or a single human could exist without that ever-present Intelligence. The Earth and everything in it are worthy of worship. Why don't we treat the whole of creation with the love, respect, reverence and adoration that we reserve for our god(s)?

The keys to paradise on Earth lie in realizing who and what you are and making it manifest on this Earth plane, making your life an offering in the full awareness that the whole of creation is sacred, not just the church, temple, mosque or synagogue, not just the soil of your country, but quite simply everything and everyone. The one process that can help create paradise on Earth is in fact not pious mouthings but the process of creation. When we discover our creativity we are at our happiest. Creativity is about newness, spontaneity and the freedom to be our authentic self.

Religions tell us heaven is always somewhere else, in some future time, never here and now. This world is a vale of tears or an endless cycle of suffering which can only be broken when we free ourselves from all desire or pleasure or joy. We are told to renounce the pleasures of the body so that we can realize ourselves and find nirvana in some place where we have paid for our sins so we don't have to come back to suffer again. We are also told we are born in original sin, for which we must always make reparation. Guilt, lamentation, suffering, oppression, that is the heritage of religion. I have to say that you were born innocent, you were and always are pristine, perfect and pure, and that joy is and always has been your birthright. The only sin is to suffer or to cause suffering, there is no other, and the quick way out of suffering is to experience joy in all the myriad ways that are possible.

I have to disagree with the path of renunciation as well. Why should we have to give up pleasure, give up sex, to be redeemed? Why should meditation and prayer be more virtuous than simply living a kind and good life? Why should suffering be glorified? Suffering is neither glorious nor virtuous. Nor are abstinence and abnegation of our bodily needs.

Twenty million rules and injunctions of how to live your life, with no thought of creating joy or happiness, only of being 'right' by someone else's rigid rules, which will enable you to reach heaven or nirvana at some future time, but never now – it is this mindset that forgets that the Earth is a conscious living entity and every bit as holy as some faraway heaven, and that mind, body and spirit are gloriously, indivisibly one and not greater or less than each other.

Do not let anyone fool you in the name of duty, piety, loyalty or sanctimony into giving up your joy. Joy and radiance are the keys to the universe. Happiness is the key to health and vitality. And material possessions alone will not give you happiness, though they may give you physical comfort and pleasure.

Mindful action, celebration of life, joyous ecstatic creation and above all love and tenderness for yourself, which will then spill out effortlessly to anyone and everyone around you, are the keys to paradise in the here and now on this beautiful, generous, bountiful Earth Mother where we happen to find ourselves through the grace of the benign Super Intelligence that is always also *you*. Make it your business to find your bliss and experience rapture, enchantment and entrancement *now*. Heaven is here on Earth in the now, in every moment.

AMc was sincere, hard-working, extremely generous, quite mercurial and quite self-critical. She was also worried. She told me that she had held her present job for six months, found it 'menial' and wanted a change. Reflecting further, this insightful 27-year-old saw that she always got restless after six to eight months in a job and that it

was a pattern that needed looking at. Something within her was getting in the way of her holding down a steady job.

I asked her what she most loved to do. She told me she was at her happiest when she was singing or songwriting, but of course it was not 'practical'. She confided that she had never told anyone about her secret desire to be a songwriter, not even her parents, although she was taking a singing class once every three weeks and wrote songs whenever she could find the time. She told me that when she was in this mode the lyrics and words for new songs came from 'thin air' and it was easy to compose them. It seemed that her creative urge was well and thriving and longing for expression.

I asked her what would happen if she were to sell a few songs. Wouldn't that be considered work? Would it be possible for work, fun and creativity to come together and help her to lead a productive and happy life? I told her that her restlessness came from a part of herself that was not satisfied with the simple mundane stuff and wanted more. Why not make some time every day or every week to feed this ache and this longing which sought expression in her life? After all, the mundane stuff would always be there, but her life would become less than what she wanted or was capable of if she always remained 'sensible'. She did not have to leave her job, just make sure she took some time for the 'serious' business of expressing her creative self. My guess was that when she did, her restlessness would become considerably less or would disappear. The niggling sense of dissatisfaction would be replaced by joyous creativity.

For AMc, this new perspective was an eye-opener. She completely understood her dilemma and saw the way out of it.

Once she decided to do something, AMc didn't hang about. I spoke to her a couple of weeks later and found she had taken a week off from her job and spent it by herself writing songs. This had been a very productive time and she was very happy with what she had produced. In fact she had just found herself very happy with the activity. She had also applied for a new job which would give her a bit less money but a couple of days off a week which she could use to indulge her passion for songwriting and developing the talent that she knew she had. She had examined her priorities and had taken charge of finding her happiness.

When she came for her next assessment she was elated and excited. She had been booked for her first big gig. She had found a musician to accompany her and was practising hard for this important event. Both she and her singing teacher had also noticed that her voice had opened up, had a much greater range and now flowed without strain. All of this had happened with ease and grace and no great effort. She also said that her feelings of restlessness concerning her 'menial' job had disappeared, though she had not got the part-time job she had applied for. Nevertheless, she had found expression for her creative self. She had originally come to heal her 'endometriosis', which disappeared after a few months of using Lumanetics, and had stayed to heal her life.

CHAPTER 19

THE QUEST FOR WHOLENESS
THE WHOLE IS AND ALWAYS WILL BE GREATER
THAN THE SUM OF THE PARTS

Today a genuine understanding is emerging of the need for wholeness. Whether in the field of health or consciousness studies or psychotherapy, there is a genuine upsurge of desire to move in that direction. On the other hand, while the intention is great, the application is less than adequate in my view. Every discipline calls for greater and greater specialization and there is no attempt to integrate this detailed knowledge into the much larger picture of which it is always a part. So it becomes dogma – codified, rigid and narrow – and therefore not inclusive but exclusive. This is the characteristic of a closed system and it is in total opposition to the principle of things coming together to form a whole. Open systems are open to modification, evolution and growth and are more likely to survive.

There is also another factor that conspires against achieving wholeness. This goes somewhat deeper. I call it the 'either-or factor'. It essentially says that if something is right, then the opposite of that is wrong. This is a limited, flawed and erroneous understanding. As Niels Bohr, the great quantum theorist, said, 'The opposite of a correct statement is a false statement. But the opposite of a profound truth may well be another profound truth.'

If one lets go of this limited either-or viewpoint and is prepared to substitute the word 'and' instead of 'or' and to consider that seemingly opposing viewpoints can both be viable and valid, then one comes to an understanding of complexity, complementarity and commonality, interconnectedness and interdependence. From this radically different viewpoint there arises the likelihood of less competition and conflict and a proportionate increase in the processes of co-operation, collaboration, integration, evolution and the creation of new ever-expanding synergistic relationships leading to an expansion in human knowledge. The spirit of the pioneer and the explorer remains alive and fresh.

A model, however comprehensive, is also by its nature limited. That is an inherent characteristic of all models unless they are constantly and consciously evolving and expanding. When that understanding dawns and that realization becomes integrated into one's belief system, one is more open to looking at other models and seeing the points of common interest that can precede co-operation.

There are two considerations that spring to mind. One is that the specialist has to be a thoroughly grounded generalist, since the interdependent, interconnected nature of the human bodymind system and in fact total interconnectedness of everything in the universe are now established beyond doubt. Tongue in cheek, if one is to be a specialist, it would be sensible to establish a new speciality: the study of wholeness. I for one would definitely consider it prudent to go to a wholeness specialist.

A related consideration would be cross-disciplinary exchanges; after all, it would only benefit the biologist to understand and integrate the insights of quantum theory, chaos theory and complexity theory and for the chemist to understand the non-local nature of human consciousness. This cross-fertilization of knowledge could form the seeds for the establishment of new disciplines of the future, where the knowledge and insights of physics, biology, chemistry, energy medicine, consciousness studies and dare I say metaphysics and philosophy could be imaginatively and coherently brought together to form new disciplines which more accurately reflected the true nature of the incredible complex human.

The Missing Link

There seems to be an unbridgeable divide between the modern allopathic approach and the holistic mindbody energy approach to health and healing. The allopathic approach very 'justifiably' insists on evidence and objectivity in the treatment of disease. There is a reliance on tests and 'hard' clinical evidence and so-called good science. Anything that does not adhere to its rigid requirements is largely dismissed as charlatanism at worst or the placebo effect at best. If it cannot be 'proven', it is not worth considering.

At the opposite end of the spectrum, the holistic approach wishes to take the whole being into account. A person's stresses and strains, vision and hopes are taken into account along with their 'symptoms' to arrive at a 'subjective' assessment of what is 'wrong' energetically or out of balance in the whole bodymind system. The intention is to restore harmony and balance to the whole. This does require a degree of intuition and judgement and is a soft approach.

The gap between the two systems is widening as they vie for clients and seek to imprint their diametrically opposed viewpoints on the world. This is unfortunate, as both have their merits as well as their disadvantages.

The objective approach can be useful and indeed life-saving when it comes to very acute physical diseases and dysfunctions. 'Diagnosis' at the physical level can be useful up to a point and the various tests can give detailed information about the pathology that seems to underlie the outward symptom or discomfort. It should remain the treatment of choice in a crisis or after an accident.

The problem with this hard approach is that despite all the tests and apparent objectivity of the diagnosis, quite often the treatment results in very unpleasant and unpredictable side effects and symptom shifts, and the 'cure' proves elusive. This is especially the case with chronic illnesses. So the objective approach is seen not to be as effective as it should be. Also, the diagnosis is often a guesstimate about what is 'wrong' and the treatment is therefore based on an incomplete understanding and will give less than perfect results.

The subjective approach, assessing the flow of energy and determining the nature of the imbalance and the blockage, sounds nonsensical and fantastic to the seekers of objectivity and evidence. Yet it often works in the most 'unreasonable' way. In addition, any holistic practitioner worth their salt would factor in variables such as emotional states, attitudinal responses and lifestyle, which will have a bearing on the disease. Yet here too there is a gap. There needs to be a degree of objectivity.

It seems to me that both approaches have validity and strengths as well as weaknesses. They are two sides of the same coin and in between is the suffering human. Yet there appears to be a missing link and no real meeting ground between the two. If only they could come together and somehow become a whole instead of two warring parts.

A sensible first step would be for these two viewpoints to find a common ground and work together. At the moment, while there are some minuscule moves in that direction, the gap is huge, with mutual misunderstanding, distrust and contempt on both sides – to the detriment of both and of course the poor suffering human caught in between. Who is telling the truth, who is to be believed and, most important of all, what is the best course of action for the suffering individual? There are no easy answers and you pay your money and take your choice.

What would have to happen for these opposing viewpoints to begin to resolve their differences, find a common ground and work together in harmony? For this to occur there would have to be a science of the subjective, a science of energy, a science of flow, a science of the invisible. Some physical evidence of this elusive energy would have to be a primary requisite, a starting point from which a workable objective parameter could emerge that was acceptable to both sides. Impossible? Almost, but not quite.

I would like to suggest that VRIC is the missing link that permits the joining of these seemingly irreconcilable approaches. It is objective, because there is something tangible – a photo – to look at. It is duplicable and reliable as it involves technology, thereby removing the personal bias of the practitioner. It is precise, because it fluctuates between only two states: a clear photo, showing the whole bodymind system moving in the direction of order, and a fuzzy photo, showing the system heading towards chaos. The guesswork is eliminated. It permits both the client and the practitioner to interact directly and objectively with the whole being, thereby factoring in the whole at the most fundamental level of expression, where the energy that is light transforms into the material form that is life.

Out of this quantum leap emerges a single workable fundamental parameter of wholeness – the photon-waveform emission of lifeforms. It offers a single parameter of wholeness fluctuating between the two easy-to-understand states of coherence-order or incoherence-chaos. This meeting of the physical dimension with the energetic one, which we know exists but have never in human history been able to access, is made visible in the altered magnetic-light field of the Luminator. This permits us to interact with both realities at the same time – the space–time reality of the physical dimension and the information flow of the energetic dimension. The dimensions can be seen to be one, not in conflict with each other but acting in co-operation, different yet totally interactive and interdependent. The age-old conflict of the opposing paradigms can be laid to rest and a new scientific art and artful science of the subjective-objective complex-simple human can emerge and benefit everyone.

Seeing the Whole Human

Let us examine for a moment what it means to see the human as a whole. If there is to be a science of wholeness that would have to be the minimum requirement.

When you think of yourself or another person, what immediately comes to mind is a physical image of yourself or the other person. And while there is no doubt that all your organs and various physical systems are unique to you, we identify a person mainly by their face. If you saw a photograph of your ear you would probably not recognize it as yours, even though it has been part of you for as long as you have existed. You might fare a bit better when it came to your eyes, but your face is instantly recognizable.

So, very logically, to assess the whole of you without an image of that which is uniquely and recognizably you has to be an incomplete exercise. X-rays and MRI scans see a part of you in a special way, perhaps in great detail, but can they give a clue about what is not seen and how it connects and interacts with the rest of you, including your thoughts and emotions, which as we know affect our physical parameters in every moment? You are constantly changing as a result of physical processes of infinite complexity, in addition to all your thoughts and intentions, feelings, moods and emotions, and the levels of information contained in your energy field, which is transacting continuously with the universe. Can you begin to see the enormity of the task of assessing a whole human scientifically?

Also, for it to be 'scientific' there has to be an observable and repeatable process involved (science's constant demand for evidence) which is accessible to the five-sensory reality, reliable and can be duplicated, hence it must involve some sort of technology. In effect we are asking for a science of the subjective – a contradiction in terms, it would seem. Given the fact of everything being in flux at the quantum level and as a result at the physical level, that science would also have to be a science of the moment, a science assessing continuous flux in its totality and reducing it to a meaningful workable and objective parameter.

The Inner Controller

Let us take things a bit further. You are not your body, you are not your mind, you are not your energy field or your meridian or chakra system. The latest theories and the most ancient say that you are consciousness. You know this at some level when you think of yourself as 'I', and you know that your body, your mind and your energy field belong to you but are not in themselves the essential you. So who is that essential you? Who is the sum totality that is in charge of keeping the infinite flowing complexity of your being in workable and running order in every milli-second of your waking-sleeping existence?

Science gets lost here and starts fumbling around for answers. But the Upanishads, philosophical texts written in India 3,000 years ago, define and describe this imperishable intelligence, the master conductor of the orchestra, as follows:

'It is neither gross nor fine, neither short nor long, neither glowing red (like fire) nor adhesive (like water). It is neither shadow nor darkness, neither air nor space, unattached, without taste, without smell, without eyes, without ears, without voice, without mind, without radiance, without breath, without a mouth, without measure, having no within and no without. It eats nothing and nothing eats it ... [It] is never seen but is the Seer, is never heard but is the hearer, is never perceived but is the perceiver, is never thought but is the thinker. There is no other seer but this, no other hearer but this, no other perceiver but this, no other thinker but this. This is yourself, the inner controller, the immortal.'

Using VRIC imaging you are in effect meeting and dialoguing with your inner controller, which communicates with you through a simple fluctuating light signal. And so through the agency of a photograph of your own image you are in direct communication with your superconscious self, the part of you that knows and controls every aspect of you in every single instant of your being. What do you call that One?

Seeing and interacting with that self can lead from the fragmented, incomplete and mechanistic understanding of twentieth-century science to an understanding of wholeness and of the magnificent, extraordinary human of twenty-first century science. This is the real possibility available to us today.

STEPPING INTO THE MAGIC
THE 6TH SENSE AND THE 7TH SENSE

Life is choice. In today's world there is a plethora of choices at every level. In fact, thanks to the Internet and Google we live in an era of infinite choice. This may sound wonderful and it is certainly better than having no or very limited choice, but choosing from an infinite variety of options is not simple, easy, accurate or fun. A choice involves making a decision of some sort or another. Which diet should I follow? Is this person good for me or not? Should I change my job now or later? There are pros and cons to every choice and our futures are shaped by the quality of our decision-making in the now. We dither and doubt and consult experts of various sorts, psychics and astrologers and of course Google, and hope that somehow we make the right choice and get what we desire.

Where you are now in your life is a direct result of the many conscious and unconscious choices made by the different aspects of yourself. At the conscious level you know but 5 per cent of yourself and the other 95 per cent – the subconscious, the unconscious and superconscious parts of yourself – also has a direct input in each choice and in the shaping of your life's unique journey. Each of these different aspects of the self has, if you like, different and often conflicting intentions as they seek to find expression for themselves. This internal unconscious conflict results in conflict in our outer lives and we are often at one level or another not happy either with the choice we have made or the end result of that choice. In other terms, the head and the heart often have different agendas, and the needs of both, plus the needs of the soul, have to be met for us to feel the sense of total rightness and the comfort that goes with it. How often do you feel this sense of total rightness when it comes to your decisions? And if you do feel it, is that feeling borne out by the result of acting on the decision? Is there a way we can make better decisions?

The 6th Sense

We access the reality of this physical third dimension largely through our five senses. However, all of us are aware of something we call the 6th sense, which is the sense that allows us to access the non-linear reality and speaks to us in the languages of gut feelings, impulses and quiet knowing. We also call it intuition (tuition from the inside), psi or ESP. This is the sense that, when used effectively, can give us access to the future or other multi-dimensional realities.

This sense is notoriously elusive, subtle and difficult to prove, at least by the standards and methodologies of so-called good science. It is, however, important and can give us clues to our real response to given situations. The gut feelings and impulses are truth indicators and the language that our emotional self uses to communicate with us. They are a non-linear internal individual response to the vast external non-linear universe.

The power of using the 6th sense well cannot be underestimated. However, the problem with it is that there is no easy verification in external reality of whether that gut feeling is real and right. Should I follow it or would I do better to just ignore it? Is it real or is it just my imagination? How many times have you experienced this soft inner voice recommending a course of action and being overruled by the reasoning, doubting mind? It does not speak the language of the rational linear intellect and is therefore not trusted by it.

The rational linear intellect and the five senses are the tools we primarily use to understand and interact with the physical reality of the third dimension, so they are the senses that are trusted most in this day and age of proof and evidence. The brain is supposed to be the command centre from which all decisions are made. The limitation of the linear mind, however, is that it often does not understand the world of feelings and it does not have the tools to understand the non-linear nature of reality. For instance, it has no way to understand how 50 trillion cells in the human body can communicate with one another on a continuum when they are not connected. How does a cell in the brain know what a cell in the foot is doing? This level of knowledge is out of the remit of the linear mind. Therefore it cannot see the big picture.

Both the linear mind and the intuitive non-linear mind are valuable and neither can be dispensed with. The problem is, they are often in conflict and give us contradictory messages, the end result of which lands us in the analysis-paralysis mode with one foot on the accelerator and the other on the brake. This unhappy situation makes decision making difficult and furthermore, having made the decision, it is difficult to be happy, as one aspect or the other feels short-changed. There is often the niggling feeling that something is not right. How can we get beyond this?

The 7th Sense

What is the 7th sense? How is it different from the 6th sense, intuition, inner knowing? Can it satisfy the demands of both the linear and non-linear mind?

The 7th sense is radically different from either the rational mind or the emotional intuitive mind. This super sense allows us to bypass or rather subsume both the rational mind and the 6th sense and gives us direct objective, systematic access to the Intelligence that controls and co-ordinates the collaborative and co-operative activities of the 50 trillion cells of your body. Do you know that each of those cells is an individual conscious entity in its own right with the power and the ability in any given moment to choose what it does from a variety of different options and actions such as maintaining its metabolism, breathing, digesting food, excreting waste, replicating itself and responding appropriately to other cells, predators and toxins in its environment? Each cell has to do this consistently and constantly as long as it is alive. Of course, each cell also has to be mindful of what each of the other 50 trillion cells minus one is doing, otherwise the whole system would collapse into chaos. It is almost impossible to comprehend the quality, the speed, accuracy and precision of the decision making needed to keep the awesome dynamic system that is your body-mind in function.

Fritz-Albert Popp's work tells us that cells communicate via faint light signals. These are binary in nature in that there are only two states – coherence or chaos, yes or no, order or disorder. There are no ifs, buts or maybes, no opinions that can be right or wrong, just the absolute truth of our being. So by accessing this state we have bypassed the limitations of the linear mind and the 6th sense, have we not?

Now we can begin to understand the magnitude of difference in the quality of this level of Super Intelligence as compared to the level of either the rational linear mind or the 6th sense. You and I certainly do not and cannot know what each of our 50 trillion cells is doing at a conscious level, yet there is a part of ourselves which does.

So, though both the conscious linear rational mind and the 6th sense are valuable assets and tools which the personality uses to interact with reality, you can understand their limitations and realize that both are contained in a bigger container of Super Intelligence, which also exists within you, or rather is you.

The truly radical possibility that emerges out of the breakthrough that is VRIC is that now we have the chance to interact with it in an objective, systematic way. With the 7th sense using VRIC imaging you are in effect meeting and dialoguing with your immortal inner controller, which is speaking to you directly in the language of light. What is the quality of the truth you access when you can talk to that One? At this level any question that you ask is answered by every single one of your 50 trillion cells speaking with one voice in an objective, systematic, direct and unequivocal way. Here there are no opinions, no ifs, no maybes, just the simple-complex truth of your entire being.

In Michael Talbot's excellent book, *The Holographic Universe,* I came across a term I had not encountered before: 'the omnijective sense'. The idea is that there is a so-called objective reality and there is a so-called subjective reality, but there is another reality where these two realities intersect and become one – in effect, where the external universe and the internal universe meet and are at one. This is the omnijective realm, neither one nor the other but both and neither, a super-intelligent realm.

Could there be a way of accessing and verifying this omnijective reality in a way that could be accepted as 'real' by the linear mind and the objective methodology demanded by so-called good science? Is there a way of using it to make the right choice for both yourself and the universe? Is there a beneficent omnijective choice?

The Random Option Process

Now let me bring you to the most magical, mysterious and miraculous yet totally exact process that uses VRIC imaging. It is the Random Option Process, or ROP for short. The ROP method allows us to bypass the linear mind and the brain, the needs and distorted filters of the personality and gives us direct access to the One aspect that knows the whole truth about us at all times, can only tell us the truth and gives us the possibility of making decisions that we can be happy with.

So how do we do this?

Up until mid-2002, if we needed to assess the coherence or otherwise of a decision, in the sense that it was beneficial or not for a client, we would ask that client to either make two opposing verbal statements or hold the two opposite thoughts, one after the other, reflecting their intention, and two separate images would be taken in the field of the Luminator. In general it worked very well – the images were often very revealing and one could see clearly which option was the really comfortable one energetically and therefore would have a beneficial end result. However, the conscious mind was involved to some extent, as the person had to hold a conscious thought or make a verbal statement. What we wanted to see was the hidden reality and the hidden opposition or resistance from the unconscious self, whose agenda might be at odds with the conscious intention and desire of that person. We wanted to talk with the unconscious directly and see what it had to say.

A friend made a simple suggestion that really resonated with me. This new method would enable us to bypass the conscious mind and the brain entirely. We would write the various options on several pieces of paper, which would then be folded and shuffled so that neither the practitioner nor the client would know which option was under consideration. The client would then hold the folded notes one by one and a VRIC image would be taken with each. That way neither the client nor the practitioner could wittingly or unwittingly influence the outcome of the imaging.

The results this method has produced have been simply staggering and have to be seen to be believed. Often they are so different from what the client is expecting that they are shocking. What that person believes to be true and what is really true for them can be revealed to be at complete variance. And yet the results cannot be gainsaid because of the total impeccability of the process. All resistance melts away in the face of the images. Now the hidden saboteur is revealed and can be looked at dispassionately and dealt with. The gap between intention and reality can be closed in a beautiful, simple and totally truthful manner.

Creating a supercoherent intent becomes a real possibility with this remarkably simple and beautifully mysterious process. The Random Option Process and VRIC imaging enable us to use the omnijective 7th sense. They align us with the supercoherent universe. We can make the right choice at the right time, with no possibility of error.

This process can be used in pretty much any circumstance where there is doubt. Doubt can be time-consuming and draining and very difficult to lay to rest. How and when does doubt become certainty? Having done this process countless times I have never yet seen a client who doubted the results of the imaging, no matter what they thought or felt before undergoing the process. All manner of decisions, from which flooring to have in the kitchen to important business decisions to meaningful personal decisions, have been made over the years using this method. Some striking examples come to mind:

'Is This a Wise Investment?'

A young client, SG, had started in the property development business in the UK. She was well educated, immensely capable, hard-working and clear-thinking. She was doing well and now she wanted to expand by investing in Florida. She said she had done her research and it looked promising. She was ready to book a flight and check out the different properties there. Could we check out this option using the ROP method?

So we did. The results were not what she was expecting. The images gave a clear no. There was nothing to be said, no discussion, and she went away clear but puzzled.

When she came back the following month for her assessment she could not wait to tell me what had happened. Apparently the Florida market had taken a dip and had she invested in it, she would not have come out of it well financially. She was amazed and relieved that she had done the imaging and received a clear answer that had stopped her from making what would have been an unwise decision.

'Should I Terminate a Painful Long-term Business Relationship?'
This client had a complex longstanding professional relationship. She had a client who had been a childhood friend; many years later a professional relationship had emerged out of this friendship. However, the person had changed over the years and had become controlling and demanding and never acknowledged anything that was done for her.

Now, several years later, my client had come to a crossroads. It was very difficult for her to let her friend go as a client – in fact it seemed unthinkable – but her behaviour had become steadily worse and now she did not know what to do. She could not forget how her friend had been, yet could not face what she had become. One day when she felt driven to desperation she decided to see whether she could actually let go of this painful relationship. The ROP process was used and she could see that if she maintained the relationship she fragmented completely.

The images worked their usual magic and she was able to sever the ties at last. She was at once sad, sorry and relieved when it was done. She had not known what a burden she had been carrying until she put it down. It is good to know when to let things and people go. It hadn't been easy for this woman to do so, but the two images reminded her of the truth of her feeling self in the now –

not what should have been or what could have been, but what really was.

'Should I Change My Job?'

M came to confirm the coherence of a decision he had already made. He had been unhappy in his job for some time and had decided to change it. But was he right to do so or not?

We started the process of exploration so I could frame the questions that were to be asked of the ROP process. He explained that his office building faced a sewage-processing station and that bothered him. He also did not really approve of the business that the company was engaged in. He had brought along a photo of the office building and I duly imaged him with it and he was coherent. He was surprised.

The next step was a simple one. Two options were written on two notes. One said it was beneficial for him to continue working for his present employer and the other said it was non-beneficial to continue working for that employer. The notes were folded and shuffled, so neither M nor I knew which one he was holding. He held one and then the other and the VRIC images were taken. When he looked at them he could not believe his eyes. They were completely different from what he had expected. It was clear that it was beneficial to continue working for that employer.

I was surprised, too, as his reasons for wanting to leave the company seemed so valid. But it struck me that he must have had some doubts or he would not have come for clarification. It was time to go deeper.

I asked him what his relationships were like at the office. Did he really like the people there? What was his boss like? M was mild in manner, soft-spoken and very capable but not particularly assertive. He had been passed over for a promotion and someone much junior and less capable had got ahead of him. M was unhappy about that but had not done anything about it. He then admitted that the same thing had happened before, when he had been working for another employer.

Here was a pattern to be discerned. In my view, which I shared with him, this was the reason why his superconscious self had faced him with the same dilemma and the imaging had given him the tough and unexpected answer that it had. Some part of him did not know how to ask for what it needed and another part of him clearly wanted that weakness to be addressed.

To check this out, M was asked to make a conscious affirmation: 'I can be in my power and speak my truth.' His image fragmented. He could see for himself that there was a part of him that did not know how to stand up for himself. There was a glaring difference between his consciously stated intention and his internal reality. M is very straight and truthful, but he had never made acquaintance with this weak, disempowered part of himself in this very direct way.

We continued by imaging him repeating the same conscious statement and holding various Lumanetic frequency combinations and when we established coherence his image cleared. M could now see for himself that he had the energetic strength to speak the truth about his needs and hold his ground. After this I coached him in various methods of handling difficult emotional situations and not walking away from them and letting them go by default.

As a result of the imaging, M continued with the same company. He also started wearing his frequencies on a regular basis. A few months later he unexpectedly got a good rise in salary as well as a promotion. The last I heard he was on a trip to Russia. He was happy in his job and happy that his worth had been recognized and rewarded in real terms. Access to the 7th sense and the awesome frequency tools had changed the trajectory of his life.

'I Could Have Danced All Night'

They came in secret, a young man in his early twenties and his mother. He was tall and well-built, but he walked like an 80-year-old. He shambled and was hardly able to put one foot before another. When he came in and took his shoes off, his mother had to bend down and untie his shoelaces.

They came into the Luminator room and sat down. The young man sat quietly while his mother did most of the talking. He could hardly keep his eyes open.

They came from an orthodox community. He was the eldest child in a family with many children and he needed to be married. That was the tradition. But he was 'not normal' and 'suffered from delusions'. He was on heavy-duty anti-psychotic medication and the doctor had advised that he would always need to be on some form of medication. The problem was that the medication was not helping, and the way he was, nobody would give their daughter to him. The family was very keen for him to give up or reduce his medication but terrified to change anything in view of what the doctor had said.

The strange thing was that when he did speak he made sense. He was not particularly communicative or articulate, but I could see he thought about things. I also noticed that his mother treated him with love, but not with a great deal of respect.

We started the process of re-establishing coherence in his energy field. As the hidden traumas were neutralized using VRIC imaging and the Lumanetics energy tools, he started changing. Within three months, with the caring co-operation of his mother, his medication had been reduced to zero. I had advised that they should not stop the medication suddenly and that it should be done gradually. As his system became stronger and more coherent it would be able to sustain itself.

As he became stronger and more functional, the pressure mounted from his father – was he ready yet to get married? I could see that he was not, that he needed more time, but I could understand their urgency. I gave my opinion that he was still too fragile, but his father was in a hurry. He was taken abroad to meet a prospective bride, but it went really badly and he regressed. The father conceded that he had been wrong and that perhaps they should have waited. But he was keen to know how long it would take. I told him that it would take as long as it took and that using pressure and force would give the same unpleasing result he had had recently.

There was no point in asking the young man whether he was ready or not. He said he was, but was he really? The impasse was resolved using ROP. Two VRIC images were taken, one with him holding a folded note saying, 'I am ready to be engaged to be married,' and the other with a note saying, 'I am not ready to be engaged to be married.' The results were spectacular, as usual. He was not ready. What the personality did not know and could not articulate was known at the supercoherent level.

His father accepted the truth of the images and this took the pressure off everyone.

The young man continued to come once a month and his progress was steady and sure. I recommended some simple dietary changes and strongly urged that he should have some physical exercise. The needs of the soul, which were attended to with the many hours of study and prayer that were part of his daily routine, had to be balanced by taking care of the needs of the body. His mother made sure that my instructions were followed. Every month we also asked him whether he was ready to be married, using the ROP process.

Then suddenly everything slotted into place. He was ready – he said so, his superconscious self said so and it was all systems go. However, now his father was not sure whether he would find a nice girl. I assured him that this young man was very special, a very pure soul with a very good heart, and that the right person would recognize this. I did not say this lightly. This young man was indeed very special – ultra-gentle, very kind and transparently good. I knew that he would make a wonderful husband.

His mother rang me a few months later to say that he had found a wonderful girl who really appreciated his special qualities and that he had got engaged to her. She thanked me and said it would not have happened without my work.

He was married a few months later. On the night of his wedding he celebrated this momentous event by dancing for several hours. His mother later asked him, 'Weren't you tired dancing for so many hours?' His response was, 'Mum, I could have danced all night!' I was as delighted as if it had been my own son.

A year and a half later I called to see how he was. He was doing wonderfully well and was thoroughly in love with his wife, who in turn was devoted to him. His studies were going extremely well, he was exercising regularly and was fitter than everyone else who went to the gym except the trainer. He was happy.

A miracle?

'Thrity, Are You a Witch?'

The phone rang and I picked it up. It was a young client who had been to see me the previous day. His first words to me were

'Thrity, are you a witch?'

I laughed and asked why he had asked me that question.

The day before he had been for an assessment and had used the ROP method to ask a certain question. He had made an offer for a specific property in Poland. He knew exactly what he was buying it for – a long-term investment – and had checked out with various experts that the price was under-market, that the area was undergoing gentrification, it was close to the centre of town and was an easy commute, etc. He had done his research and knew what he was going to do with it: divide it into two apartments and rent them out. He was looking for long-term capital growth as part of his pension plan. It all sounded very plausible and well-thought-through.

We did the imaging with the folded notes following the ROP method and the answer was no, it was not beneficial to buy that property. He was definitely not expecting that answer and was disappointed and puzzled. We discussed the various possible reasons why the answer had turned out as it did and I asked him to research it further.

The next morning he had a call from his lawyer in Poland who informed him there was a clause in the contract that would make it very difficult to divide the property as he had planned. It was fortunate he had not committed to buying the property and had not signed a contract or he would have been in serious trouble.

Why had the lawyer phoned him the very morning after he had asked the question of his supercoherent self? Is it a listening universe?

Coincidence or the 7th sense in action?

'Five Lights or Eight?'

Five lights or eight? Wardrobes on the long wall or short wall? Carpets over the whole area or carpets with wooden surround around the radiators in case they leaked some day and ruined the carpet? Should the bath be placed central to the window or on another wall? Questions, questions, questions, doubts, doubts, doubts, and no resolution in sight! Doubts, debates, dilemmas, but no clear decision and therefore no action. Whichever option he considered, the other appeared to have equal merit. There seemed no way out of the mental quagmire that he had got himself into.

D was a very talented and sought-after interior designer and project manager and his latest project was his own house, which he shared with his wife. This was the start of the project and the first bedroom suite was being remodelled. The whole house was to be refurbished and at the rate he was going, it would take forever. D could plan right down to the very last detail (which by itself can be a gift and a very good thing), but he wanted everything to be right – perfectly right, with no possibility of error. He was a perfectionist who was very hard on himself if he made a 'mistake'. Now he was driving himself crazy and had got really stuck in the analysis-paralysis mode. He just could not progress to the next step unless he could resolve these seemingly innocuous choices with some degree of peaceful acceptance that the choice he had made was right. But no matter which choice he considered, another part of him said it was wrong. Not a fun place to be.

As I saw it, he had no consideration for his time – a precious commodity that we take for granted. Moreover, the stress of this constant inner conflict was making him anxious, unhappy and unwell. He might end up with a 'perfect' house – if he ever managed to complete it – but all the joy would be lost in the process.

I reminded him that he was expending precious life-force energy – his most fundamental resource – with no thought or awareness of its value. These questions were important up to a point, but in the larger scheme of things did not seem of earth-shaking consequence.

He agreed with everything I said, but I could see clearly that for him this quandary he had got himself into was actually quite distressing. So I offered to do the ROP process with one qualification: he could use it for four choices and no more. I guessed that if he could, he would want to ask many more than four questions – in fact, it would be questions with no end in sight. He agreed to this rather reluctantly and I could almost see other questions arising even as we spoke.

The results were amazing as usual. As D consulted his supercoherent self, the answers were clear and unequivocal. As soon as he saw the images, I could see the relief on his face. The doubts were gone, the quagmire had become a clear pathway and he could see the light at the end of the dark tunnel of his doubt.

Where there is doubt, creativity dries up – they cannot co-exist. Excessive doubts drain energy and prevent progress. Here they were miraculously, magically taken care of in a few minutes – the 7th sense in action!

After D had obtained relief from his turmoil as a result of ROP, we went more deeply into the reasons for his unproductive behaviour and explored his unconscious fears of being wrong and failing. These had come from painful experiences in the not-so-distant past which were still lingering in his cellular memory and his energy field.

'Is This the Right Office?'

M had worked from home for several years and had built a successful business from zero. Now she wanted to expand and get herself an office. So the search was on.

After looking at many options she had boiled them down to two. The first office was larger and had two rooms, which she really wanted. It was not in very good decorative order and needed a fair bit of work. The rent was a bit higher than that of the other one. The landlord was OK, but not particularly helpful or generous. The building, the entrance and the general appearance were OK but not great. The location was good.

The second one had only one large room and was in much better decorative order. The room was big enough to be divided into two, but again there would be work involved. The landlord, however, was amenable, friendly, helpful and generous. The room would have a beautiful new floor, a chandelier and many upgrades at no cost to M. The location was good and the building was very well looked after.

M had more or less decided to take the larger office, but still wanted to confirm that it was the right choice. What did I think? My opinion was exactly the opposite. I knew she would be in trouble if she chose the first one and would be happy in the second one.

M was happy to leave the decision to the ROP method. So we did the notes with the hidden options and the second one was the one that made her coherent. It was clear that there was a disparity between what she wanted at the conscious level and what her supercoherent self wanted. She was not best pleased with the result, but had learned to trust the process over a period of time and so went with it.

What transpired after that was amazing. The landlord gave her far more than he had promised (very unusual) and she got a whole year rent-free. That was a huge bonus. In the other option she would have had no rent-free period and would have had to spend a substantial sum. The magic of the 7th sense in action!

After M had been in the office a few years, very happily, it was time for a rent review. She was resigned to the fact that her rent would rise, but there was another surprise in store: she was offered a new lease with no rise in the rent. She was the only person in the building who was offered that deal.

Today M concedes that renting that office was the best thing she could have done and yet it could have been completely different had she gone with her first choice, the one she was 'sure of'.

Resolving Doubts – Dithering – Dilemmas
The ROP Method Using VRIC Imaging
Clear Coherent Decision Making

Five lights in the bedroom, says the folded ROP note –
coherence.

Eight lights in the bedroom, says the folded ROP note –
incoherent.

SUPERCOHERENCE – THE 7TH SENSE IN ACTION!
THE ROP METHOD
MAKING A COHERENT CAREER CHOICE

Choice 1 – work for present company –
incoherent.

Choice 2 – change to new named company in the same profession –
incoherent.

Choice 3 – change of career –
coherent.

Within days of this process client unexpectedly got an offer for a completely different career much more in line with his talents and his inclination.

THE 7TH SENSE IN ACTION – STEPPING INTO THE MAGIC
BEYOND THE BRAIN – THE ROP METHOD

Client holding folded note with hidden option 1 –
coherent.

Client holding folded note with different
hidden option 2 – incoherent.

CHAPTER 21

THE UNLIMITED MODEL
THE INFINITE HUMAN

Everything that you understand, everything that you do, every action that you take, every response that you make, every belief system that you have is based on a model of understanding. It is your unique understanding of the way reality is.

Every model, whether you take the biological model, the physiological model, the mathematical model, the astrological model, the genetic model, every model has a limitation. It is bounded, it is not boundless. Some models are larger than others and can give us a larger and more inclusive view and more options. Other models are smaller; they are extremely restricted and therefore restricting. Humans have always accepted models of limitation. Our understanding of the finite nature of the physical reality, bounded by death and destruction, is an example of one such model.

Let us take ourselves to a model of limitlessness – the greatest model of all, the model of ceaseless change, of absolute certainty, of infinite newness, of creation. By what is this model bounded? It changes even as you seek to contain it. It cannot be contained, it is an open model. Can an open model exist? Yes, it can, if you start to understand the true nature of the reality that is.

Why do we need models anyway? They are a way of understanding our physical reality, our lives, our place in the scheme of things. They give us frames of reference and point the way to making the choices and taking the actions that are necessary to meet our various needs. If we are ill, our model will determine whether we seek the help of a medical doctor or a homoeopath or some other type of assistance. The actions that we take come from the set of beliefs that form our model and these are beliefs that we will live and die by. We create our reality at every level, or rather our reality is created for us by our model.

If your life challenges you and you wish to create a different reality, examine the model you are operating by. Change the model and a different set of options will appear. Make sure when you do this exercise that you choose a much larger model, one that is open (meaning open to the new and open to change) and preferably one that is a limitless one. Change to a model of evolution, a model of creation. If you do so, your reality will expand.

This expanded reality is not somewhere out there, it is the reality that exists within you and is the reality that is you. After all, the impulse of intelligence that surges through your 50 trillion cells doesn't equivocate. It doesn't question what its options are, it knows in every instant, figuring and factoring in immeasurably vast amounts of the impossibly complex information about the universe that is you. Is this a model based on limitation of any sort? It is the model of instant knowing, instant coherent response to the infinite flow of change. Why don't we look upon that model and come to terms with the fact that that is the model of what we are, what we can seek to be and what it is possible to be?

We get glimpses of this model in the non-linear models based on divination and intuition, but the rational objective mind cannot easily reconcile to this reality and hence the self becomes conflicted and limited. The model then has to shrink to the level of the mind's understanding and acceptance or a compromise has to be sought.

But when the intellect comes face-to-face with this model of bound-lessness and realizes this in its own terms, it can unconditionally accept that expanded model as the true one. Then you will have access to this place of limitless knowledge and wisdom in an objective way that your rational mind can accept and feel comfortable with. When this happens, will you live from that boundless creative place that exists within you and is you? What possibilities will emerge for you as a result? What are the possibilities of creation that can unfold in your life?

Unconditional belief in this model, when it gets seared into your cells, your psyche and your DNA, allows you to breathe more easily and feel your comfort, safety and certainty expand at every level of your being. As you become acquainted with the superconscious you, the unlimited you, the you of total possibility, the you of awesome intelligence, and manifest that in every aspect of your life in every moment, starting from now, which is the only moment that really is, what will you do? What will you create?

Go to the model of limitlessness. Don't be bound by any of the lesser models. By all means factor them in, but know that they are limited. And you are not. You are not limited by your genes, you are not limited by your astrological sign or chart or your personal life circumstances. You are more, more than you can ever imagine in your wildest dreams, and you can become it now. You are it now. Know that with every fibre of your being, at every level. Understand it, accept it, hold it to your heart, to your emotions, to your intellect. Filter every single thing that you think, say and do through that limitless model and see what happens to the physical, mental, emotional and spiritual reality that is your life.

SUPERCOHERENCE AND THE FUTURE
THE HIGH-FREQUENCY HUMAN
HIDDEN POWER, HIDDEN STRENGTH

Baseline VRIC image Two months' old –
coherent.

Baseline VRIC image Mother –
incoherent.

SUPERCOHERENCE AND THE FUTURE
THE HIGH-FREQUENCY HUMAN
HIDDEN POWER, HIDDEN STRENGTH

Mother and baby – both coherent.

Question – who is stronger, the little 'helpless' baby or the mother?

SUPERCOHERENCE AND THE LIVING LASER
TWENTY-FIRST-CENTURY HUMAN

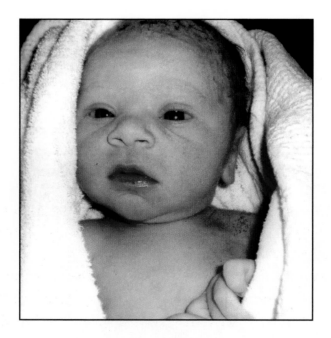

Within moments of birth
clear – cognizant – coherent.

TWENTY-FIRST-CENTURY HUMAN

This little one is the daughter of one of my long-term clients. Her mother has experienced Biolumanetics and the Monocrom colour-light, in effect the living laser or supercoherence process.

As I knew that this baby would have had the benefit of her mother's energy organization or fine-tuning and toning 'treatment' from the very start, I was intrigued to see how she would turn out. Would she be somehow different? What would this little living laser be capable of? I had no particular expectations, but I did advise her mother to have a natural birth and asked her to take a photo of the baby as soon as she was born. The photo opposite was taken just after she had come out of her mother's womb and been wiped down to remove the blood from the birthing process.

Her mother reported that when she was born she did not cry. Instead she came out with her hand in her mouth and calmly surveyed the scene. Look at her face. It is a strong face. There is no fear there. Just a couple of minutes ago she made the extraordinary journey from the safety of her mother's womb to the unfamiliar environment of a hospital theatre and she was not fazed by it in the least. She was clear and cognizant at birth.

I went to see her less than a week after her birth and was amazed to see she could already hold her head up. Her progress to date has been simply astonishing.

What does the future hold for this little 'Photo sapiens' and what does this extraordinary process mean for humankind? The future looks bright!

When she was eight weeks old I invited her mother over with her for a short assessment. The VRIC photos from that time speak for themselves. The mother's baseline image is incoherent, but the little one's baseline is coherent. When her mother picks her up, she makes her mother coherent. Who is the stronger? What is the frequency of this little twenty-first-century human?

ALL IS ONE
ALL IS ONLY THE ONE

In my early teens I became an atheist. I flatly refused to say any prayers or go to any temple. I could not understand why there could be such injustice and suffering in the world. If there was a god 'up there', why and how was this permitted?

Now, though I cannot claim to have found all the answers, Biolumanetics, VRIC imaging and the supercoherence process have made me understand beyond the shadow of a doubt the utterly awesome nature of the Intelligence that is always present in every being, no matter what their physical or mental state appears to be. Its nature is truth, purity, clarity, super function and infinite possibility. I have seen it in people who are extremely ill and have been so for years. I have seen it in people who are extremely mentally disturbed or just plain unhappy. I have seen it, in people of every age, from the tiniest baby to the very elderly. The certain knowledge of the constant presence of this extreme Intelligence is seared into my cells, my psyche and my consciousness, and is now my unconditional belief. I cannot forget it is there for an instant, no matter how hopeless a person's circumstances or how seemingly helpless they appear to be. It goes beyond 'good and bad', 'right and wrong' and is present in the serial murderer and the saint. It reminds me of its awesome, benign and extraordinary presence in everything and everyone that I see, no matter what their appearance is at the physical level. I know with absolute unequivocal certainty that all is one and that all is only THE ONE. Everything, from a single atom to the mightiest galaxy to you and to me, is the face of a thinking, feeling, loving, supercoherent, Superconscious Intelligence – for how can it be anything other?

I say this not with blind faith but with the knowledge of personal experience. And this knowledge has led me to understand that there is hope for humanity and that truth and love will always prevail.

AFTERWORD
WHAT NOW? THE WAY FORWARD

If the ideas and revelations in this book have touched you, raised your curiosity and awakened your sense of wonder, then I will consider my job well done. You will probably have a lot of questions for which you will need answers. Where do you go from here? How do you take this forward? How do you participate in this new adventure?

You will have noticed that this is not a 'how to' book in the conventional sense. It will not tell you how to reach your goals. No exercises, mental, physical or spiritual, are recommended. There are no recommendations of pretty much any sort. The rules of success and happiness have changed forever and you will need new tools – the power tools of the twenty-first century – to have super success on your own terms.

Will these tools help you to make a million bucks? Will they help you to get the girl/boy/man/woman of your dreams? Is this all you want?

Since the reality that is the Luminator came into my life, I have found that our dreams and hopes are way too small and what is possible is a magnitude of scales greater than you could dream of right now. While it is wonderful and indeed essential to have dreams, hopes, plans and goals, I want to say that there is an expanded reality of possibilities out there/in here that you are most likely not aware of, have never had access to and therefore have never dreamed about. I did not dream of finding the Luminator, I did not know of its existence or its capabilities until it came to me. Not in my wildest dreams could I have imagined it. So I can take no credit for this event. It was engineered by an extraordinary Intelligence which I also had no clue about at the time. But the magic was always happening, regardless.

These are the immediate steps you can take to start opening to that magic:

Step 1: Please leave your questions or comments for me at www.SuperCoherence7thSense.com/blog. I value your feedback and would love to hear from you.

Step 2: Come and interact with me at the free teleseminars that we run to keep people abreast of the latest developments. Find the details at www.SuperCoherence7thSense.com/teleseminars.

After dipping your toe in the water with the three steps above, if you want to dive in, then the place to go to is www.TheSuperCoherence Program.com. This programme is squarely about reconnecting each person to the extraordinary resources of intelligence and function that are hidden within each cell and atom of their being. Harnessing unlimited authentic personal power, energy and vitality with almost no effort and having the wisdom to use it to become a self-responsible, self-accountable universal human is a real goal to aspire to. You can learn the skills and acquire the frequency tools to be a fearless pioneer, a creator, an authentic, independent, clear-thinking, deeply feeling unlimited human.

A gentle caution: this programme is not about teaching leadership skills and being a great leader in either business or government. I do not particularly care for hierarchical systems and have no interest in perpetuating them. In the present challenging times you will need to be your own person first, to see clearly past your own conditioning and blind spots – an almost impossible but completely necessary and extremely rewarding task.

If this makes sense to you and stirs you, then welcome aboard. You are in for a wild ride.

I really look forward to connecting with you.

Recommended Reading

These are some of the books that helped me in my research and exploration and might be of interest to you. Please visit the website www.ThrityEngineer.com for my latest recommendations.

* Brian Breiling *et al* (eds), *Light Years Ahead*, Celestial Arts, 1996
* Fritjof Capra, *The Tao of Physics*, Shambala Publications Inc., 1975
* —, *The Web of Life*, Anchor Books, 1996
* Deepak Chopra, *Quantum Healing*, Bantam Books, 1989
* —, *Ageless Body, Timeless Mind*, Crown Publishers Inc., 1994
* Masaru Emoto, *The Message from Water*, HADO Kyoikusha, 1999
* Richard Gerber, *Vibrational Medicine*, HarperCollins, 2000
* Malcolm Gladwell, *The Tipping Point*, Little, Brown and Company, 2000
* —, *Blink*, Little, Brown and Company, 2005
* James Gleick, *Chaos*, Penguin, 1987
* Valerie Hunt, *Infinite Mind*, Malibu Publishing, 2000
* Jacob Liberman, *Light: Medicine of the Future*, Bear and Company, 1991
* Bruce Lipton, *The Biology of Belief*, Mountain of Love/Elite Books, 2005
* Lynne McTaggart, *The Field*, HarperCollins, 2001
* James Oschman, *Energy Medicine: The Scientific Basis*, Harcourt Publishers, 2000
* John Ott, *Health and Light*, Pocket Books, 1973
* Candace Pert, *The Molecules of Emotion*, Touchstone, Simon and Schuster Inc., 1997
* Dean Radin, *The Conscious Universe*, HarperCollins, 1999
* Matt Ridley, *Genome*, Fourth Estate Ltd, 1999

- Keith Scott-Mumby, *Virtual Medicine*, Thorsons, 1999
- José Silva, *The Silva Mind Control Method*, Pocket Books, 1978
- Jane and Grant Solomon, *Harry Oldfield's Invisible Universe*, Thorsons, 1999
- Michael Talbot, *The Holographic Universe*, HarperCollins, 1991
- M. Mitchell Waldrop, *Complexity*, Touchstone, Simon and Schuster Inc., 1992
- Danah Zohar, *The Quantum Self*, William Morrow and Co., 1990
- Gary Zukav, *The Dancing Wu Li Masters*, William Morrow and Co., 1979
- —, *The Seat of the Soul*, Fireside, Simon and Schuster Inc., 1989

Monocrom: Colour, Light and Sound for the Enhancement of Human Function

Many of the case studies in this book mention Monocrom. Since mid-1998 I have been using the Monocrom light-colour dome and the Monochord sound table in conjunction with Biolumanetics. Valerie Hunt and many others advocate the use of colour and sound to nourish the human energy field, and the research at 3S bears this out. Masaru Emoto's work also shows the effect of music on water and, as you know, the body is 70 per cent water.

VRIC imaging shows that the Monocrom light-colour dome and the Monochord sound table create and enhance coherence in the human energy field. Light and sound are the building blocks of life and affect our emotions and state of being very immediately and directly. Both of these technologies, which I call 'the technologies of happiness', are tools of wellness and wholeness and can tune and tone the bodymind in amazing, effortless and enjoyable ways. Find out more about them at www.ThrityEngineer.com.

YOU CAN HEAL YOUR LIFE, the movie,
starring Louise L. Hay & Friends
(available as a 1-DVD set and an expanded 2-DVD set).
Watch the trailer at **www.LouiseHayMovie.com**

****

The 8th Chakra, by Jude Currivan

The Law of Attraction, by Esther and Jerry Hicks

It's the Thought that Counts, by David R. Hamilton

The Divine Matrix, by Gregg Braden

The Spontaneous Healing of Belief, by Gregg Braden

HAY HOUSE PUBLISHERS

For the most up-to-date
information on the
latest releases, author
appearances and a host
of special offers, visit

www.hayhouse.co.uk

Tune into **www.hayhouseradio.com**
to hear inspiring live radio shows daily!

292B Kensal Rd, London W10 5BE
Tel: 020 8962 1230 Email: info@hayhouse.co.uk

We hope you enjoyed this Hay House book.
If you would like to receive a free catalogue featuring additional
Hay House books and products, or if you would like information
about the Hay Foundation, please contact:

Hay House UK Ltd
292B Kensal Rd • London W10 5BE
Tel: (44) 20 8962 1230; Fax: (44) 20 8962 1239
www.hayhouse.co.uk

***

Published and distributed in the United States of America by:
Hay House, Inc. • PO Box 5100 • Carlsbad, CA 92018-5100
Tel.: (1) 760 431 7695 or (1) 800 654 5126;
Fax: (1) 760 431 6948 or (1) 800 650 5115
www.hayhouse.com

Published and distributed in Australia by:
Hay House Australia Ltd • 18/36 Ralph St • Alexandria NSW 2015
Tel.: (61) 2 9669 4299; Fax: (61) 2 9669 4144
www.hayhouse.com.au

Published and distributed in the Republic of South Africa by:
Hay House SA (Pty) Ltd • PO Box 990 • Witkoppen 2068
Tel./Fax: (27) 11 467 8904 • www.hayhouse.co.za

Published and distributed in India by:
Hay House Publishers India • Muskaan Complex • Plot No.3
B-2 • Vasant Kunj • New Delhi – 110 070.
Tel.: (91) 11 41761620; Fax: (91) 11 41761630.
www.hayhouse.co.in

Distributed in Canada by:
Raincoast • 9050 Shaughnessy St • Vancouver, BC V6P 6E5
Tel.: (1) 604 323 7100; Fax: (1) 604 323 2600

***

Sign up via the Hay House UK website to receive the Hay House
online newsletter and stay informed about what's going on with
your favourite authors. You'll receive bimonthly announcements
about discounts and offers, special events, product highlights,
free excerpts, giveaways, and more!
www.hayhouse.co.uk